Black Slaves, Indian Masters

BARBARA KRAUTHAMER

Black Slaves, Indian Masters

Slavery, Emancipation, and Citizenship

in the Native American South

THE UNIVERSITY OF NORTH CAROLINA PRESS

CHAPEL HILL

This book was published with the assistance of the Fred W. Morrison Fund
for Southern Studies of the University of North Carolina Press.

Set in Minion and The Serif

by codeMantra

Manufactured in the United States of America

The paper in this book meets the guidelines for permanence and
durability of the Committee on Production Guidelines for Book
Longevity of the Council on Library Resources.

The University of North Carolina Press has been a member
of the Green Press Initiative since 2003.

Library of Congress Cataloging-in-Publication Data

Krauthamer, Barbara, 1967–

Black slaves, Indian masters :

slavery, emancipation, and citizenship in the Native American south /
Barbara Krauthamer.

pages cm

Includes bibliographical references and index.

ISBN 978-1-4696-0710-8 (cloth : alk. paper)

1. African Americans—Relations with Indians. 2. Slavery—United States—History.
3. Choctaw Indians—History. 4. Chickasaw Indians—History. 5. Slaveholders—
United States—History. 6. United States—Race relations. I. Title.

E98.R28K73 2013

305.800973—dc23

2013004070

17 16 15 14 13   5 4 3 2 1

To Noah, Max, and Zora

Contents

Illustrations

Acknowledgments

When I began working on this book, I imagined that writing the acknowledgments would be a most enjoyable moment. It would mean, of course, that the book was complete and the time had come to relax, reflect on my journey, and happily thank everyone who assisted and encouraged me. As it turns out, this may be the hardest part of the process. So many friends and colleagues have helped me over the years, and now I cannot imagine how to convey the depth of my gratitude.

This book has been with me for a very long time. I am forever grateful to Nell Irvin Painter for her wisdom and guidance. It was Nell who first suggested I consider researching the history of slavery and emancipation in the West. She told me I might find something interesting if I looked into the history of Oklahoma. She was right. Thank you also to Christine Stansell, Leslie Rowland, and James McPherson.

More recently, my colleagues at the University of Massachusetts–Amherst have been wonderfully supportive and encouraging. I am especially grateful to Joye Bowman, Heather Cox-Richardson, Jennifer Fronc, John Higginson, Laura Lovett, Joel Wolfe, Whitney Battle-Baptiste, Kym Morrison, and Ron Welburn for their friendship and support.

Early in my career, I had the good fortune to meet Tiya Miles, Celia Naylor, Claudio Saunt, David Chang, and Circe Sturm, fellow travelers in the study of African American and Native American histories. Over the years, we have attended conferences together, shared our research with each other, coauthored publications, and shared the milestones of our personal and professional lives. I have learned so much from them and greatly appreciate the time they have taken to read and comment on my work. They are truly outstanding friends and colleagues. In my ideal world, Tiya, Celia, and I would get to spend much more time together.

Many friends have helped and encouraged me along the way. Thank you to Laylah Ali, Stephanie Batiste, Herman Bennett, Daina Ramey Berry, Jennifer Brier, James F. Brooks, Nicole Eustace, Stephanie Camp, Lisa Gail Collins, Laura Edwards, Venus Green, Martha Hodes, Anthony Kaye, Deborah K. King, Elizabeth McHenry, Ken Mack, Paula Massood, Ted Melillo, Joseph Miller, Jennifer Morgan, Dylan Penningroth, Jenn Richeson, Andrew Shankman,

Nicole Shelton, Jonathan Smith, Sharra Vostral, and Daryle Williams. I greatly appreciate Ned Blackhawk's enthusiasm about this project. Special thanks to Rashauna Johnson Chenault, Kendra Field, Leslie Harris, Dawn Peterson, and Liz Pryor for wonderfully provocative and insightful conversations about race, slavery, identity, and southern history. Kristin Roth-Ey is a model scholar and a true friend.

I owe tremendous debts of gratitude to Evelyn Brooks-Higginbotham, Frances Jones-Sneed, Robin D. G. Kelley, Wilma King, Colin Palmer, and Deborah Willis. They have been kind and generous mentors, often on short notice.

Fellowships from a number of institutions provided me with the time and resources needed to research and write this book. A year-long fellowship from the National Endowment for the Humanities allowed me to spend a considerable amount of time in the archives in Oklahoma. Additional research was completed during a short-term fellowship at Yale University's Gilder Lehrman Center for the Study of Slavery, Resistance, and Abolition. I completed portions of this project at Stanford University's Research Institute for Comparative Studies in Race and Ethnicity. Of course, I would not have been able to accomplish very much of anything without the assistance of the archivists and research staff at the University of Oklahoma's Western History Collection; the Archival Research Room in the Washington, D.C. branch of the National Archives; the Oklahoma Historical Society; the Beinecke Library; the Kansas Historical Society; and the interlibrary loan office at the University of Massachusetts–Amherst.

I am at a loss when it comes to thanking Mark Simpson-Vos for shepherding this book through the publication process. He seemed to appear out of nowhere, and suddenly there was a book manuscript taking shape on my desk. I suspect that he might have psychic powers. Every time I was certain that I could not write another sentence, an encouraging e-mail from Mark appeared in my in-box. I am so grateful to Mark, Zachary Read, Jay Mazzocchi, Beth Lassiter, and everyone else at the University of North Carolina Press. The two anonymous readers of my manuscript offered insightful and useful comments, questions, and suggestions for revisions. I thank them for their thoughtful engagement with my work.

As joyous as I am to see this book in print, I am sad that Nancy Grant and Claudia Tate are not here to share this moment with me. I would have liked to thank them and tell them how glad I am to have known them. They were brilliant scholars, teachers, and mentors. And they are missed.

It is not an overstatement to say that this book would not exist were it not for the love, support, and help of my family. My parents instilled in me a profound appreciation for both intellectual creativity and academic rigor. I hope my mother sees this book as a loving tribute to my grandfather Eugene McIntosh. My sisters and brothers have provided crucial encouragement, inspiration, distraction, entertainment, and love. I am very grateful to my brother the Honorable Peter Krauthamer and Tanya Chutkan for their hospitality during my research trips to Washington, D.C.

Until recently, my children have not known a time when I was not working on this project. They routinely asked, "Have you sent your book to your editor yet?" I am eternally grateful to Max and Zora for their patience and also for the inspiration I derived from their impatience.

I trust that Noah Elkin knows how truly grateful I am for all that he has done.

Black Slaves, Indian Masters

Introduction

In the summer of 1937, nearly seventy-one years after her emancipation from slavery, Kiziah Love welcomed a field-worker from the Oklahoma office of the Federal Writers' Project into her home. Love was one of approximately 7,000 black people who had been enslaved and emancipated by a Native American master.[1] Benjamin Franklin Colbert, a Choctaw slaveholder and cotton planter, owned Kiziah Love, her mother, and at least twenty-four other black people as slaves in Indian Territory, the place we now know as Oklahoma. Ninety-three years old, blind and bedridden, Love assured her guest that her memory remained sharp and that she could recall a great deal about her life in slavery. Jessie R. Ervin, one of the eight writers assigned to the Oklahoma Slave Narrative Project, interviewed Love, using the standard list of questions given to interviewers and also adhering to the guidelines for rendering the subject's account in so-called black dialect. After speaking with Love about her work, religion, health, and family life during slavery, Ervin concluded the interview with questions about emancipation. Love said that, yes, she "was glad to be free." She continued, "What did I do and say? Well, I jest clapped my hands together and said, 'Thank God Almighty, I'se free at last!'" Almost as an afterthought, Love added: "I live on the forty acres that the government give me."[2]

Kiziah Love's recollections evoke a history of slavery and emancipation that is simultaneously familiar and unexpected. This book is a study of slavery, emancipation, and freedom in the Choctaw and Chickasaw Indian Nations that traces the intricate points of connections between the Indian nations and the United States. The history of slavery in the Indian nations is very much a part of southern history and U.S. history. To be sure, we cannot fully understand the meanings and consequences of slavery, emancipation, and citizenship in the Indian nations without paying attention to the complicated history of Indian sovereignty. Kiziah Love's description of emancipation as a moment of jubilee and deliverance reflected the universal sentiment of black people across the United States and throughout the African Diaspora. But her passing mention of receiving the fabled "forty acres" of land from the government gives one pause by calling attention to the distinctiveness of black people's history of slavery, emancipation, and citizenship in Indian Territory. Despite a brief wartime flirtation with the notion of granting land to former slaves in coastal Georgia, the U.S. government did not authorize land redistribution to freed slaves. Yet at the end of the nineteenth century, federal efforts to terminate Indian sovereignty entailed appropriating the Indian nations' public domain and allotting the land not only to Indians but also to their former slaves and the descendants of slaves.

Indians, Race, and Slavery

From the late eighteenth century through the end of the U.S. Civil War, Choctaw and Chickasaw men and women held people of African descent in slavery. Like their white southern counterparts, Indians bought, sold, owned, and exploited black people's labor and reproduction for economic and social gain. Choctaws and Chickasaws purchased slaves—men, women, and children—to work on their Mississippi farms and plantations and to serve in their homes. Slaveholders and those who did not own slaves embraced a racial ideology that affirmed black people's inherent difference and inferiority and thus justified their enslavement. Whether they owned only a few slaves, rented a slave for seasonal labor, or operated a large plantation with hundreds of slaves, Choctaws and Chickasaws understood that slavery allowed for the accumulation of personal wealth. Enslaved people cleared and plowed fields, hauled logs, drained swamps, planted and harvested crops, drove wagons, built homes, wove fabric, sewed clothes, cooked meals, and cared for Indian children, all for their masters' benefit. Choctaws and Chickasaws purchased slaves in private transactions with other slaveholders and at public venues in cities such as New Orleans, conducting their business with white traders and slaveholders as well as with other Indians. While most Choctaw and Chickasaw slaveholders owned only a few slaves, the majority of enslaved people were owned by a small contingent of wealthy and socially and politically influential men. Clustered in neighborhoods dominated by large farms and plantations, enslaved people worked to create durable and meaningful family and community ties with each other. They eluded their masters' surveillance, circumvented laws and customs governing their speech and mobility, and sometimes successfully liberated themselves by running away.

Many historians who have written about the nineteenth-century Choctaws and Chickasaws have noted the existence of chattel slavery and simply linked it to Indians' increased participation in the early nineteenth-century American market economy. Discussions of slavery have not concentrated on enslaved people's lives or their relationships with their Indian masters but instead have focused on the nature of Indians' relationship to the American market economy.

In the early decades of the nineteenth century, Euro-American settlement surged across the Deep South, pressing up against the Choctaw and Chickasaw peoples, who had long laid claim to millions of acres stretching from present-day Alabama to the Mississippi River. While the United States recognized Indians' right to the soil based on their prior occupancy, the federal government was nonetheless wholly committed to extinguishing Indian land claims. In the early decades of the nineteenth century, federal officials pursued measures designed to alter and eradicate Indians' social and economic practices, especially their land-use patterns. Framed as "civilization" policies, lawmakers and reformers imagined they might remake Indian people and assimilate them into the American mainstream. One key component of assimilation policies entailed dispatching Christian missionaries to Indian communities. Missionaries often regarded themselves as benevolent friends to Indians and sought to instruct them in the ways of Euro-American society. U.S. policy pressed Indians to abandon hunting and take up settled agriculture, a shift that most officials hoped would lead Indians to cede their uncultivated land to the United States. To this end, the federal government also regulated trade with Indians, establishing trading factories that supplied Indians with credit and manufactured items.

Indians' gradual shift away from hunting, a largely collective enterprise, and toward more individually oriented agricultural pursuits was coeval with their changing understandings of property. Increasingly, individuals accumulated goods, whether crops or manufactures, rather than looking to traditional headmen to distribute food and other items. To the extent that historians have recognized the rise of chattel slavery among the Choctaws and Chickasaws during this period, the issue has been explained simply in terms of Indians' heightened individualistic engagement in market-oriented activities. Decades ago, historian Richard White simply attributed slavery to the rise of an economically and politically powerful class of "rich mixed-blood planters." White characterized their willingness to embrace commercial agriculture as an ill-advised turn away from indigenous values and practices that resulted in the destruction of Choctaw culture and institutions and left the Choctaw people impoverished, dispossessed, and dependent.[3]

Much of the current literature on southern Indians' adoption of market-oriented endeavors, such as commercial farming and raising livestock, has dispensed with the notion of dependency. So, too, have many scholars moved away from an uncritical equation of biology, ancestry, "blood," or racial identity with specific and supposedly innate traits, viewpoints, and behaviors.[4] Rather, a new generation of ethnohistorians has argued for seeing these economic shifts through an optic of continuity. That is, scholars have argued that rather than treating the rise of animal husbandry and cotton agriculture among the Choctaws and Chickasaws exclusively as evidence of the crushing weight of the American market on indigenous cultures, we should consider these changes from the vantage of Indians. We should investigate the meanings and values that Indians attributed to their new activities. This attention to the staying power of indigenous beliefs as enacted in Native peoples' daily lives makes an important argument for appreciating the complexity and nuance of southern Indians' engagements with and responses to U.S. policies and institutions. Studies that foreground Native people's ideas and actions offer an important analytical counterbalance to those that only consider the weight of external economic and political forces upon Indian communities.

In this vein, ethnohistorians have treated slavery principally as a mechanism that facilitated cultural continuities without giving serious consideration to the dramatic changes necessarily embedded in the purchase and ownership of black people as property. In such analyses, scholars argue that acquiring slaves allowed Indian men to refrain from fieldwork—historically the province of Native women. Men could pursue new market-oriented endeavors, such as the cultivation of commodity crops like corn and cotton, but remain true to the old ways in which men did not play central roles in agriculture.

Yet analyses that either emphasize the demise of indigenous culture and the concomitant rise of Indians' dependency on the market or foreground the durability of indigenous beliefs and adaptability of indigenous practices do not adequately account for the emergence of chattel slavery within Choctaw and Chickasaw communities. In both cases, slavery is presented as an inevitable and unremarkable outcome of Indians' participation in the American market. Buying and selling enslaved people, however, was not like other forms of property accumulation and circulation but marked a dramatic shift in Choctaw and Chickasaw ideas and practices of property, race, and gender.

Arguments that frame slavery principally as a strategy for sustaining indigenous ideals and practices fall short if we pay careful attention to the relations of power embedded in slavery. Slavery in the Choctaw and Chickasaw Nations rested on intersecting racial and gender ideologies that justified the enslavement and exploitation of black men's and women's bodies, labor, and reproduction. By the end of the eighteenth century, Choctaw and Chickasaw slaveholders, as well as those who did not own slaves, came to embrace those elements of Euro-American racial ideologies that identified people of African descent as an inherently and permanently inferior group. Among Choctaws and Chickasaws, racial identification and status—slave or free—were largely synonymous. Racial chattel slavery in the antebellum Indian nations was not simply a more-extreme variant of older indigenous practices of holding war captives as subordinates and servants. War captives—Indians captured by other Indians—were held in servitude only temporarily and were ultimately executed or incorporated into their captors' communities. Black slaves, by contrast, were held in lifelong and hereditary bondage. Racial identity and status passed from mother to child.

Indigenous concepts of gender necessarily changed as both Indian men and women owned male and female slaves and exploited the agricultural labor of both black men and women. If slaveholding allowed Choctaw and Chickasaw men to abstain from agricultural labor and preserve a sense of their traditional gender roles, what did that mean for Indian women who were displaced from fieldwork by black people? How did the presence of black *men* as agricultural workers inform Indian men's and women's definitions of their gender roles? What did these shifts in gender and labor patterns among elite Indians mean for those Choctaw and Chickasaw women and men who did not own slaves? Unfortunately, the archives are not especially cooperative when it comes to answering these questions. Documents produced by slaveholders and other Indians make reference to some of these issues of race, gender, labor, and slavery but do not answer all of these questions. Still, simply by raising the question, by considering the meanings and consequences of racial and gender ideologies not only for enslaved black people but also for the Indians who owned them, we can better understand the complexity of race and slavery in the antebellum South.

Choctaw and Chickasaw slaveholders clearly embraced a racial and gender ideology of black inferiority that informed their relationships with each other, with their slaves, and also with nonslaveholding Indians. Their adoption of this racial ideology in some ways aligned their social and economic interests with those of their white neighbors. Both Indian and white slaveholders sought to maintain a social and economic order premised on the commodification and degradation of black people's bodies and labor. But this does not mean that Indians either accepted Euro-Americans' ideology of white superiority or saw their interests as identical to those of white southerners.

Indian Removal, Sectional Crisis, and the Civil War

Until the 1830s, an estimated 15,000 Choctaws and some 3,000 to 4,000 Chickasaws claimed millions of acres of land across the Black Belt prairie of northern and central (present-day) Mississippi and western Alabama. Choctaws and Chickasaws, moreover, organized and governed themselves as entities mostly apart from either the state or federal governments. U.S. laws recognized the boundaries of Indians' territory and prohibited U.S. citizens from violating those boundaries. Yet a wide range of observers from the United States objected to Native peoples' self-governance and also charged that Choctaws and Chickasaws claimed an excess of land to the detriment of white Americans. That the Choctaw and Chickasaw peoples each held their land in common as public domain fueled white Americans' frustration and hostility. In 1810, for example, some 450 white squatters on Chickasaw land refused to relocate, protesting to Congress that the "heathan" Indians left their "fine fertile countrys lying uncultivated."[5] Many federal policy makers, too, cast Indians in ethnocentric and racist terms, challenging their right to self-governance and their land claims in the South.

That some Choctaws and Chickasaws owned slaves and operated plantations did not serve as an adequate defense against federal pressures to give up their southern lands. Indeed, in some instances, white observers charged that Indians failed at the task of slaveholding because they were too lenient with their slaves and did not adequately exploit or abuse their slaves. For example, one observer from the early 1840s wrote: "The full-blood Indian rarely works himself and but few of them make their slaves work. A slave among wild Indians is almost as free as his owner."[6] Such pronouncements, however, may tell us how Euro-Americans characterized Indians in racial terms that justified U.S. domination, but they do not reveal much about the lives of enslaved people owned by Indians.

It is a cruel irony in Native American history that Indian people's adoption and adaptation of Euro-American institutions ultimately did little to shield them from U.S. domination. Choctaws' and Chickasaws' embrace of chattel slavery and the attendant racial ideology of black inferiority, for example, did not stem the tide of white intruders—illegal squatters—on their Mississippi lands. Similarly, Choctaw and Chickasaw leaders' respective efforts to model their systems of governance on U.S. institutions did not protect their people or land from federal assault.

In the early nineteenth century, Choctaw villages were located around the watersheds of the Tombigbee, Pearl, Big Black, Chickasawhay, and Pascagoula Rivers in east-central Mississippi. The Chickasaws lived mainly to the north of the Choctaws, in villages spread out over the upland prairies in northeastern Mississippi and western Alabama. In 1708 Thomas Nairne, a British diplomat and trader from the Carolina colony, praised the Choctaw and Chickasaw region in romantic terms as "pleasant open forests of oak chesnuts [*sic*] and hickery so intermixt with savannas as if it were a made landscape."[7] Choctaws and Chickasaws identified themselves as separate peoples; indeed, for a long time under the seventeenth- and eighteenth-century British, French, and Spanish colonial regimes, Choctaw and Chickasaw warriors regarded each other as bitter enemies. Until the 1820s, governance among both the Choctaws and Chickasaws was local, with headmen, or chiefs, presiding over the groups of villages that comprised local chiefdoms. One account from 1732 described the Choctaws as consisting of "so many little republics."[8] Largely in response to the pressures and demands of the U.S. federal government, Choctaws and Chickasaws gradually reorganized their systems of governance.

Historians James Taylor Carson and Greg O'Brien chart the consolidation of the Choctaw chiefdoms and the emergence of a self-identified "nation" in the 1820s. While the Chickasaws have not been the subject of similarly focused studies, historians Wendy St. Jean and James R. Atkinson have written studies that offer broad coverage of eighteenth-century and early nineteenth-century Chickasaw political and diplomatic history.[9] They, too, locate the emergence of a single Chickasaw polity in the early decades of the nineteenth century. Both the Choctaws and Chickasaws came to identify themselves as single entities or "nations" by the 1820s. Leaders of the Choctaws' three divisions came together in the late summer of 1826 to establish a single constitutional government. In 1828 David Folsom, a distinguished Choctaw warrior and leader, declared: "Our nation . . . is rising."[10] By the early 1820s, the Chickasaws' system of governance by hereditary leaders, called minkos (sometimes written as "mingos"), underwent similar changes. In 1822 the U.S. agent responsible for overseeing affairs with the Chickasaws reported that they had built a "house for a National purpose."[11]

Even as Choctaw and Chickasaw leaders adopted largely centralized government structures with bicameral legislatures, state and federal lawmakers continued their assault on southern Indian governments. Andrew Jackson's election to the presidency in 1829 ushered in a new era of federal Indian policy that favored a brutal campaign of dispossession and forced removal over assimilation and gradual land cession. In the spring of 1830, Congress approved an Indian removal bill that affirmed a federal policy of compulsory relocation. In the autumn of 1830, Choctaw leaders signed the Treaty of Dancing Rabbit Creek, which ceded the Choctaw people's Mississippi land to the United States in exchange for land west of the Mississippi River in Indian Territory. Likewise, Chickasaw leaders ceded their remaining territory east of the Mississippi River to the United States under the 1832 Treaty of Pontotoc Creek.

The federal government's expulsion of the Choctaw, Chickasaw, Cherokee, and Creek Nations opened the door to the rapid growth of plantation slavery across the Deep South. But Indian removal also pushed chattel slavery westward, setting the stage for future conflicts over the expansion of slavery into western territories and states. The histories of chattel slavery and Indian removal intersect and overlap in complicated and often painful ways. In many respects, considering these histories together and paying attention to the complex dynamics of power and brute force that underlay both slavery and removal allows for a more nuanced understanding of the antebellum South. Recognizing the presence and participation of Native actors, communities, and nations in southern slavery, for example, challenges images of the South as an exclusively white-dominated space. Yet delving into the history of black slavery and Indian removal yields moments that illuminate the fundamental ways in which the history of slavery defies scholarly logic and remains unimaginable. For example, the military personnel responsible for removing parties of Choctaws, Chickasaws, Cherokees, and Creeks to Indian Territory routinely debated whether or not enslaved people should be counted as people or property for the purposes of allocating blankets and food.

Much of the history of federal Indian policy during the era of Indian removal has been well told by other scholars and is not discussed in depth in this work. It is, however, important to note the specific consequences of removal policies for the Choctaws and Chickasaws. From the 1830s until 1855, the Choctaws and Chickasaws were compelled to stand as a single nation under one government and legal code, including the laws governing slaves and slavery. President Andrew Jackson and an array of bureaucrats and military officials pressed for this unification during and after the negotiations of the Choctaw and Chickasaw removal treaties. An item in an Arkansas newspaper characterized the views of those who supported unification as follows: "The two nations, from contiguity and intermarriage, have become so closely identified in language, in habits, in manners, and in customs, that they could not well live apart from each other."[12] Choctaws and Chickasaws did share mutually intelligible Muskogean languages, and some scholars argue that their respective origin myths tell of common progenitors. Government officials, however, characterized the merger as one that would promote the "civilization" of two peoples who seemed well poised to adopt American social and economic values. According to two officials, the Choctaws and Chickasaws had the potential to become "one of the strongest, wealthiest and most respectable communities of aborigines on the continent of America with the means in their own hands of soon becoming civilized, educated, independent American citizens."[13]

Choctaw and Chickasaw leadership initially opposed unification. Chickasaw leaders declared their desire to preserve the independence of "our Nation and our names" and briefly contemplated negotiating with Mexican authorities for land.[14] Ultimately, an 1837 treaty unified the two nations. It established a Chickasaw district on the western edge of the Choctaw Nation in Indian Territory and guaranteed Chickasaw representation in the National Council.[15] In 1855 another treaty formally separated the nations, and the Chickasaws then reestablished their own government and legal code, including slave laws.

For the black people held in bondage by Choctaw and Chickasaw masters, the merging and separating of Choctaw and Chickasaw governments had little immediate consequence. Enslaved people lived under laws and customs that sought to control their reproduction, labor, mobility, and speech. To the extent that legal codes and social norms were documented, there appears to be little difference among Choctaws' and Chickasaws' views and expectations of enslaved people. While Choctaw and Chickasaw political history is not at the center of this study, it remains a relevant topic of discussion in the context of slavery.

Indians were physically removed from the Deep South, but they were never isolated or distant from the prevailing debates and concerns over the future of southern slavery. Through the 1840s and 1850s, the mounting sectional crisis over slavery in the United States extended to Indian Territory and the Choctaw and Chickasaw Nations in a number of ways. Indeed, the 1854 Kansas-Nebraska Act effectively delivered the U.S. sectional crisis to the Indian nations' doorstep. The creation of the Kansas Territory directly north of Indian Territory entailed stripping Native peoples in Kansas of their land and relocating them to Indian Territory. Moreover, the bloody conflicts among proslavery and free-soil settlers in Kansas greatly alarmed Choctaw and Chickasaw leaders, who worried that Indian Territory might become the next battleground for white mercenaries and expansionists.

Disputes among Indian and white slaveholders over the U.S. Fugitive Slave Law of 1850 call our attention to both the ways Indians were caught up in U.S. debates over slavery and the ways that enslaved people's resistance sparked some of those controversies. When enslaved people fled their Indian masters by crossing the border between Indian Territory and the United States, they not only challenged their masters' authority but also set off debates among Indian and U.S. lawmakers over the reach of federal authority and the property rights of Indian slaveholders. Indian Territory rarely if ever appears in studies of the U.S. sectional crisis and the fights over slavery's westward expansion. Yet it is clear that Indian Territory, black slaves, and Indian masters were very much on the minds of many Americans, including white proslavery expansionists, free black abolitionists, and federal lawmakers and judges. By the same token, black people and Indians in the Choctaw and Chickasaw Nations acted in ways that informed the tenor and outcome of these prevailing controversies over slavery as they played out within the Indian nations and in U.S.-Indian relations.

The dense web of issues and people linking the Indian nations to the U.S. South during the period of the sectional crisis becomes most evident with the Choctaws' and Chickasaws' 1861 alliance with the Confederacy. Though many Indian leaders debated the implications of severing their ties to the Union, Choctaw and Chickasaw leaders almost universally cast their lot with the Confederacy. When the war ended, Indian leaders, U.S. policy makers, and black men and women in the Choctaw and Chickasaw Nations confronted a new set of questions about the meanings of black freedom and Indian sovereignty.

Black people's history in Indian Territory, especially in the Choctaw and Chickasaw Nations, calls into question aspects of what we assume to know about American slavery and emancipation. For the enslaved men, women, and children in the Choctaw and Chickasaw Nations, the end of the Civil War offered little cause for celebration. The Choctaw and Chickasaw governments, unlike their Cherokee, Creek, and Seminole counterparts, did not abolish slavery at the close of the war. Because the Indian nations existed as autonomous political entities, Union victory did not automatically liberate black people from bondage. Neither the Emancipation Proclamation nor the Thirteenth Amendment to the U.S. Constitution applied to Indian Territory. Only in the course of negotiating a new treaty with the United States during the spring of 1866 did Choctaw and Chickasaw leaders grudgingly consent to acknowledge slavery's demise and affirm the emancipation of slaves in their nations.

Despite having separate governments, the Choctaw and Chickasaw Nations entered a joint treaty with the United States in the spring of 1866. This treaty laid the groundwork for the abolition of slavery in the two nations and outlined the terms of black people's freedom and citizenship in the two nations. The treaty also set the stage for the federal government's late nineteenth-century dismantling of Indian governments and appropriation of Indian lands. Steeped in the language of natural rights, the Choctaw/Chickasaw 1866 treaty mirrored facets of Congressional Reconstruction legislation regarding black people's freedom and rights. The treaty reflected Republicans' efforts to consolidate federal power over the former Confederate states by establishing the primacy of national citizenship in lieu of previous relationships between masters and slaves or states and citizens.[16] This assertion of greater federal authority over sovereign

Indian nations, however, was embedded in a new campaign to eradicate Indian governments and land claims.[17] Yet despite the apparent contradiction between defending black people's freedom and rights and undermining Native people's political and territorial autonomy, both aspects of federal policy emerged from the same set of Reconstruction-era ideologies and visions of the future.

Postemancipation wrangling over the meanings and limits of freedom and the relationship between freedom and citizenship points to the slippery nature of the concept itself. The meanings of freedom were never static, and the rights associated with it emerged from different conditions for different constituencies at any given moment. The work of historians such as Edmund Morgan, Eric Foner, Dylan Penningroth, and Amy Dru Stanley has cautioned us to be mindful of freedom's historically contingent nature.[18] The history of emancipation and freedpeople's citizenship in the sovereign Indian nations casts a new light on Reconstruction-era discussions of freedom and citizenship.

When considering their 1866 treaty and the prospect of extending citizenship to their former slaves, vocal Choctaw and Chickasaw leaders equated race (Indianness) and nation (political autonomy) to galvanize Native peoples' sense of unity and purpose in opposing U.S. colonialism.[19] Former slaves in the Choctaw and Chickasaw Nations also perceived the ways the 1866 treaty had welded their citizenship to the issue of Indian sovereignty. And they, too, engaged ideas about race, nation, and identity as they negotiated with Indian leaders and federal authorities in their efforts to secure their citizenship rights. In this regard, freedpeople in Indian Territory appear not unlike their counterparts in the states: both demanded that the federal government make good on the promises inherent in Reconstruction legislation. This is not to suggest, however, that the freedpeople were uninterested in or opposed to the longevity of Indian sovereignty. Thus they had to balance carefully their cultural and political identification with indigenous peoples against their determination to win out over the Indians who sought to block their citizenship.

Freedpeople and Indians alike had little choice but to assess the nations' domestic issues within the larger context of the federal drive to erode sovereignty and claim indigenous people's land for white American settlers and commercial ventures. Yet when freedpeople negotiated with Indian leaders or inserted themselves into U.S.-Indian affairs, they constantly sidestepped and straddled the categories of race and status that others had attempted to impose upon them for nearly a century. In slavery and freedom, they insisted upon organizing their lives in line with both their particular experiences in the Indian nations and their understandings of conditions and events in the United States.

Federal policy makers linked the issues of black people's freedom and rights in the Choctaw and Chickasaw Nations to the very dissolution of the Indian nations' territorial and political autonomy. Until the close of the nineteenth century, Indian leaders and freedpeople responded in kind. They framed their arguments about black people's rights in the nations and the nation's rights to self-governance in racialized and often racist language.

Historians need not follow their lead. Rather than simply accept the framing of black people's rights and Indian sovereignty as seemingly opposing poles, we might do better to understand the complexity and inconsistency of Reconstruction. So, too, paying closer attention to events and debates over race, citizenship, and governance in Indian Territory reveals Reconstruction's continental scope and again reminds us that the history of emancipation and the subsequent efforts to redefine freedom and citizenship in a postslavery age were never simply matters of black and white. Indeed, as Congress and the U.S. Supreme Court withdrew the federal defense of black people's citizenship rights in the United States, federal policy makers devoted ever more attention to debates over Indian citizenship. Ultimately, black people's status as citizens of the Choctaw and Chickasaw Nations was only fully realized in the moment when the federal government terminated the nations' governments and extended U.S. citizenship over the nations' people, both Indian and black, in the early years of the twentieth century.

One of the central issues addressed by scholars interested in the history of race, slavery, emancipation, and citizenship in Indian Territory is the question of racial self-identification. How did Indians and people of African descent define themselves and each other in terms of race and national belonging? There is an extensive scholarship on the history of race, and much of it owes a great debt to historian Barbara Fields's insistence that we recognize race as a socially and historically constructed set of ideas. Numerous scholars have investigated the history of race and have paid close attention to the dynamic intersections of race, gender and class. Despite heightened attention to the ways in which various constituencies have fashioned the meanings of race in American history, the correlation of African descent with blackness as a self-evident racial category continues to hover in the background. Thus the binaries black/white and slave/free continue to inform but also constrain approaches to the history of slavery, emancipation, and citizenship in the United States. Focusing on black people's lives, including their relationships with Native peoples, allows us to consider the complex meanings and sometimes shifting boundaries of blackness as defined by people of African descent. Black people in the Choctaw and Chickasaw Nations identified themselves in ways that reflected their understandings of the Diasporic condition of racism and slavery as well as the particularities of their personal, familial, and historical experiences among Indian peoples.

Book Overview and Chapter Outline

This book is principally a work in the field of African American history. Its primary aims are to present a detailed history of black people's lives in the Choctaw and Chickasaw Nations and to consider how this material can inform our understandings of the history of black people's enslavement, emancipation, and citizenship. Readers interested in other aspects of this history, such as more-detailed studies of the Choctaw and Chickasaw peoples or works that focus more on the history of U.S. Indian policy, are advised to consult the footnotes for suggested works. There is so much we do not know about black people's lives in the Indian nations, and this work is offered as an effort to present and discuss the extant source material and relevant historiography. As part of ongoing scholarly conversations about race, gender, slavery, and freedom in the Americas, I hope it adds new dimensions and new questions to our understandings of slavery and the transition to freedom in the Indian nations and the United States.

Beginning with the early history of slavery and the lives of the enslaved, chapter 1 focuses on the late eighteenth-century emergence of chattel slavery in Choctaw and Chickasaw communities and enslaved people's lives in the Indians' Mississippi towns. Earlier generations of scholars interested in this topic mainly attempted to chart a clear and causal relationship between Native practices of captivity and subordination and chattel slavery. I take a different approach by highlighting the rupture and differences between captivity and chattel slavery, especially the centrality of a racial ideology that posited black inferiority and established slavery as a lifelong and heritable condition. Paying close attention to the bedrock ideologies of race and gender allows us to recognize the force and violence embedded in chattel slavery.

Even though the first two chapters focus on slavery and the lives of enslaved people, the discussions of race, property, power, and violence also consider the ways Native people were construed as inferior or uncivilized by both land-hungry white southerners and federal policy makers. Thus a brief history of Indian removal is included in the first chapter to highlight Native people's importance to southern history and to illustrate the points of intersection between the histories of slavery and Native dispossession. As Indians were forcibly relocated west of the Mississippi, slavery moved westward with them.

Chapter 2 presents a detailed look at enslaved people's religion and community relations. Early nineteenth-century federal "civilization" programs aimed at southern Indians entailed dispatching Christian missionaries to Indian communities. By the 1810s, the interdenominational American Board of Commissioners for Foreign Missions sponsored Presbyterian and Congregationalist missionaries to the Choctaws and Chickasaws. Northern missionaries eagerly welcomed enslaved Christians into their fold, especially when their efforts to convert Indians faltered. Missionaries struggled mightily with the issue of slavery. While they opposed the institution of bondage, they were hardly advocates of racial equality. They expected black people to work hard and remain subordinate to white people, if not Indians, even in freedom. Fortunately for historians, missionary men and women kept lengthy and detailed records. Missionaries' records—their official and private correspondence—thus offer a wealth of information about enslaved people's lives, though they must be read carefully and critically.

The theme of enslaved people's resistance efforts begins in chapter 2 and is developed in chapter 3. It is discussed in the context of the growing sectional crisis over slavery in the United States. At no point were the Indian nations isolated from people and events in the states, especially in regard to slavery. Enslaved people's resistance in the Choctaw and Chickasaw Nations often raised alarms about their ties to enslaved people in the neighboring states of Texas and Arkansas. It also sparked concern about their relationships with missionaries suspected of abolitionism. While Indians' concerns about enslaved people's unruly behavior were not unfounded, their fears reflected anxieties about both black people's unrest and white Americans' incursions into Indian Territory.

By the 1850s, debates over the territorial expansion of slavery were the most inflammatory topics of the day in the United States, and they often focused on whether or not proslavery Americans should expand into Indian Territory. Thus Choctaw and Chickasaw leaders paid close attention to the Fugitive Slave Law of 1850 and the Kansas-Nebraska Act of 1854. In chapter 3, I consider the ways enslaved people's resistance in Indian Territory reflected their keen awareness of Indian politics and U.S.-Indian relations. This chapter follows the increasingly tense political climate in the Choctaw and Chickasaw Nations and considers the ways leaders framed their conflicts in terms of race, slavery, and ties to U.S. political factions. This chapter ends with a discussion of the Choctaws' and Chickasaws' 1861 alliance with the Confederacy to illuminate the ways Indians understood their defense of slavery as part of a larger campaign to defend their sovereignty.

In the second half of the book, I examine the history of ema
black people's struggles to create meaningful lives in Indian Ter
finally came to an end in the Choctaw and Chickasaw Nations
the two nations entered a joint treaty with the United States. T
moment of emancipation is the main subject of chapter 4. This
lights the violence directed at emancipated black people in the months after
the war's end and considers their strategies for enlisting federal assistance
against recalcitrant slaveholders. The discussion of the Choctaw/Chickasaw
1866 treaty centers on the convoluted provisions for establishing black people's
citizenship in the two Indian nations. While the treaty reflected the interests
and goals of the federal government, its provisions were influenced at least in
part by Choctaw and Chickasaw delegates and their attorneys. Chapter 4 thus
considers the views and aims of both federal policy makers and Indian political leaders as they sought to rebuild their nations in the wake of the Civil War.

Black people struggled for some four decades to secure their status and
rights as citizens in the Choctaw and Chickasaw Nations. This seemingly bi-
zarre fact has fascinated many scholars but has not been explored in depth in
the current historiography. Chapters 4 and 5 follow the debates and conflicts
that arose among freedpeople, Indian leaders, and federal lawmakers over the
issue of black people's citizenship in the Choctaw and Chickasaw Nations.
Rather than chart every twist and turn in this stunningly convoluted history,
chapter 5 highlights black men's efforts to organize their communities and assume a visible and vocal position in the back-and-forth between Indian and
federal lawmakers through the 1870s and 1880s.

Chapter 6, likewise, offers a brief discussion of the federal government's
final push to terminate the Indian nations' governments and land claims. This
chapter does not delve deeply into the history of the Dawes and Curtis Acts,
which authorized the federal appropriation and allotment of Indian lands and
the dissolution of Indian governments. Rather, this chapter focuses on black
people's efforts to negotiate relationships with newly arrived black settlers from
the states as well as with federal and Indian authorities. The book thus ends in
that moment when Kiziah Love and thousands of other former slaves and their
descendants received land allotments—their "forty acres"—from the federal
government.

In the end, this book aims to provide a narrative overview of the history
of black people's slavery, emancipation, and citizenship in the Choctaw and
Chickasaw Nations that is situated in a broader context. The history of slavery, emancipation, and freedom in the Choctaw and Chickasaw Nations is an
inescapable and necessary piece of a larger history of American slavery and

_dom. Slavery and freedom, especially in the Deep South, were never simply or strictly matters of white over black, and focusing closely on the Choctaw and Chickasaw Nations can allow us to understand both the distinctiveness of this case study and its fundamental connections to the larger context in which it unfolded.

1

Black Slaves, Indian Masters
Race, Gender, and Power in the Deep South

In the early nineteenth century, Choctaw and Chickasaw men and women embraced the idea of acquiring black people as property, equating blackness with lifelong, hereditary, and degraded servitude. First in Mississippi and then after their removal in the 1830s to Indian Territory (now Oklahoma), wealthy and middling Choctaws borrowed, bartered, and paid cash on the barrel to buy enslaved black people from nearby white slave owners, professional slave traders, and each other. Through the antebellum period, growing numbers of Choctaws and Chickasaws calculated their personal wealth by counting the slaves they had purchased.[1]

The practice of owning people of African descent as property—slaves—emerged in large measure from Choctaws' and Chickasaws' heightened participation in the antebellum market economy and, like other market-oriented endeavors taken up by southern Indians, altered social and economic relations within Indian communities and among Indians and their white neighbors. But buying, selling, and owning African-descended people as property was not simply like other market practices that took root in southern Indian nations. Slaveholding, and the associated transactions of profiting from owning and exploiting black people's labor and reproduction, required that Native peoples engage decidedly new meanings of property, race, and gender that had lasting consequences for Indians and African Americans alike. Slaveholding Choctaws and Chickasaws did not blindly adopt and imitate the racial ideology of their Euro-American neighbors in Mississippi but instead crafted and refined their own ideologies of racial identification and differentiation that reflected the particular social, economic, and political conditions of their time and place. Racial categories, which encompassed not only blackness but also conceptions of Indianness and whiteness, were never static but were made and remade from the late eighteenth century through the antebellum era. During this time, Choctaws and Chickasaws engaged new forms of property ownership, personal wealth, and shifting gender roles, and also contended with the mounting local and federal assaults on Indian sovereignty and land title in the southern states.

CHATTEL SLAVERY DID NOT EMERGE in the Choctaw and Chickasaw Nations until the early years of the nineteenth century, but neither the institution of human bondage nor its bedrock ideology of racial hierarchy materialized out of thin air in Indian communities. Beginning in the late seventeenth century, generations of Choctaw and Chickasaw men and women became well acquainted with the social and economic dynamics of the European colonial slave societies taking shape around them. This chapter begins with an overview of indigenous practices of unfreedom and captivity and Indian enslavement in the French and English colonies. The aim is not to suggest a clear and unbroken trajectory from captivity to slavery. Nor is the intention to imply that antebellum chattel slavery in the Choctaw and Chickasaw Nations was a largely benign variation of older, indigenous forms of unfreedom. Rather, the brief discussion of indigenous captivity and Indians' own enslavement by European colonists is meant to suggest a historical narrative that recognizes a meaningful and shifting Native presence in the long history of American chattel slavery.

Through the first quarter of the century, Choctaws and Chickasaws gained a familiarity with slavery in the French and British colonies that was intimate and brutal. By the time the French built their posts at Biloxi and Mobile at the turn of the seventeenth century, English traders from Carolina had already made their way along Cherokee and Creek paths to the Tombigbee River and the Chickasaw villages hundreds of miles west of the Eastern Seaboard. European colonial authorities pursued trade alliances with southern Indians as part of an imperial strategy to advance their own business interests while constraining their European rivals' territorial and commercial expansion. Late seventeenth-century and early eighteenth-century English alliances with the Chickasaws established Chickasaw male warriors as "commercial slave traders," and within a few decades, Chickasaws earned the lasting reputation of being fearsome and superior warriors.[2] Starting in 1702, French authorities, seeking to thwart the expansion of British-Indian trade farther into the lower Mississippi valley, negotiated alliances with Choctaws that included provisions for the purchase of Indian slaves.

British and French traders obtained Indian slaves by tapping into existing indigenous practices of raiding and captive taking. Choctaws and Chickasaws had long seized male and female captives during wartime as a means of obtaining spiritual and physical replacements for loved ones lost in war.[3] Like other Native peoples, such as the Cherokees, Choctaws and Chickasaws usually put male captives to death after a period of ritualized torture. On one occasion in 1752, for example, Choctaws whipped a captive Chickasaw warrior for three days and planned on burning him to death on the fourth day, but he escaped. In the same year, Chickasaws tortured two captive Choctaw warriors "in a most barbarous Manner, takeing of their Scalps and cutting out their Bowels before they were dead."[4] Captive women and children were spared such a bloody fate and instead were adopted into their captor's kin group to bolster the population and symbolically replace those who had been killed in war. Because clan membership and descent followed the female line, Choctaw and Chickasaw women, especially those who had lost kin in war, bore the responsibility of determining captives' fate. They decided whether a man should be spared from execution and which women and children should be adopted as kin or held as subordinates or servants.

Armed and compensated by colonial authorities, Indian warriors in the lower Mississippi valley increasingly sought captives not to avenge the loss of kin but to gain valuable objects—the captives themselves—that could be exchanged for European manufactures such as duffels, guns, metal wares, liquor, and jewelry.[5] Through much of the eighteenth century, European traders supplied these goods to Choctaw and Chickasaw headmen, local leaders who wielded political and spiritual power in their communities. Ethnohistorians have shown that in the Southeast, Indian headmen adapted long-standing indigenous diplomatic protocols to accommodate trade and military alliances with colonial partners. Powerful headmen had long achieved their status, established their spiritual power, gained the respect of their communities, and confirmed their authority through demonstrated success as hunters and warriors. Leaders bore the responsibility of distributing resources—the bounty of a deer hunt and also communal food crops—and thus demonstrated their power through the circulation of goods rather than their accumulation. In the eighteenth century, Choctaw and Chickasaw headmen, like their Creek and Cherokee counterparts, received trade goods from colonial allies and oversaw their distribution to warriors, their families, and the other members of the community. From the vantage of Native peoples, foreigners and the goods they bore possessed spiritual power, including the potential for chaos. Local leaders thus sought to rein in and access that power through their diplomatic relationships with outsiders and also through the circulation of exotic European goods among their people.[6]

British officials in Carolina armed and rewarded Chickasaw and Creek war parties for destroying Choctaw settlements and turning over Choctaw captives for enslavement in the British colonies. In 1708 Carolina trader and diplomat Thomas Nairne found that the Chickasaws enjoyed "the Greatest Ease" taking enemy captives to "get a Booty" from the British.[7] French authorities, in turn, compensated Choctaws for the Indian captives they seized. In 1721, for example, during a period of warfare between Choctaw and Chickasaw settlements, Louisiana authorities sought "to incite [Choctaw warriors] to do well" by paying handsomely for every Chickasaw scalp and each of "the slaves that they bring in."[8] Chickasaw and Choctaw warriors targeted any number of indigenous peoples within an approximately 200-mile radius of their settlements in northeastern and central-eastern Mississippi. These slaving expeditions wreaked havoc on indigenous communities, disrupting local economic and demographic stability and precipitating lasting changes in the organization of local and regional populations.[9] Colonial intrusions also dramatically altered Indians' motives for taking captives and the consequences of capture.

Once in the hands of British traders, Indian captives, mainly women, were taken to Charleston and sold to planters who enslaved them alongside African women and men on South Carolina and Barbados rice and sugar plantations. The predominance of Indian women among the captives sold to British planters is suggested in the inventory of the slaves owned in 1715 by John Wright: fifteen black men and seventeen women, of whom thirteen were identified as Indians.[10] A pamphlet promoting settlement in South Carolina instructed Anglo-American men of modest means to purchase "a good *Negro* man and a good *Indian* woman." Wealthier colonists were directed to acquire African men, along with "Fifteen *Indian* women to work in the Field" and another "Three *Indian* Women as Cooks" and to attend to "Household-Business."[11] According to historian Alan Gallay, an estimated 24,000 to 51,000 Indians, including approximately 2,000 Choctaws, were sold into the British slave trade between 1670 and 1715. During this period, Carolina enjoyed a lively trade in Indian slaves, as the number of the colony's exported Indian slaves exceeded the number of its imported African slaves.[12]

Beginning in the 1720s, the colonial trade in Indian captives/slaves quickly gave way to a thriving transatlantic trade in enslaved Africans. The number of enslaved Africans imported to North America swelled in the middle of the eighteenth century, with close to 19,000 Africans enslaved in Louisiana by 1769 and nearly 40,000 in South Carolina by 1750. The extensive transatlantic and domestic importation of black slaves into the lower Mississippi valley meant that the black population expanded alongside the burgeoning white population. Indeed, like South Carolina, Mississippi had a black majority that remained in place well into the nineteenth century.[13]

With this dramatic expansion of the enslaved African population, Choctaws' and Chickasaws' roles in the context of colonial slavery shifted. Increasingly, enslaved Indians, and also the children born to enslaved Indian and African unions, were described in racial terms of blackness, a reflection of the hardening association of blackness and enslavement.[14] No longer desired as slaves by colonial planters, Indians were instead often pressed into service as slave catchers, policing both the territorial divide between the colonies and Indian country and the ever-more-rigid distinctions of race and status that defined colonial slave societies. Hoping to preclude any concerted acts of resistance or rebellion among Africans and Indians, Carolina and Louisiana lawmakers routinely demanded that their Indian allies catch and surrender runaway African slaves, often including this requirement into their treaties and diplomatic agreements with southern Native peoples. In 1726 French officials urged Louisiana's lawmakers to "take prompt and sweeping action against runaway [African] slaves" by employing "neighborhood Indians" to capture them.[15] Not long after England gained control of the French territory east of the Mississippi River, Choctaws and Chickasaws received the following directive at a 1765 assembly with the English governor of the newly designated West Florida: "We farther Expect you will agree to bring in any Negroes who may desert their Masters Service, for which a proper reward will be allowed to the Person who Shall execute this Service."[16]

Though Indians generally had little choice but to follow French and British authorities' demands that they capture and return fugitive slaves, they were never simply hapless pawns in a colonial game of dividing and conquering subjugated peoples.[17] To the contrary, many southern Indians routinely discerned opportunities to pursue their own interests while making good on their commitments to their colonial allies.[18] This is well illustrated by Choctaw warriors' tactical responses to the 1729 Natchez attack on Fort Rosalie, a French outpost along the eastern banks of the Mississippi River just north of New Orleans. In the winter of 1729, Natchez Indians in Louisiana, distressed by the spread of disease and alcohol that too often accompanied the expansion of French settlement and had diminished the Natchez population by half since the arrival of the French, attacked the nearby French settlers at Fort Rosalie. The raiding parties killed about 240 French men, women, and children and seized another fifty French women, along with approximately 300 enslaved Africans. French commanders of the besieged fort reported that the Natchez warriors "did no harm to the negroes, having them feast on the cattle of the French, intending to go and sell them later to the English of Carolina."[19] Three African captives who escaped from the Natchez corroborated this account, informing French authorities that their captors had intended to deliver them to the English-allied Chickasaws for sale to Carolina slave traders.[20]

Not long after the attack, French authorities dispatched their Choctaw allies to retaliate against the Natchez by sacking their villages and retrieving the African captives. Like the Natchez, Choctaw warriors calculated the Africans' value in the context of colonial slavery. They assessed their own ability to use the recovered captives to tip the balance of power in their trade and diplomatic relations with the French. Choctaw leaders thus held out for favorable ransoms before handing over the recaptured Africans. One Choctaw leader, for example, informed the French that he would not "return the negroes who had been captured from the Natchez" unless the French supplied him with goods "at the English prices." Alibamon Mingo, a prominent Choctaw leader of the Chickasawhay towns—the southernmost of the principal Choctaw divisions and one that had been battered by Chickasaw raiders—stood firm when demanding compensation. He maintained that his warriors would only relinquish the Africans after he had received "4 pieces of limburg cloth, besides a coat, a gun, a white blanket" and many more items that the French calculated as "goods in proportion to their worth for each negro."[21] Caught up in the web of geopolitical alliances and enmities that linked Choctaws and Chickasaws to the French and British colonies, enslaved African women and men became valuable objects of exchange in Choctaw and Chickasaw trade and diplomatic relations with colonial authorities.

Records of the Choctaw headmen's negotiations with the French suggest that their reasons for holding on to the African captives went beyond simply improving their bargaining position and point to the complex genesis of chattel slavery among southern Indians. Some Choctaws retained the African captives to use as servants in their own villages. One Choctaw leader, "little chief of the Yellow Canes," indicated that he intended to hold on to his captives "for the purpose of serving his warriors." As late as April 1730, French authorities learned that Choctaw warriors "had carried away a number of negroes to their country."[22] Notably, Choctaw warriors retained African men and not women to be their servants, which was a change from the previous custom in Indian raiding and captive taking. The African men held by Choctaw warriors endured physical hardships and violence that rivaled the onerous conditions of enslavement under French masters. In 1731 three African men under the command of Alibamon Mingo sought out the French authorities while en route to Mobile. The men asked to be reclaimed by the French because, they explained, "The Indians make us carry some packages, which exhausts us, mistreat us much, and have taken from us our clothing." The officer who spoke with the three men noted that one "had a tomahawk wound on the head which went as far as the bone."[23]

Any Choctaw deliberations that informed the decision to spare the lives of these male captives are lost to the historical record, but the captives' indisputable subordination to Choctaw warriors suggests a changing conception of servitude. Not only were male captives kept alive and pressed into servitude, but Choctaw men rather than women, as had once been the custom, appear to have made the decision to spare the captives' lives and retain them as subordinate laborers.[24] This was certainly not the first time southern Indians had spared the lives of male captives. But considering this instance in tandem with Choctaw leaders' insistent negotiations with the French over the price of their African captives suggests the germination of new ideas about servitude and market practices among the Choctaws.[25] Choctaws' and Chickasaws' eighteenth-century interests in chattel slavery were refracted through their trade and diplomatic relations with the colonies, and they capitalized on Euro-Americans' flowering commodification of black bodies as a strategy for advancing their own trade and diplomatic interests.

Through much of the eighteenth century, Choctaw and Chickasaw men inserted themselves directly into the business of chattel slavery, working not only as slave catchers but also as traders in early iterations of the domestic slave trade, shuttling slaves between colonial entrepôts from New Orleans to Charleston. One Carolina master, for example, purchased an African woman from a Chickasaw trader and described her as speaking "good English, Chickasaw, and perhaps French, the Chickasaws having taken her from the French Settlements on the Mississippi," suggesting the trajectory of the woman's enslavement in colonial and Native hands.[26] Southern Indians need not have embraced the emerging colonial racial ideology about the inferiority of blackness to have appreciated both enslaved Africans' market value to colonists and the ways they might profit from acquiring and exchanging this embodied currency so highly valued by colonial traders and slaveholders.

It is impossible to pinpoint the exact moment when Choctaw and Chickasaw men and women began thinking about themselves as potential slaveholders and Africans and African Americans as people they could own as property. It is clear, however, that by the turn of the eighteenth century, Choctaws and Chickasaws were less inclined to regard enslaved Africans and African Americans primarily as objects of negotiation in transactions with Euro-Americans and more likely to consider them as property to be accumulated, sold, and exploited for individual prosperity. This shift toward buying, selling, and exploiting black people's bodies and labor for material gain accompanied broader, ongoing changes in the ways southern Indians acquired and valued goods.

From the middle of the eighteenth century, especially after the French departure from the region in 1763, through the period of the American Revolution, licensed and unlicensed British traders poured into southern Indian villages, bypassing established protocol that routed trade and diplomacy through local headmen. Traders instead conducted business directly with individual hunters and others who had goods and services to offer for exchange. The gradual erosion of the headmen's role as the conduit of trade goods and the wider availability of European items sapped foreign goods of their supernatural power. Southern Indians, both men and women, acquired ever more merchandise on their own rather than relying on headmen to orchestrate its circulation, and Indians more than ever before valued their possessions as personal property and not communal resources. Indeed, as historian Clauio Saunt has shown, Indians started buying and using locks during this period to ensure the exclusivity of their property.[27]

While eighteenth-century imperial rivals had courted Indian hunters and warriors as crucial trading partners and military allies, the U.S. government regarded Indian men and women as potentially volatile subjects who needed to be brought under control.[28] Almost immediately after the Revolution, federal policy makers, looking to strengthen the United States' hold on the distant reaches of the Deep South, bore down heavily on Choctaws and Chickasaws, pressing them to give up hunting and trading in deerskins, along with their communal hunting grounds, in favor of commercial agriculture and individual ownership of private property. Government officials aimed to "civilize" or assimilate Native peoples by forcibly channeling them farther into the market economy and transforming their material conditions.

Beginning in 1785, the federal government developed and pursued an Indian policy largely engineered by Henry Knox, the secretary of war under George Washington, that set forth two interrelated goals: peaceful land acquisition and programs to "civilize" and assimilate Indians. His policies, which flowered during Thomas Jefferson's presidency, laid much of the foundation for the future of nineteenth-century U.S. Indian policy.[29] Knox conceded that the United States was morally bound to recognize Indians' rights to the soil based on their prior occupancy, but he also argued that their uncivilized use of the land warranted direct intervention. Consequently, officials devised plans that aimed to consolidate the United States' hold on the remote Deep South, a region inhabited principally by indigenous people and lingering French and Spanish settlers, by acquiring Indian lands and repopulating the area with people described by one official as "real Americans."[30] Like the backcountry squatters who illegally moved onto Indian lands, American policy makers contended that Indian nations claimed an excess of land that they failed to use appropriately, devoting too much time and space to hunting and not enough to farming. U.S. Indian policy, consequently, aimed to secure land cessions from Indians by pushing them to adopt the social and economic practices of American yeomen farmers, believing that as Indians abandoned the deer hunt, they would also abandon their hunting grounds and cede that land to the United States.[31]

It was not simply Indians' choice of economic activities—hunting and subsistence farming—but also how they organized and divided their work that attracted policy makers' attention. As among other southern Native peoples, Choctaw and Chickasaw women bore the primary responsibility for agricultural labor, which included growing food crops; gathering nuts, berries, and tubers; making salt; and catching fish. Additionally, they accompanied Native men during the hunting season, building winter camps, preserving meat, and preparing deerskins for trade in the Euro-American market. The scope of women's labor and its fundamental importance to Native economic and social relations led many Euro-American observers to assert that Indian women were drudges or beasts of burden.[32] Although nineteenth-century writers employed the imagery and language of oppression and even slavery to describe Native women's work, Indian women were not necessarily depicted as *naturally* inferior and defeminized by virtue of their race and thus were not seen as inherently suited for the backbreaking physical labor and exploitation of chattel slavery as black women were.

Early American policy makers and reformers, drawing on Enlightenment ideas about mankind's potential for progress, envisioned Indians—unlike Africans and their American-born descendants—as one day moving closer to white Americans on the higher rungs of civilization.[33] Yet if Native women labored in the fields, white observers reasoned, then Native men could not be engaged in much, if any, productive labor. In the eyes of both elite policy makers and local white populations in the South, Native men who spent their time hunting rather than farming demonstrated their racial inferiority through their backward and stunted gender roles. Anglo-American men, believing in the economic and social values of agrarianism, regarded hunting as a leisure activity and did not apprehend either its place in Native peoples' subsistence and trade economies or its metaphysical meanings in Native cosmologies.

Shortly after the Presbyterian missionary Joseph Bullen arrived in 1799 in Big Town, a Chickasaw village on the upper Tombigbee River near Tupelo, he wrote about the town's inhabitants: "Labour is done by the women, hunting by the men."[34] That Indian men seemed content to remain idle and dependent on Indian women's labor was not the only problem; the men's apparent failure to transform "nature into property" also warranted swift and dramatic federal intervention.[35] Native men's apparently excessive reliance on women's productive labor, coupled with the absence of private property ownership, clashed with the early republican political discourse and ideology that linked the well-ordered patriarchal household to an orderly society governed by laws and reason.

Choctaws and Chickasaws, like Creeks and Cherokees, were matrilineal, tracing descent and kinship through women's male relatives rather than along the paternal line. Maternal uncles, not fathers, assumed leading roles in children's lives, overseeing their nieces' and nephews' upbringing and bestowing upon them access to the status and prestige of their mother's family. Choctaws and Chickasaws, furthermore, often practiced sororal polygamy, with sisters marrying the same man. When federal policy makers and other observers took stock of Indians' land use, labor patterns, and social relations, they saw sexual chaos rooted in the absence of private property and patriarchal authority.[36]

Knox and his contemporaries, most notably Thomas Jefferson, contended that with the appropriate guidance and instruction, Indians could evolve from men of savage hearts to civilized souls. Eventually, Indian men could assimilate into the American economic and social mainstream as independent and productive men, a transformation that would also facilitate the cession of vast expanses of land to the United States. In the spring of 1796, to hasten economic and social changes within Indian communities, Congress established federally licensed trading factories. The plan was to afford Indians access to a variety of material goods and the ability to acquire them on credit in order to cultivate both the desire to own private property and indebtedness. Eventually, the U.S.-backed trading companies would require that Indian nations cede their land as payment for the sizable debts incurred by individuals.[37] During the early decades of the nineteenth century, the federal government dispatched agents and called for missionaries to live among southeastern Indians and train Native men and women in the arts of animal husbandry, settled agriculture, and domestic labor in addition to Christianity.

Faced with a depleted whitetail deer population, an increasing presence of white squatters on their land, and the determination of the United States to impose social and economic change, Choctaws and Chickasaws conceded that they could no longer rely primarily on hunting for either subsistence or trade. More and more, Choctaw and Chickasaw women and men looked for ways to alter their patterns of producing and acquiring food and manufactured goods. In 1801 Choctaw delegates convened at Fort Adams in the Mississippi Territory to meet with envoys from the United States who sought their consent for the construction of a major road, the Natchez Trace, which would link Nashville to

New Orleans by cutting across Choctaw and Chickasaw territory. When asked by the American representative to present their requests for compensation "to better your condition in trade, in hunting, in agriculture, manufactures and stock-raising," a Choctaw chief of the Eastern Division, Mingo Homastubbee, asked that the federal government supply female teachers "to learn our women to spin and weave" and also requested "ploughs . . . weeding hoes, grubbing hoes, axes, handsaws, augers, iron wedges, and a man to make wheels, and a small set of blacksmith's tools for a red man."[38] Within a year, the federal government opened a trading factory at Fort St. Stephens in western Alabama, and Indian hunters supplied American traders with deerskins and cowhides in exchange for hoes, saddles, cotton cards, whips, and cowbells. Two decades later, Choctaw chiefs reflected on the changing economic conditions in their country, concluding: "We cannot expect to live any longer by hunting. . . . Our game is gone."[39]

Buying and selling goods through federally engineered conduits of credit and commerce did not leave Choctaws and Chickasaws hopelessly dependent on American manufactures, nor did it strip them of the ability to direct the production and distribution of resources within their communities. Though they were under tremendous political and economic pressure to take up market-oriented endeavors and the practices of "civilized" life, Choctaws and Chickasaws made calculated and deliberate decisions about the form and meanings of their acquisition of property and production of resources.[40] Many southern Indians started slowly, producing only a small surplus for sale and concentrating the rest of their energies on subsistence farming. But growing numbers of Choctaws and Chickasaws forged ahead, devoting extensive tracts of land to commodity crops, namely cotton and corn, and raising large herds of livestock for sale as well. By 1810 Choctaws' production of cotton cloth demonstrated what federal officials deemed "substantial evidence of the progress of manufactures."[41]

Through the 1830s, federal agents enthusiastically reported that Choctaws sold cloth, livestock, and food supplies to their white neighbors and also to travelers passing through Choctaw towns along the Natchez Trace on their way to and from New Orleans. Choctaw and Chickasaw women established themselves as producers and purveyors of cotton cloth, planting seeds, tending crops, and weaving thousands of yards of cloth each year—enough to outfit their families and sell to American buyers. Chickasaws, too, gained the approbation of Indian agents, who praised their "large herds of cattle, swine, sheep and goats, and poultry of every description" and noted that Chickasaws were "well adapted to the culture of cotton, corn, wheat, oats, peas, potatoes &

beans."[42] The Reverend Jacob Young, writing of his travels through the area, re-called in 1807: "Almost every Indian we passed had something to sell, especially corn at two dollars per bushel, corn blades at a bit, pumkins for a quarter, and hickory-nuts, walnuts, hazel-nuts for a bit."[43] American travelers and settlers, explained Indian Agent William Ward, also obtained livestock and other provisions from Choctaw vendors. According to Ward, Choctaws often provided "the neighboring whites with pork and beef." One newcomer to Mississippi recalled in 1818: "We procured all our provisions from our Chahta neighbors on very good terms."[44] During the early decades of the nineteenth century, the frontier exchange economy of earlier generations had given way to a market economy in which Indians manufactured and sold items for profit.[45]

As they waded deeper into the antebellum American market economy, Choctaw and Chickasaw women and men also became enmeshed in networks of commerce that reached across the southern states and linked the African Diaspora, Native America, and the Deep South. Transactions between Choctaws, Chickasaws, and their white neighbors brought enslaved women and men into the Indian nations via the transatlantic slave trade, the inter-American slave trade, and the domestic slave trade. African-born women and men who disembarked from the fetid holds of slaving vessels to be sold in southern port cities such as Charleston were purchased by both Indian and Euro-American slaveholders. In the winter of 1805, for example, Cherokee slaveholder James Vann purchased a Guinean woman in Charleston who walked barefoot from the city to his estate in northwestern Georgia and lost her feet to frostbite as a result.[46] An enslaved man described only as "a native of Africa" had been enslaved in Georgia before "several changes of masters" landed him in the hands of a Choctaw owner by 1821. In the 1830s, a Chickasaw slaveholder owned "an old African man." Up to the Civil War, travelers and missionaries would document the presence of African-born slaves in Indian communities.[47]

Family ties and trade connections in other port cities, such as New Orleans, facilitated Choctaw and Chickasaw slaveholders' acquisition of slaves, some of whom were imported not from Africa but from other points in the Americas. Spanish efforts to invigorate immigration to the lower Mississippi valley included granting permission in 1776 to French merchants for the importation of enslaved people from St. Domingue and other islands. In subsequent years, U.S. merchants doing business in New Orleans invested their capital in importing enslaved people from Jamaica and other English Caribbean colonies to sell in Louisiana and west Florida.[48] An enslaved woman named Catrene, for example, was born in the West Indies in the 1770s and then lived in Mobile and New Orleans before the Choctaw Leflore family purchased her.

Only after Catrene's arrival among the Choctaws and subsequent contact with white missionaries in the Choctaw Nation did the French-speaking woman learn English.[49] Though the Indian peoples of the lower Mississippi valley were so often buffeted by the political and economic exigencies of waning Atlantic empires in the late eighteenth century, Indian slaveholders navigated the developing market economy and tapped into the various capillaries of the Atlantic slave trade.

When the United States created the Mississippi Territory from the former Spanish Natchez District in 1798, it banned the importation of slaves from overseas, but the domestic slave trade quickly pumped slaves from other parts of the United States into Mississippi. Tens of thousands of enslaved people were brought into Mississippi from across the southern states, and they endured extensive journeys over land and on riverboats before landing in Choctaw and Chickasaw towns. Choctaws and Chickasaws owned black people who had been born in Virginia and Tennessee and were sold to traders and masters who brought them farther south, into the expanding cotton kingdom of the early nineteenth century. Many African American men and women were "sold from place to place" and had "several changes of masters" before Choctaw and Chickasaw masters purchased them in Mississippi.[50]

U.S. Indian agents tracked Choctaws' and Chickasaws' acquisition of slaves and did not discourage them from buying slaves, as many federal officials believed that purchasing slaves and exploiting their labor might enhance Indians' understandings of the dynamics of property ownership and commercial gain. In a 1790 scouting report submitted to Secretary of War Henry Knox, Major John Doughty wrote that the Chickasaws owned "a great many Horses & some families have Negroes & Cattle." By 1830 the agent to the Chickasaws observed that they used part of the profits gained from the sale of cotton, horses, beef, and hogs for "the purchase of [necessaries] and luxuries of life, slaves, sugar, and coffee, as well as dry goods."[51]

Through the antebellum period, white American observers took stock of slaveholding patterns among the Indians, noting who owned how many slaves. The Reverend Young wrote of meeting Chickasaw George Colbert, "a half breed Indian," who with his brother owned forty slaves.[52] Oliver Stark, a missionary stationed in the Choctaw Nation, concluded: "Slaveholding is confined to the whites, halfbreeds & those who have intermarried with the Chickasaws."[53] It is not surprising that missionaries and other white observers from the states focused intently on slaveholders of Euro-American ancestry in the southern Indian nations. Among reformers committed to the project of "civilizing" Indians were those who believed that Indians' assimilation might be hastened, at least in part, through intermarriage with white Americans. Toward the end of his presidency, Thomas Jefferson said to delegates from northeastern Indian nations: "You will unite yourselves with us, and we shall all be Americans. You will mix with us by marriage. Your blood will run in our veins."[54] For those who entertained the possibility of intermarriage as a viable plan for assimilating and eventually effacing Indian peoples, the children born to marriages between southern Indians (mainly women) and Euro-Americans (mainly men) stood out as shining examples of the salubrious effects of whiteness.[55]

Long after visions of Indian assimilation gave way to the harsh realities of dispossession and forced removal to Indian Territory, Euro-American observers credited white traders, interpreters, and diplomats with introducing chattel slavery to southern Indians and cultivating the institution in Indian country. Again, notions of white superiority informed this view among those who could not imagine that Indians might share white Americans' market-oriented acquisitiveness.[56] Slaveholding, it seemed, ran in the veins of their "mixed blood" offspring. In his 1842 report on the findings of his tour through Indian Territory, Major Ethan Allen Hitchcock wrote about Indian slaveholders and their black slaves: "[A]mong the half-breeds and the whites who have married natives, they become slaves indeed in all manner of work."[57] The obsessive preoccupation with the racial demography of slaveholding in the Indian nations and individual slaveholders' racial makeup echoed assimilationists' view that intermarriage might expedite Indians' advancement toward "civilization" and the underlying belief in white superiority.

Southern Indians did not share this outlook on racial identity and slaveholding with the American reformers in their midst. As historian Theda Perdue has illustrated, southern Indians drew more from Native categories of identification than Euro-American conceptions of racial identity and hierarchy, at least when considering their own intimate relationships with Euro-Americans. To illustrate the ways in which Indians eschewed the dominant American racial ideology, Perdue points to the marriages between Indian women and white men and the social conventions that cast their children as "Indian" rather than "mixed blood" or "half breed," pejorative terms routinely employed by antebellum observers.[58]

The sons born to the unions of Euro-American men and Indian women rose to prominence in southern Indian nations not because their fathers were "white" but because they were related to politically powerful men through their mothers. David Folsom, for example, was a son of Euro-American Nathaniel Folsom and a Choctaw woman who was a cousin of Mushulatubbee,

Peter Perkins Pitchlynn, speaker of the National Council of the Choctaw Nation and Choctaw delegate to the government of the United States. (LC-USZ62–58502, Library of Congress Prints and Photographs Division, Washington, D.C.)

an acclaimed war leader and chief. In 1826, it was Folsom's maternal link to political leadership that allowed him to succeed Mushulatubbee as chief of the Choctaw's Eastern District. Peter Pitchlynn, who served as chief of the Choctaw Nation in the mid-1860s, was the son of British trader and interpreter John Pitchlynn and Sophia Folsom, a daughter of Nathaniel Folsom. Much of Peter Pitchlynn's political authority derived from his matrilineal connection to Mushulatubbee.[59] In the Leflore family, similarly, the matrilineal tie to Pushmataha, a prominent war chief and contemporary of Mushulatubbee, rather than a notion of racial patrimony opened the way for Greenwood Leflore's political ascendancy in the Choctaw's Western District.[60] Chickasaw George Colbert was one of the many sons of Scottish trader James Logan Colbert and his three Chickasaw wives. George Colbert rose to political prominence in the antebellum period not because of his paternal ancestry but because of his success as a warrior during the American Revolution.[61] Maternal ties and other measures of male achievement helped elevate men to prominence.

Choctaws and Chickasaws did not necessarily prize Euro-American ancestry in terms of racial ideology, specifically white superiority, but they did value and profit from the wealth and property derived from slavery that flowed from Euro-American fathers to their children and grandchildren. John Pitchlynn, for example, bequeathed fifty-six enslaved men, women, and children to his sons, daughters, and grandson.[62] Whether as inheritance or gifts, ownership of enslaved people as property was transferred within families from one generation to the next. Chickasaw Overton Love, a descendant of the British slaveholder Thomas Love, gave his daughter an enslaved girl named Mary Lindsay as a wedding gift.[63] By the early years of the nineteenth century, growing numbers of southern Indians regarded individual material wealth, including slaves and the products of their labor, as the foundation of political and social power. Choctaw and Chickasaw conceptions of racial identity and hierarchy grew in tandem with their changing conceptions of property and power. If matrilineal ties to prominent leaders elevated the sons of Euro-American men and Indian women, so, too, did the acquisition of paternal estates that often included enslaved African American women, men, and children.

While southern Indians may have dispensed with the aspects of the dominant American racial ideology that exalted white superiority and posited Indian inferiority, they firmly embraced a racial hierarchy that degraded blackness and associated it exclusively with enslavement. During an 1828 visit to a Creek settlement, Peter Pitchlynn was dismayed "to find people of my own color (Indians)" socializing freely with black people at a dance. "There is no distinction between them and the Negroes," he continued. "They mingle together in Society upon an equality."[64] Southern Indians developed their own ideas about racial hierarchy that did not stem merely from inherited predilections or unthinking imitation. As Nancy Shoemaker argues, Indians, like Europeans, had "the intellectual equipment to construct knowledge."[65]

Owning people of African descent as property rested on ideas about the inferiority of blackness that came to be expressed as timeless and natural differences between Indians and black people. By the 1830s, as the late William McLoughlin explained, southern Indians' origin myths asserted the separate creation of red, black, and white people.[66] Racial language, furthermore, worked to entrench the notion of inherent and hierarchical difference between Indians and black people. On one occasion, Choctaw Loring Folsom bemoaned his financial difficulties in racialized language, complaining that "the blackest of the black and I am brought about equal."[67]

In Choctaw and Chickasaw communities and across the southern states, the ideologies of racial hierarchy that buttressed chattel slavery were intertwined with and inseparable from understandings of gender.[68] As the definition of property and racial identity evolved in the early nineteenth century, so, too, did understandings of gender. This is perhaps most clearly evident in the changing meanings of agricultural labor. Historian Jennifer Morgan has shown how the development of chattel slavery in the British colonies precipitated a monumental shift in the definition of "laborer" with the regular presence of enslaved African women working in rice, sugar, and cotton fields. The category of "laborer," once reserved for free and unfree men, expanded to include enslaved African women, as slaveholders turned away from established English "cultural meanings of work" and "inverted the gender ideology that they applied to white women and work."[69] In the southern Indian nations, by contrast, the critical shift in the gendered and racialized meanings of agricultural work occurred with the addition of enslaved black *men* to a predominantly female (Indian) agricultural workforce.

Indian men and women who had the means and the opportunity purchased enslaved black men and women to cultivate subsistence and commodity crops and directed both to work in the fields. Enslaved men and women worked together in the cotton fields and performed other labor necessary to ensure the successful operation of commercially oriented farms.[70] In 1824 John Pitchlynn sent his son Peter a list of instructions for managing the family's plantations and slaves: "When you send the boys to saw plank send cart with provisions and keep them there until they finish sawing." By 1831 John Pitchlynn employed a white overseer and reported owning fifty slaves and having 200 acres under cultivation. Decades later, enslaved men on the Pitchlynn plantations picked and ginned cotton and raised and harvested corn. On other plantations, enslaved men cultivated and harvested wheat.[71]

In a society that had long defined agriculture not simply as women's work but as an integral component of female identity that garnered respect, the inclusion of enslaved men in the workforce marked an important new direction in the meanings of agricultural work, necessarily altering older, positive associations of horticulture with female identity. Slaveholding Indian men owned and controlled enslaved women and men and their labor, as well as the goods they produced, in ways they had never possessed Indian women and their work. By directing enslaved men to work in cotton and corn fields, slaveholding men may have successfully dodged the stigma associated with Indian men's agricultural work, but they did so primarily by stigmatizing the racialized, laboring bodies of black men and women.[72]

Slaveholders reworked the meanings of labor and gender in tandem with their understandings of racial hierarchy. Indian men and women defined themselves in relation to each other but also to the enslaved black women and men whose commodified bodies and labor they owned. In 1820 Choctaw chiefs wrote to the Reverend Worcester, praising the success of the recently established Elliot mission school in the Choctaw's Western District. "We are pleased to see our boys go into the woods with their axes, and into the fields with their hoes," they said. The chiefs then added that they were also heartened that Choctaw girls would "learn to cook and sew like white women."[73] Such praise was surely calculated to convey a willingness to adapt to the ways of their white neighbors and hopefully thwart local and federal efforts to erode their land base. Only two years earlier, the two chiefs had rebuffed President James Monroe's proposal that the Choctaws cede land to the United States, responding to the president that they had no land to give and did not intend to leave Mississippi. When they described their people as able and willing to embrace Euro-American gender roles, the chiefs employed language and imagery that framed Indians in terms of gender and race, deliberately likening them to white people.

Within a few years, other Choctaw leaders were far less enamored of the missionaries and the vocational training component of the "civilization program." In 1825 the embattled Robert Cole, who was caught up in the strife over how best to respond to external pressures on Choctaw territorial and political autonomy, blasted the missionaries as "cheats and liars" who mismanaged the Indians' money and goods. Even worse was the fact that missionaries put Choctaw boys to work in the fields, where they were "driven . . . in the same manner that negroes were on the plantations in the Southern States."[74] Like those leaders who had sought to reassure federal officials of Indians' capacity for assimilation, Cole framed his rejection of American reformers explicitly in terms of gender and race. Cole and his cohort were not protesting that Choctaw boys performed the fieldwork historically associated with Indian women. They objected to their children performing the tasks that were associated with and extracted from enslaved black people.

Choctaw and Chickasaw conceptions of race and gender difference and hierarchy found their clearest expression in the laws governing property ownership and legal status in the nations. In the summer of 1826, Choctaw leaders drafted a constitution and organized a central legislative body. This marked a decisive departure from the old governing structure in which decision making and conflict resolution rested in the hands of respected and accomplished chiefs, warriors, and female orators. Among the most dramatic changes implemented with this new legal system was the development of law governing the ownership and inheritance of private property.[75] At subsequent sessions, the legislature adopted a legal code that applied to both Choctaws and Chickasaws and elaborated on the issues of race, slavery, and property. A law adopted in 1835 confirmed that upon a man's death, his estate passed to his widow and children. Widows who remarried and squandered their children's inheritance, specifically slaves, would not be allowed to continue serving as the guardian of their children's property. In the case of orphans who inherited slaves, their guardian was required to hire out the slaves "to the highest bidder for the benefit of the orphans." Laws also addressed the issue of enslaved people's ownership of property, stating that by the end of 1836, no "negro slaves shall be in possession of any property or arms," and any property or arms seized from slaves would be auctioned for the benefit of the Choctaw Nation. Legal distinctions between Indians and black people extended beyond slavery, as the Choctaw constitution of 1840 held that "no free negro, or any part negro" could settle in the Choctaw Nation. By contrast, other laws held that white men— by definition "free"—only needed to "procure permission in writing from the Chief or the United States Agent" to reside in the Choctaw Nation.[76]

Racial categories came into sharper relief in the constitutional provisions regarding sex and citizenship. In the early decades of the nineteenth century, Choctaw and Chickasaw lawmakers embraced a racial ideology that linked race with legal status—free or enslaved—and citizenship. While Indians from other nations might be naturalized and adopted as Choctaw citizens and white men could gain citizenship after marrying a Choctaw woman, "a negro or descendant of a negro" was not eligible for naturalization. The 1840 constitution elaborated on the subject of race and citizenship, barring anyone "who is any part negro" from holding office.[77] Chickasaw laws, too, protected Chickasaws' right to own slaves, prohibited slaves' ownership of property, and barred anyone of African descent from citizenship, suffrage, and office holding in the Chickasaw Nation.[78] The right to own property instead of being owned as property was thus a cornerstone of Choctaw and Chickasaw conceptions of citizenship, which was defined in terms of race. The racial construction of citizenship was, furthermore, asserted as a natural distinction that should not be transgressed. Indian legislators condemned sexual relationships between Indians and black people and punished Choctaws and Chickasaws for "publicly tak[ing] up with a negro slave" with fines, whippings and, ultimately, expulsion from the nation.[79] Proscriptions against interracial marriage or "public" relationships between Indians and black people not only naturalized the notion of racial difference but also helped define and maintain the boundaries of race and citizenship.[80]

Physical dominance and violence often served to mark and maintain the distance and differences between free and enslaved people. Choctaw and

Chickasaw slaveholders defined their control over slaves as a particular form of power that could, and should, be enacted through violence. Organizing their households under a male head already marked a significant change from older practices of matrilineality, and vesting the male head with expansive control over the people and property in his household only underscored the shift. According to missionary Cyrus Kingsbury, Choctaws equated owning slaves with owning other types of property, and he expected that younger generations would learn that one day they, too, "may lawfully buy them & mark [slaves]." Many slaves' bodies bore the marks of whippings and physical abuse inflicted by Indian slaveholders and the white men they employed as overseers. In 1822 Choctaw slaveholder Anthony Turnbull "hired a white man to drive his negroes." In 1824 the U.S. Indian agent posted in the Chickasaw Nation noted that white men were hired as overseers not only on large plantations but also on smaller farms, where they monitored and punished enslaved workers. Choctaw and Chickasaw planters did not rely exclusively on white overseers to direct and correct their slaves. When Peter Pitchlynn traveled away from his plantation, for example, he relied on his brother to manage his slaves and "whip them" if necessary.[81] Ex-slaves Matilda Poe and Kiziah Love each spoke of owners who whipped and punished their slaves.[82] With the expansion of chattel slavery in the southern Indian nations, slaveholders relied on violence as a routine means of punishment, and physical abuse became an uneventful daily occurrence in the lives of the enslaved and slaveholders.

Violence directed toward enslaved people differed significantly from the physical correction and even executions prescribed by the legal code as punishments for crimes committed by citizens or other free people in the nations. The violence and coercion leveled against enslaved people went largely unchecked beyond individual slaveholders' calculations of the gains or losses that might be incurred as a result of bodily domination. Physical violence against slaves served not simply as a mode of correction but as a demonstration of slaveholders' power and mastery. In 1816 the agent to the Chickasaws reported to his superiors that "several negroes have been lately murdered in this nation in a most barbarous, cruel, and unprovoked manner." In one case, an Indian master killed one of his slaves and defended the attack by stating that he owned the slave and thus could kill him.[83]

Violence against enslaved women stretched across time and space when slaveholders laid claim to enslaved women's future children and when they sold children away from their mothers and families. In her 1859 will, Sophia Pitchlynn, Peter Pitchlynn's mother, bequeathed a number of enslaved boys and girls to her own adult children, making no mention of the enslaved parents from

RACE, GENDER, AND POWER IN THE DEEP SOUTH

whom these children had been taken. Ex-slave Anna Colbert said her master, Sam Colbert, "bought and sold slaves," separating families and directing the men and women left behind to take new spouses. Looking back on her life in slavery, Matilda Poe, once owned by Chickasaw Isaac Love, remembered a day when a neighboring slaveholder sold "several babies to traders" who stopped at the Love plantation. Poe's mother and other enslaved women took care of the babies for two days, trying to teach them to drink from cups or bottles now that their mothers could no longer nurse them. It was the babies' crying for their mothers, Poe recalled, that was especially brutal to witness.[84] Slaveholders' violence against the enslaved becomes more visible when we consider selling and bequeathing enslaved people alongside whipping, raping, or branding them.

In the late 1820s and 1830s, Choctaws and Chickasaws relied on their government's newly drafted legal code to protect their ownership of slaves, detailing the distribution of estates in their wills and pursuing complaints against their fellow citizens to clarify the rights of ownership. In the Choctaw and Chickasaw Nations, individuals did not own land as private property but instead claimed their improvements, along with household items and slaves, as personal possessions. In this context, slaves stood as a tremendously valuable form of property that usually represented a sizable investment and also promised significant returns.[85] After his father's death, for example, Peter Pitchlynn called upon the chief of the Choctaw Nation to ensure that John Pitchlynn's estate was properly divided among his heirs. According to Pitchlynn, this entailed ordering the lighthorsemen (policemen) to seize at least two Pitchlynn slaves from someone who was not entitled to retain them.[86] In another case, a Chickasaw chief worked to restore a young enslaved woman named Mason and her child to Hannah and Jessey, two minors who had inherited Mason from their father.[87] Southern Indians also turned to the federal government of the United States to ensure that they received similar protection in their dealings with American slaveholders.

When unscrupulous Americans attempted to steal slaves from Indian masters or defraud Indians looking to buy or sell slaves, Indians brought their complaints to federal authorities, protesting the theft of their property. In 1824, when "some armed white men" seized the slave that Choctaw Molly McDonald had purchased on credit, her son James registered his complaint with the U.S. secretary of war. James McDonald argued that the enslaved person in question "was clearly the property of my mother." McDonald maintained that his mother ultimately had been robbed of both the slave and the money she had paid toward the final price—crimes, he argued, that fell under federal regulations of trade between Americans and Indians.[88] McDonald complained bitterly about the unfair treatment Indians received at the hands of their white neighbors and local officials, arguing that Indians had property rights that white people should be bound to respect. The outcome of the McDonald case is not known, but James McDonald's lament about the absence of justice in Indians' property disputes with white Americans portended the tenor of U.S.-Indian diplomatic relations in the late 1820s after the election of Tennessee planter and famed Indian fighter Andrew Jackson to the presidency.

Ongoing local and federal efforts to extinguish southern Indians' land title reached a boiling point with Jackson's 1828 presidential election. In his first State of the Union address, Jackson set forth his plan for Indian removal, arguing that ceding their southern homelands for western territory would ultimately prove beneficial for Native peoples, distancing and protecting them from conflicts with white Americans. Not long after Jackson's election, Mississippi lawmakers finally succeeded at enacting legislation that extended state law over Choctaw and Chickasaw land, though not over Choctaw and Chickasaw people. The Mississippi law, of course, was not the only one of its kind; Alabama and, most notably, Georgia enacted similar measures in the same period. The passage of these laws set off heated debates in Congress and among reformers, many of whom opposed coercing Indians off their land and characterized the laws as unjust and oppressive. President Jackson, however, supported the states' efforts to drive Indians out of the South. With Jackson's support, Congress drafted the Removal Act of 1830. It confirmed the president's authority to exchange land in the West for Indians' land in the East and appropriated half a million dollars to cover the costs of expelling and relocating southern Indians. Jackson signed the federal Indian removal bill into law on May 29, 1830. Around the same time, Mississippi governor Gerard Brandon signed into law measures that brought Indian men and women under the state's laws by criminalizing chiefs' exercise of authority and barring all Indian customs, except marriage, not acknowledged by the state law. Though the Mississippi law did grant Indians the same rights and privileges as white people in the state, "no one," writes historian James Taylor Carson, "expected the Choctaws to remain long enough to exercise their new rights."[89]

In the autumn of 1830, federal commissioners John Eaton and John Coffee met with Choctaw chiefs and captains, as well as a contingent of politically influential Choctaw women, to negotiate the terms of a removal treaty. When this meeting failed to reach an agreement, Eaton and Coffee met with a smaller group, including Greenwood Leflore, Mushulatubbee, Nittakaichee, and David Folsom, and issued a threatening ultimatum that they agree to remove from

Mississippi. Under the Treaty of Dancing Rabbit Creek, the Choctaws ceded their remaining 10 million of acres of Mississippi land to the United States.[90] The treaty granted sizable allotments of land in Mississippi to a number of Choctaw leaders, which most would sell before setting out for Indian Territory. By the end of 1831, Eaton and Coffee set their sights on the Chickasaws, seeking to convince them to join the Choctaws in the West.

In 1830 Chickasaw leaders had agreed to the Treaty of Franklin, which provided for the cession of Chickasaw lands and their removal only if they found an acceptable western site for relocation. Chickasaw surveyors, led by Levi Colbert, maintained that the land in Indian Territory was not suitable and thus voided the Treaty of Franklin. After the Choctaw's Treaty of Dancing Rabbit Creek was finalized, however, President Jackson instructed Eaton and Coffee to bring the negotiations with the Chickasaws to a close. Eaton and Coffee were to convince the Chickasaws to join with the Choctaws under one government, a proposal initially rejected by both Choctaw and Chickasaw leadership. Despite not having found land in the West and their continued opposition to merging with the Choctaws, Chickasaw leaders eventually accepted the Treaty of Pontotoc Creek (October 20, 1832), ceding to the United States their lands east of the Mississippi River. The treaty recognized the wealth that individuals had accumulated, including wealth in slaves. Under the treaty, Chickasaws received allotments of their Mississippi land, with additional allotments going to those who owned slaves. The allotments were to be sold at the time of removal to underwrite the costs of land surveys, transportation, and rations. Finally, in January 1837 the Treaty of Doaksville effectively merged the Chickasaw Nation with the Choctaw Nation. Under this treaty, the Chickasaw Nation paid $530,000 to the Choctaw Nation to open some 5,000 square miles on the western edge of its land in Indian Territory to the Chickasaws, creating the Chickasaw District of the Choctaw Nation and giving its Chickasaw residents equal legal standing and political representation in the Choctaw Nation.[91]

In anticipation of Choctaw removal, federal personnel took censuses of the Choctaw districts under the leadership of chiefs Netuchache, Mushulatubbee, and Greenwood Leflore. Preparing for the public sale of Choctaw land to U.S. citizens, census takers compiled information regarding land cultivation and slave ownership. An 1831 census of Choctaw towns enumerated 512 enslaved black people in a total population of almost 18,000. Discrepancies in the records, however, leave open the likelihood that this number is inaccurate and that there were more enslaved people in the nation.[92] Chickasaw removal records paint a similar picture. Muster rolls and census records compiled in the autumn of 1837 enumerate close to 1,200 slaves and 255 owners, of whom only twenty owned more than ten slaves.[93] A handful of outsiders, such as U.S. Indian agents, living in Indian country owned slaves, but the vast majority of owners were recognized members of Choctaw and Chickasaw society.[94]

The sons, and to a lesser degree the daughters, of Euro-Americans predominated among Choctaw and Chickasaw slaveholders, but the boundaries of the slaveholding class in the Choctaw and Chickasaw Nations, as in the southern United States, were flexible. Slaveholding was widely distributed across the population and not determined by ancestry. Slaveholders included the few wealthy cotton planters who owned between fifteen and fifty slaves and middling farmers who owned anywhere from one to fifteen slaves. But others who either did not own slaves or needed additional seasonal laborers often hired slaves.[95] While considerable scholarly attention has focused on the demography of slaveholders in the Choctaw, Chickasaw, Creek, and Cherokee Nations, far less attention has been focused on enslaved and free black people.[96]

The majority of enslaved people, approximately 450, lived in the Mushulatubbee and Leflore districts, with only sixty-two enslaved people identified in Chief Netuchache's district. In each district, however, at least half of the enslaved population lived on farms or plantations with fifteen or more slaves. In the Mushulatubbee and Leflore districts, one-quarter to one-third of the enslaved population lived on farms or plantations with five to fifteen slaves.[97] This means that the vast majority of enslaved people lived and worked alongside their peers rather than in isolation from other slaves. Enslaved people likely also came into contact with the handful of free black people identified in the 1831 Choctaw census. Included in this group were the members of the Beams family, who lived in Leflore's district, and another extended free black family in Mushulatubbee's district. A "free woman" named Sally Tom lived two miles from the factory and headed a household that included one unidentified "slave"; her two daughters and their "white" and "mulatto" husbands, Thomas Ware and Joshua O'Rare, respectively; and their young children. Jack Tom and Moses Tom, who were listed on the census but not identified by race, and Jim Tom, described as "Half breed negro; has an Indian wife," were likely related to Sally Tom, as well. The Toms were not the only free black people living near the U.S. trading factory. Jacob Daniel (not identified by race) lived near the factory with his "half negro and half Indian wife," as did William Lightfoot, classified as "a mulatto; half Indian and half negro," and James Blue, a free black man married to a Choctaw woman.[98] Whatever linked this community to the factory is not known, nor is it clear whether or not they left Mississippi and relocated to Indian Territory.

Malmaison, Mississippi plantation home of Choctaw Greenwood Leflore. (Malmaison, Carrollton, Carroll County, MSHABS MISS, 8-CARL.V, 1-, Library of Congress Prints and Photographs Division, Washington, D.C.)

The histories of chattel slavery and Indian removal overlap and intersect in complex and uncomfortable ways. They are not simply parallel or even competing narratives but are intertwined histories of destruction and dislocation. The expulsion of the Choctaw, Chickasaw, Cherokee, and Creek Nations opened the way for the rapid territorial and economic expansion of plantation slavery into the Deep South. Through the 1830s, the land that had once been Indian country quickly became the United States' "kingdom" of cotton, as white slaveholders and black slaves flooded the region. From the 1830s until the Civil War, hundreds of thousands of enslaved African Americans were sold from the Upper South to work and die on the mostly white-owned plantation labor camps that covered former Indian towns and hunting grounds.[99]

Still, the image of the postremoval Deep South as exclusively white and black is misleading because some Native people remained even after removal.[100] For example, Greenwood Leflore, one of the signers of the Choctaw removal treaty, elected to remain in Mississippi, where he eventually owned some 15,000 acres of land and 400 slaves.[101] In 1833, after large numbers of Choctaws had already removed from Mississippi, Samuel Garland remained in Mississippi and intended to remain "as long as I can raise one ear corn." Garland, who owned seven slaves in 1831, did not grow his own corn but relied on his slaves to raise corn and cotton. In 1833 he expected that his "first rate overseer" would ensure that his slaves, along with those owned by his male relatives, cultivated 200 to 250 acres of cotton.[102]

While Indian removal cleared a path for the growth of the U.S. plantation complex, Indian emigrants pushed the boundaries of chattel slavery even farther west. In the months leading up to their departure, some Choctaws and Chickasaws, especially those of means, purchased slaves to take with them to Indian Territory. Men and women who had been granted land reservations under the removal treaties sold their property to white speculators who paid in cash and human chattel. Choctaw chief Mushulatubbee, who already owned ten slaves, sold his allotment to a white man for six more. His sons, James and Hiram King, also sold their land and purchased three enslaved children.[103] Federal officials reported that a "great many Chickasaws sold their homes, and reservations that were reserved to them under the treaties, for negroes, . . . believing they were good property."[104] Choctaw leader Peter Pitchlynn sold off the land he received in the treaty for cash, which he then used to purchase five enslaved girls for amounts ranging from $275 to $450.[105] Purchasing slaves was a strategic investment that enabled many people to profit from their land reserves in Mississippi. Because Choctaw/Chickasaw land in Indian Territory would be held in common by the nation's citizens, as it had been in Mississippi, enslaved people remained an especially valuable form of privately owned property.

Once in the possession of Choctaw and Chickasaw owners, enslaved women, men, and children—some of the "many thousands gone"—soon found themselves embarking on another journey of dislocation: Indian removal. Susan Colbert and her mother, for example, went to Indian Territory with their new Choctaw owner, Bob Shields, who had used his land to buy them from a white slaveholder.[106] Though Colbert does not speak directly about the family and loved ones they left behind, the separation of enslaved families by sale was commonplace in the antebellum years. For some of the black people purchased by Indians before removal, there was another layer to their experiences of separation and dislocation: kidnapping. The most heavily documented case involved the purchase of six enslaved children by Mushulatubbee and his sons. After the exchange of land for slaves was complete, allegations arose that five of the children were free and had been stolen from their mother in Kentucky.[107]

Charges of fraud and malfeasance arose, often in the flurry of transactions involving land, slaves, cash, and credit. Disputes over the sale of land and slaves arose among Indians, as well as between Indians and white people. For example, a Choctaw woman who had not yet left Mississippi disputed her father's sale of "a negro woman and ninety head of cattle" that the woman claimed as her property.[108] In another case from February 1832, Molly Nail protested that she had entered a contract to sell her reservation in exchange for "four young negroes and one hundred dollars" but had not yet received this payment. She accused the men who had promised her the slaves of defrauding her and demanded the contract be voided. By the end of the year, however, Nail had apparently received both her slaves and cash and declared herself ready to leave Mississippi.[109] The conflicts that emerged from the buying and selling of black people drew the attention of the federal personnel in charge of removal. As a means of providing "better security with respect to slaves, and stronger evidence as to their identity," the officers in charge of removal were directed to include descriptions of slaves along with other itemized lists of Indian property.[110]

The contradiction at the heart of chattel slavery—defining people as property—added to the tumult of removal. Federal agents in the Cherokee, Choctaw, and Chickasaw Nations found themselves unsure about how to calculate the disbursement of food, blankets, and money to Indian households that included slaves. Should slaves be classified as "mere portable property" or as *people*? That was the question facing the military personnel directing the daily operations of removal. After receiving inquiries from agents in 1831 and 1832 about whether and for how long they should provide enslaved people with food, federal authorities answered in the affirmative: "rations would be issued to slaves, the property of emigrating Indians." Choctaws who chose to travel on their own rather than under the direction of the United States were to receive a payment of ten dollars for each member of their household, including slaves, who traveled "without the aid of the Government." But federal agents, looking for a way to keep costs down, decided that slaveholders would not receive the commutation allowance for "negroes not owned in the nation at the time of the treaty."[111] As a federally driven project executed by military personnel, Indian removal generated letters, reports, and censuses that enumerated the human and financial costs of forced relocation. Records intended to account for the movement of Indians and their property also unmistakably reveal the presence of the black people owned as property by Choctaw and Chickasaw slaveholders.

Rather than traveling under the direction of the U.S. military, Peter Pitchlynn led members of his family and forty-five of the black people they owned from Mississippi to Indian Territory in 1832. Another independent party of Choctaw emigrants included eleven enslaved people. Chickasaw George Colbert, too, left Mississippi at his own expense, leading a party of Chickasaws, including their slaves, to the West. Pitman Colbert also guided a party of Indians and slaves west to Doaksville in the spring of 1838. Over the next two years, hundreds more enslaved people left Mississippi and Alabama with their Choctaw and Chickasaw owners to resettle in the new Choctaw/Chickasaw Nation. An 1842 Chickasaw removal party, for example, consisted of 138 slaves and fifty Chickasaws; an 1844 removal party included 138 Chickasaws and fifty-six slaves.[112] Jack Campbell remembered that his mother "belonged to an Indian, and was moved from Alabama to the Choctaw Nation." Joe Nail, similarly, left Mississippi with his Choctaw owners, and Chaney Colbert moved west as property of the Chickasaw Colbert family.[113] On the journey west, enslaved people's labor shielded their owners from some of removal's travails and facilitated the transport of the rest of their belongings. Enslaved men drove wagons loaded with household goods and tended horses and livestock while enslaved women prepared meals. The U.S. Army personnel in charge of removal also relied on enslaved laborers, hiring them from Indian and white owners to push boats, care for horses and cattle, drive wagons, and work as personal servants.[114]

Disease and privation shadowed removal and resettlement for all emigrants, both enslaved and free.[115] Massive flooding of the Arkansas River in June 1833 destroyed the nascent farms and settlements in the eastern part of the new Choctaw/Chickasaw Nation, where slaveholder Mushulatubbee and people from his district, including Peter Pitchlynn, had settled. The swollen river nearly reached the roof of the storehouse at the federal government's Choctaw Agency near Skullyville and wiped out its food stores. The flood drowned livestock and swept away houses. In the wake of the flooding, disease ripped through a population already weakened by malnutrition. This population, of course, included the enslaved people who had been put to work constructing buildings, tending cattle, clearing fields, and putting in the corn crop that was wiped out by the flood. Chronic food shortages and waves of cholera continued to batter emigrants through the 1830s and well into the next decade.[116] Notations in the October 1837 muster rolls of Chickasaw removal parties reveal the toll taken on enslaved families: "1 Negro boy deceased"; "1 Negro child deceased"; "1 Negro man deceased."[117] Writing from Mississippi in 1834, the aging John Pitchlynn expressed his reluctance to move west to the place his adult children called "the Land of Death."[118]

Slaves' deaths and births occupied the attention of Indian slaveholders. Enslaved women's reproductive health was always of paramount importance to antebellum slaveholders because the women's ability to conceive and deliver healthy enslaved babies ensured their owners' future wealth. In times of hardship and crisis, enslaved women's fertility and enslaved children's health became all the more important.

Writing in the late summer of 1841, Rhoda Pitchlynn (wife of Peter Pitchlynn) reported on the illness and deaths among their children and slaves. At the end of August, one enslaved baby died from a "fever," and at least three other enslaved children fell ill, along with one of the Pitchlynn daughters. Three weeks later, fifteen enslaved children had influenza. By the end of October, young Lycurgus Pitchlynn and a number of enslaved children came down with whooping cough, which claimed the lives of many people in the region.[119] Undoubtedly, disease and hunger hit everyone hard in the years after removal. Though sick enslaved babies and sick Pitchlynn children appeared in the same lines of Rhoda Pitchlynn's letters, their illnesses and deaths had distinct meanings and consequences for the Pitchlynns.[120] Long after removal, generations of enslaved people in the Choctaw and Chickasaw Nations would also remember the early days in Indian Territory as a time scarred by sickness and death.[121]

THE EMERGENCE OF CHATTEL slavery marked the ascendancy of a new set of ideas about what constituted property and who could own or be owned in the Choctaw and Chickasaw Nations. Slaveholding necessarily engaged conceptions of race, specifically the degradation of blackness, even as Indians resisted embracing notions of white superiority. As increasing numbers of Indian men and women relied on the forced labor of African and African American men and women to generate both subsistence and commodity crops, the meanings of gendered labor shifted to accommodate the presence of black men in the agricultural workforce and to allow for Indian men's domination of enslaved male and female workers. Focusing on Indians' ownership and exploitation of enslaved black people need not diminish our awareness of the pressures exerted by local white populations, state governments, and federal officials on southern Indians' land, cultures, and governments. To the contrary, a better understanding of slavery in the southern Indian nations can illuminate the complex and contradictory ways in which southerners—Indian, white, and black—struggled over the meanings of property, race, slavery, and freedom in the nineteenth century.

2

Enslaved People, Missionaries, and Slaveholders
Christianity, Colonialism, and Struggles over Slavery

Enslaved people sold from the southern states to masters in Indian country brought with them the faith, skills, and practices central to the distinctive African American religious traditions taking root and flowering in other southern locations from the late eighteenth century through the early decades of the nineteenth century. Scholars of slavery and the African Diaspora no longer debate whether newly arrived African slaves and their American-born offspring retained memories and knowledge of their lives prior to the Middle Passage and enslavement. Rather, we now pay careful attention to the myriad ways in which Africans of diverse ethnic backgrounds came together on slave ships, auction blocks, and plantations throughout the Americas and forged common cultures and collective identities by reviving and adapting African customs and values. Of course, the process of drawing on African antecedents to build new cultures and communities in the Americas entailed selecting and modifying cultural elements from both the Euro-American and Native American peoples they encountered. Enslaved people, for instance, coalesced around familiar spiritual beliefs and ceremonies and brought African understandings of the spirit world to bear on Euro-American Christianity.

Through the antebellum period in the southern states and Indian country, the organized, collective expression of spiritual belief stood as an important component of many enslaved people's lives. For those women and men who wound up on the Mississippi farms and plantations of Choctaw and Chickasaw slaveholders and faced the task of creating their families and communities anew, religious faith and practice were important elements in the recreation of meaningful lives and relationships. Individual and communal devotion helped preserve the connections, knowledge, and memories of people and places left behind in the states, the West Indies, and Africa.[1] Not all enslaved people in the Indian nations or anywhere else in the United States embraced Christianity, nor was religion a panacea against the rivalries, animosities, and betrayals that divided friends, families, and communities everywhere. Still, focusing on the enslaved Christian community in the Choctaw and Chickasaw Nations reveals some of the contours of enslaved people's lives and allows us to see how they understood what it meant to be enslaved by peoples who were themselves facing institutionalized forms of domination.

Black people's religious lives in the antebellum Choctaw and Chickasaw Nations were closely linked to the churches and schools established by white missionaries in the 1820s. Christian missionaries arrived around 1820 in the Choctaws' and Chickasaws' Mississippi territory with the express goal of "civilizing" and assimilating Indians, preparing them for the seemingly inevitable extension of white settlement and U.S. governance. A shared faith drew many enslaved people and missionaries together but rarely aligned their understandings of the meaning and consequences of religious devotion in life and death. Relationships among white missionaries, Indians, and black slaves took shape in complex, contradictory, and sometimes expected ways. For most southern Indians, the connections between missionization and U.S. expansion were inescapable. Initially, few Choctaws or Chickasaws heeded missionaries' calls to Christianity, but they did permit their slaves to worship at the missions. Slaveholders, including those who converted to Christianity, rarely initiated or promoted Christianity on their farms and plantations. That impulse came from within the slave quarters.

Though slaveholders tolerated slaves' religious fraternization with missionaries, relations between slaveholding Indians and missionaries were frequently contentious. Choctaws and Chickasaws were perpetually watchful for the ways missionaries might seek to advance the ideals that informed and justified an increasingly aggressive and land-hungry U.S. Indian policy. Some missionaries' antislavery sentiments further antagonized Indian slaveholders. For enslaved people, however, these tensions between missionaries and Indians could be beneficial. By establishing close ties to missionaries, enslaved people located resources and opportunities to curb their master's authority and mitigate, or even terminate, their bondage.

A great deal of what is known about the lives of the early generations of black slaves in the Choctaw and Chickasaw Nations comes from the records of northern missionaries, evangelical Protestant men and women who understood themselves as benevolent reformers and hoped to "civilize" Indians through the spread of Christianity. Missionaries did not intend to preserve individual life stories or compile a collective history of enslaved people. They dutifully recorded their efforts to run the mission stations, and in the course of writing personal reflections and generating official correspondence, they penned both general and detailed images of the enslaved people who prayed and worked at the missions. The "invisible institution" of enslaved people's Christianity and the larger community in which it took shape becomes at least partly visible on the pages of missionaries' journals and letters.

Early in the nineteenth century, some of the most prominent northern reformers and clergymen, such as Lyman Beecher, turned their attention to the plight of Indians, establishing the interdenominational American Board of Commissioners for Foreign Missions in 1810. On their preliminary visits to southern Indian towns, northern ministers were heartened to find men raising corn crops rather than hunting for subsistence and women engaging in domestic labor such as spinning and weaving. The Cherokees, Choctaws, and Chickasaws, one visitor concluded, seemed primed for successful missionization. In 1816 Cyrus Kingsbury, a Congregational minister from Massachusetts, wrote to Secretary of War William H. Crawford about establishing a mission school among the Cherokees. Kingsbury and his fellow missionaries believed that their work was more than a "duty enjoined by the Gospel"; it was also an "act of justice" toward Indians.[2]

Members of the American Board concerned themselves not only with converting Indians but also lobbying Congress and federal officials to treat Indians justly and humanely. Board founders and supporters included prominent reformers and politicians, such as Theodore Freylinghuysen and Jeremiah Evarts, who were especially distressed by what they perceived as the lack of justice and humanity at the core of the federal government's ongoing efforts to usurp Indian land and press Indian peoples to move west. By the end of 1816, the Choctaws, Chickasaws, and Creeks had already ceded millions of acres of their Mississippi lands to the United States.[3] The men and women associated with the American Board bristled at federal efforts to winnow southern Indians' landholdings and feared that forced removal was an affront to the laws of man and God. Missionaries and supporters of the American Board vociferously denounced Indian removal as cruel and oppressive. A letter printed in a Methodist newspaper asked about the Choctaws in 1829: "What account will our people render to God, if, through their neglect, this people, now ripe for the gospel, should be forced into the boundless wilds beyond the Mississippi, in their present state of ignorance?"[4]

The American Board concentrated its efforts on the Choctaws rather than the Chickasaws. Circuit riders and other missionary societies picked up the slack in Chickasaw country. In 1817 the Reverend Elias Cornelius toured the Chickasaw, Choctaw, and Cherokee Nations to assess their receptiveness to missionization. Cornelius, the corresponding secretary of the American Board's Prudential Committee, was "kindly received" and felt the Choctaws and Chickasaws displayed "not only a readiness but an ardent desire" for mission schools.[5] In June 1818 the Reverend Cyrus Kingsbury arrived with Loring and Matilda Williams at the site of their new mission, called Elliot, near the Yalobusha River in the Choctaw Nation's Western District.

From the outset, the newcomers depended on the hospitality of their Indian hosts. When they first arrived, Kingsbury and the Williamses lived in a house owned by Levi Perry, a local leader and large slaveholder.[6] The mission was far from the main areas of Choctaw settlement near the Chickasawhay, Pearl, and Pascagoula Rivers, but it was close enough to the Yalobusha River to receive deliveries of needed supplies. By August, the missionaries had constructed their own fifteen-by-eighteen-foot dwelling. A year and a half later, Elliott consisted of "seven commodious cabins," along with a kitchen, a dining hall, and a schoolhouse. The station also included a mill, a blacksmith's shop, stables, and other farm and mechanical outbuildings. Sixty Choctaw students were enrolled in this first mission school, which relied heavily on the support of Choctaw leaders. Many politically powerful Choctaw men came out in support of mission schools, and Puckshanubbee, the chief of the Western District, committed $200 of the nation's funds to the school at Elliott .[7]

In June 1799 the New York Presbyterian missionary society sent the Reverend Joseph Bullen to visit with Chickasaw leadership to gauge their willingness to host missionaries. Though he gained leaders' permission to teach and preach to Chickasaws as well as their slaves, Bullen failed to win converts during his four-year stay. Historian James Atkinson concludes that Bullen's mission floundered because he did not develop organized and lasting schools and churches. As in Choctaw country, missionaries to the Chickasaws relied on local support, especially from wealthy and prominent families, to launch their schools and churches.

In 1820 Levi Colbert, one of three wealthy slaveholding brothers who were prominent Chickasaw leaders, hosted a young missionary at his home at Cotton Gin Port. The Presbyterian Synod of South Carolina and Georgia had sent the Reverend Thomas C. Stuart to the Chickasaws as their first missionary. In the same year, Colbert permitted missionaries from the Cumberland Presbyterians to conduct their school in his home until the buildings went up at a nearby site. The school, called Charity Hall, boasted a log classroom building, housing for students, outbuildings, and a farm for agricultural training. Missionaries offered "Bible and hoe" instruction, combining a standard academic curriculum with agricultural and vocational training. By 1822 Thomas Stuart's Monroe mission school, named after the president of the United States, opened near the town of Tockshish. During the next few years, Chickasaw leaders committed $5,000 to the construction of two more schools and also promised an additional $2,500 annual payment to support the faltering school system. Under Stuart's direction, the Martyn and Caney Creek schools were established, bringing the total number of schools to four. The American Board of Commissioners for Foreign Missions assumed control of the struggling schools in 1826 and slowly boosted their enrollments until Mississippi and the federal government initiated their Indian removal campaign.[8]

Many Indians were wary of the missionaries, regarding them as surrogates of the federal government who would advance its land-hungry, assimilationist agenda and profit from Indians' losses.[9] For example, the large and expensive compound at Elliot fueled Choctaws' early suspicions about the missionaries' motives. Historian Clara Sue Kidwell explains that the missionaries appeared to be "enriching themselves at the expense of the Choctaws."[10] At the same time, however, many of the most powerful Choctaw and Chickasaw leaders facilitated the missionaries' presence in their towns, donating land and supplies for the construction of mission stations. Choctaws and Chickasaws who lent their support to missionaries weighed the possibilities for gaining more than they risked by inviting these outsiders into their communities. Indians courted, funded, and patronized mission schools for pragmatic reasons, hoping to gain the linguistic and cultural fluency necessary to interact with their white neighbors and federal and state officials.[11]

Still, the connections between missionization and U.S. expansion were inescapable. In October 1820 John C. Calhoun, the secretary of war, tapped General Andrew Jackson to negotiate a new land cession treaty with the Choctaws. Jackson, an esteemed war hero and Indian fighter, set aside his contempt for Indian treaties and went to Mississippi to meet with Choctaw leaders. The first sentence of the Treaty of Doak's Stand reads: "WHEREAS it is an important object with the President of the United States, to promote the civilization of the Choctaw Indians, by the establishment of schools amongst them; and to perpetuate them as a nation, by exchanging, for a small part of their land here, a country beyond the Mississippi River, where all, who live by hunting and will not work, may be collected and settled together." Under the terms of the treaty, the Choctaws ceded approximately 6 million acres of their territory in exchange for approximately 13 million acres west of the Mississippi River. The treaty's seventh article directed that a portion of the ceded land would be sold and the proceeds used to underwrite Choctaw schools "on both sides of the Mississippi river." The treaty did not force the issue of removal, but it brought white settlement even closer to what remained of the Choctaws' Mississippi

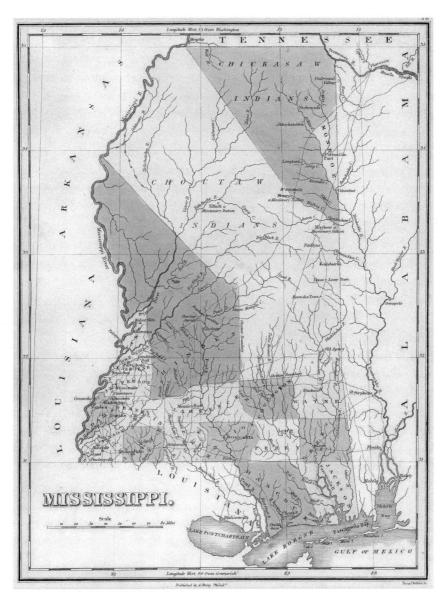

Map of Choctaw and Chickasaw territory in Mississippi. (Anthony Finely, map of Mississippi [1824?]; courtesy of the Mississippi Department of Archives and History)

territory and fomented discord among the nation's leadership over how to best handle the mounting pressures on their land and people.[12]

With the issues of land cessions and removal foremost in their minds, the Choctaws and Chickasaws who attended or sent their children to mission churches and schools did not clash with missionaries over conversion or religious beliefs. Instead, Indians were perpetually at odds with missionaries over the issue of slavery. Human bondage did not accord with the missionaries' vision of a Christian society. In their eyes, Indians' ownership of slaves and reliance on their labor to generate food and commodity crops did not signal their warm embrace of American ideals of private property and market-oriented production. Instead, missionaries argued that slavery highlighted Native people's laziness, cruelty, and resistance to "civilization." Slavery, Kingsbury wrote in 1844, was "one of the greatest obstacles to the progress of the Gospel [and] civilization" in the Indian nations. In subsequent correspondence, Kingsbury elaborated on the subject of Indians as slaveholders, writing: "The indolent slave of an indolent, ignorant Indian . . . is an unfortunate being. . . . Negroes raised in the states & especially those raised under the Gospel are much more intelligent & industrious than those raised among the Indians."[13]

The harsh criticism Kingsbury and his colleagues directed toward Indian slaveholders certainly reflects their disdain for slavery but also signals their paternalist ideas about Indians as a racially backward and uncivilized people. Missionaries' eagerness to build up thriving churches and schools in Choctaw country required a certain intellectual flexibility regarding issues of race. Many missionaries, especially those coming from northern antislavery communities, abhorred slavery and deemed Indian slaveholders unenlightened.

Yet they also identified a number of pragmatic and spiritual motives for commending Indian slaveholders who converted and welcoming Indian slaveholders into the church. Conflicts over the question of admitting slaveholders to mission churches roiled the American Board for decades. Public debates on this issue gained widespread attention in the United States and created major rifts among the American Board leadership and also in its constituent churches. In the 1820s, however, the issue was addressed at the local level. Missionaries did not want to alienate slaveholding Indians as potential converts and so received them at prayer meetings and granted church membership with the hope of enlightening them through discussion and prayer. One missionary to the Cherokees explained that because their "opportunities for knowledge" about the wickedness of slavery had "not been as great as white people's," Indians should not be held fully accountable for their participation in the sinful institution of bondage.[14] Moreover, missionaries to the Choctaws surely could not afford to estrange the wealthy slaveholding leaders who committed funds from their nations' annuities to help cover the costs of running the missions.

The simultaneous toleration, condemnation, and exculpation of Indian slaveholders point to the complicated and often contradictory nature of Euro-Americans' early nineteenth-century racial thinking. In the early decades of the nineteenth century, Euro-American reformers routinely compared and contrasted the experiences and possible futures of Indians and black people. Thomas Jefferson, of course, addressed the subject of racial hierarchy and Indians' and Africans' positions relative to each other and also to white people in *Notes on the State of Virginia* (1787).

While Jefferson ranked Africans firmly below Indians in terms of intellect, morality, and beauty, his was never the only word on the subject. By contrast, Henry Clay, a longtime member of the U.S. Congress and Senate and also an ardent supporter of African colonization, held a different view. Clay, who was elected president of the American Colonization Society in 1836, believed in African Americans' potential to thrive intellectually, socially, economically, and politically once they were removed from the United States. African Americans, he contended, were more intelligent and advanced than Indians but could not flourish in the United States. Like other reform-minded Euro-Americans in the early nineteenth century, the American Board missionaries who went to the Choctaws and Chickasaws did not advocate racial egalitarianism. Rather, they contemplated both the inferiority and potential of the black and Indian peoples they encountered. Missionaries often compared their intellectual and moral capacities and wondered whether habitual behavior or innate traits informed the differences between them.

The notion that black people, especially those steeped in Christianity, were intellectually and morally sounder than non-Christian Indians, especially those without Euro-American ancestry, prevailed among the missionaries.[15] Consequently, in their efforts to uplift both the slave and slaveholder in Indian country, missionaries welcomed enslaved people into their flock and hoped they would assist in spreading the word of the Gospel and "civilization" among the Indians.

Enslaved people in the Choctaw and Chickasaw Nations responded favorably to the missionaries, glad for the opportunity to attend prayer meetings. Not long after Kingsbury and the Williamses had established Elliot, Loring Williams moved on to open Bethel mission on the high prairies between the Pearl and Big Black Rivers, not far from the Natchez Trace. In the spring of 1822, "an unusual number of people, chiefly blacks" gathered for prayer meetings at Bethel. That summer, Loring Williams found that enslaved people were far more serious about prayer and salvation than either the Indian children or women in the area.[16]

In 1823 South Carolina missionary Hugh Dickson established a church to complement the school at the Monroe mission to the Chickasaws. Three of the earliest members were the slaves Dinah, Abraham, and Esther.[17] Attending church services organized by missionaries, meeting on their own, and exhorting nonbelievers to find their faith bound enslaved believers to one another, revitalizing their spirits and consoling their weary hearts.[18] For those who had been sold from masters in the states to Choctaw and Chickasaw slaveholders, rebuilding their religious lives in the Indian nations sustained a sense of connection to the kin and communities that had been left behind. Recreating a religious community also provided the opportunity to build new family and community ties. Attending prayer meetings and studying with missionaries were acts largely initiated by the enslaved and reflected their beliefs and interests.

Among the slaves that Choctaws and Chickasaws purchased from Georgia masters were a number of African, African American, and West Indian (Caribbean) women and men who had previously been members of black churches in and around Savannah. The regional and ethnic diversity of the African-descended population in Choctaw country is best understood in a broader regional context. Until 1810, approximately 22 percent of the enslaved population in the United States had been born in Africa. While that percentage fell off during the following decade, African-born people still comprised a significant proportion of the enslaved, and their presence remained especially salient for the next generation born into slavery in America. In the years leading up to the 1808 ban on the transatlantic slave trade to the United States, South Carolina and Georgia enjoyed a brisk trade in African slaves, principally from central and western Africa, with approximately 40,000 Africans imported to Charleston between 1804 and 1807; Charleston's slave markets, in turn, supplied Georgia slaveholders.[19]

In the South Carolina–Georgia Low Country and throughout the Diaspora, heterogeneous communities of enslaved Africans drew on shared elements of their spiritual beliefs and ceremonies as one means of forging a common culture and identity that encompassed the diversity of African ethnicities and their American iterations. Historian Michael Gomez describes this process as a "move away from ethnicity and towards race as the primary category for inclusion."[20] Generations of historians, anthropologists, and archaeologists have illuminated the ways religion became one of the central axes in Africans' acculturation to enslavement in the Americas. Enslaved Africans came into contact with Christian religions and synthesized selected elements of Christianity with African spiritual beliefs. They did not submit to the religion of their enslavers as much as they Africanized it, infusing the words and rituals with African-derived meanings that often eluded Euro-American observers.[21]

In coastal Georgia and South Carolina, Africans and their American-born progeny encountered the expressive religiosity of white Baptist and Methodist revivals. In the late eighteenth century, the growing Euro-American Baptist and Methodist evangelical movements preached spiritual equality of the races, and, although the churches' white members clashed over the issue of slavery, both free and enslaved black people were welcomed into the fold. The singing and falling into trances that signaled white converts' surrender to the power of their faith resonated with many enslaved Africans, whose spiritual worldview acknowledged the dynamic connections between the world of the living and the spirit realm.

In the earliest years of the nineteenth century, free and enslaved black people in and around Savannah formed their own Baptist congregations, sometimes joining the white congregations that were open to them and participating in the region's denominational associations. Enslaved men and women from the Savannah area established the Great Ogechee Colored Church in 1802, the same year that free black people and enslaved people hired out in Savannah formed the Second Colored Church. In 1813 a black minister, the Reverend George Sweet, assumed the leadership of the Great Ogechee Colored Church.[22]

As enslaved people of diverse backgrounds coalesced around mission churches in Indian country, they transformed mission spaces from sites of co-lonial domination into meeting grounds where they continued the ongoing process of forging a collective identity. Missions served as the space where enslaved people melded their African past with their lived experiences of slav-ery in the U.S. and Native South. Women and men born in Africa, the United States, and the West Indies came together at mission churches to build bonds of friendship on earth as well as to connect with the spiritual world. At the Monroe mission, for example, "An old African man" joined the church in 1832. Also at Monroe, Sarah, an elderly African-born woman who had been raised in the West Indies and also had lived in New Orleans, attended prayer meet-ings at Monroe.[23]

The first cohort of enslaved evangelicals that gravitated toward the mission churches in the Choctaw Nation in the early 1820s included a number of people who had previously belonged to Georgia's thriving black Baptist communities. Thirty-year-old Rosa, owned by the Leflores, was originally from Georgia, "where she became Baptist." Another elderly enslaved woman had also been a "church member in Georgia" before she was purchased by a Choctaw master. An African-born man indicated to Kingsbury that he, too, had found salvation in Georgia. The black evangelical community in the Choctaw Nation included at least one enslaved man who had previously belonged to the Reverend Sweet's Baptist church in Savannah.[24] Coming from communities saturated with black Baptist organizations, the enslaved worshippers in the Choctaw Nation were hardly novice initiates. They did not seek instruction from the missionaries as much as a space where they could continue their own brand of faith under the direction of skilled preachers and adept leaders from within their own ranks.

The missionaries who received them, however, believed that enslaved Baptists needed close supervision and instruction to ensure they did not backslide into sinful or heathenish ways. In his early correspondence with the leadership of the American Board, Cyrus Kingsbury credited himself with bringing education and salvation to both Indians and black people, scarcely acknowledging the religious education, practices, and institutions that enslaved Baptists had already developed on their own. In the winter of 1820, Kingsbury noted in his journal that he had preached to a number of black people who "appeared very thankful for the instruction." That spring, he concluded that the number of black attendees at Sabbath services was on the rise because "they have an opportunity to learn to read in the morning."[25] But Kingsbury and his colleagues in the Choctaw and Chickasaw Nations were not exclusively or even initially responsible for spreading literacy among the enslaved in the nations.

A number of enslaved people already knew how to read, having acquired the skill prior to their arrival in Indian country. Enslaved preachers and laypeople in Choctaw and Chickasaw communities read the Bible on their own and to each other, offering thoughts, interpretations, and reflections that linked them more closely to each other than to the missionaries. Teaching enslaved people to read was a fairly common component of early nineteenth-century efforts to spread the Gospel in slave quarters in the southern states, explains historian Janet Duitsman Cornelius. Numerous Baptist and Methodist ministers and missionaries in the southern states, many of whom supported slavery, taught enslaved people to read the Bible but generally did not teach people how to write. In the hands of southern clergymen and slaveholders, biblical instruction served the social and economic interests of slavery. Though southern clergymen and slaveholders did not teach slaves to write, enslaved people located other sympathetic teachers who would advance their education. As the authors of antebellum slave narratives attest, learning to read and write was a precious gift that opened doors to the world beyond slavery. In her autobiography, Harriet Jacobs reflects fondly on her childhood mistress, a kind woman who taught the young Harriet to "read and spell," a "privilege, which so rarely falls to the lot of the slave." Frederick Douglass, too, first learned to read from a sympathetic mistress, and after his master prohibited these lessons, Douglass befriended white boys in the neighborhood and persuaded them to teach him.

The religious schooling provided to slaves in the Choctaw and Chickasaw Nations, therefore, does not necessarily distinguish the missionaries or Indian slaveholders as kinder or more lenient than their counterparts in other parts of the South. Kingsbury and other missionaries positioned themselves as champions of the enslaved, but they nonetheless adhered to a racial hierarchy of white superiority that reflected their own interests in the Indian nations. They did not offer religious instruction with the intention of training black preachers or empowering black congregants. Nor did they preach a proslavery message of black subordination to their Indian masters. Instead, missionaries taught reading as a means of instilling in black people virtues such as humility and obedience to white people, especially missionary preachers. Missionaries also taught enslaved people to read with the principal goal of preparing them to assist in the campaigns to Christianize and civilize Indians.[26]

A number of enslaved men and women did assume the role of intermediary between missionaries and Indians, serving mainly as interpreters and mostly in the Chickasaw Nation. In the Choctaw Nation, Cyrus Kingsbury bemoaned the shortage of interpreters, which precluded him from devoting as much time as he would have liked to preaching and evangelizing. During his 1799 tour of the Chickasaw Nation, the Presbyterian missionary Reverend Joseph Bullen engaged the services of a black interpreter in Big Town, a Chickasaw village known to its residents as Chaguiliso. An enslaved Christian woman named Dinah worked as an interpreter for missionary Thomas C. Stuart at his Monroe mission. Dinah had been born in the Chickasaw Nation but was fluent in both English and the Chickasaw language, probably the consequence of her being owned by James Gunn, a British man who married a Chickasaw woman.

Dinah's spiritual awakening began before the missionaries appeared, leaving open the possibility that Chickasaw and possibly African spiritual beliefs helped shape her early thoughts about the divine. She first contemplated the meaning of life after the New Madrid earthquakes in the winter of 1811–12. A series of exceptionally powerful earthquakes began in the middle of December 1811 and continued off and on for more than four months. The earthquakes centered in the boot-heel region of Missouri in the city of New Madrid on the Mississippi River, and the earth shook as far away as Boston, Canada, and Mexico. Thousands of tremors rocked the Mississippi valley, including the Chickasaws' territory in northeastern Mississippi. Many people across the region attributed the earth's undulations to divine but not necessarily Christian causes. Many Indian peoples in the South, for instance, attributed the quakes to supernatural forces that were reacting to white people's taking of Indian lands.[27]

Dinah's retrospective account is the only one to offer a glimpse of the earthquakes' effects in Chickasaw country. Once missionaries arrived and began preaching at Monroe, Dinah understood that the ground's pitching and swaying beneath their feet heralded the Judgment Day. When the church at Monroe was established, Dinah joined, and it was there that she learned to read and write. Because of Dinah's linguistic skills and professions of faith, Stuart relied on her for many years to translate his sermons.[28]

It is hard to know what enslaved people like Dinah thought about their roles as proselytizers, which they either chose themselves or were cast to play by missionaries. Certainly, by tapping slaves to assist with the religious education of Indians, the missionaries drew them into the assimilationist project and directed slaves to act in ways that would have been unthinkable in the southern states.[29] In the Indian nations, enslaved people participated in the education of the ruling class, assuming positions of intellectual and moral authority over free people and slaveholders. In some instances, enslaved believers felt moved to testify to their faith and exhorted their masters without missionaries' guidance or oversight. Because many Choctaw and Chickasaw slaveholders already spoke English, enslaved converts did not necessarily face language barriers when they spoke to their masters about religion. On one occasion, the power of the Holy Spirit filled an enslaved woman in the Choctaw Nation, causing her to enter a trance before getting up to preach to her master and a group of forty or fifty of her fellow bondspeople.[30]

What did these moments of elevation mean to enslaved translators and interpreters? Did the enslaved imagine themselves preparing for a day when they were no longer held in bondage? Did preaching independently or as the missionaries' proxies create momentary but meaningful experiences of autonomy and authority? Did interpreters and other enslaved converts pray for their masters because they saw them as sinners, as slaveholders, or as "savages"?

Well into the twentieth century, former slaves spoke of their Indian masters in the racial lexicon of the day, identifying Indians as "full blood" and "mixed blood" and often associating specific personality traits, such as kindness, cruelty, and avarice, with these classifications. For example, Choctaw freedman Edmond Flint said of Indian slaveholders: "There were humane and inhumane masters [and] . . . as a rule the slaveowning Indians were of mixed blood."[31] The ex-slave narratives of the 1930s tell us a great deal about how later generations of enslaved people thought and spoke about Indians in their interviews. These assessments, however, should not simply be projected back 100 years to the 1830s.[32]

In the early antebellum period, enslaved believers seem to have given little thought to whether their masters were "civilized" by the standards of white Americans. Instead they focused on whether Indian slaveholders were saved in the eyes of God. After hearing Reverend Bullen preach in 1799, one elderly woman owned by Chickasaw William Colbert proclaimed her joy at hearing the Gospel after having lived "long in heathen land."[33] Missionary Loring Williams reported: "Negroes are praying for their masters." But sometimes when enslaved people called loudly and openly for their masters to repent and seek salvation, the meanings of their prayers could be ambiguous, cloaking visions of deliverance from bondage in the evangelical language of faithful devotion to the Lord. At an 1822 prayer meeting, for example, one older woman testified: "Long time have I prayed for this wicked people. I first used to pray that Judgements of afflictions might bring them to repentance."[34] Echoing biblical calls to repent, this woman's testimonial hints at the anticipation of the judgment that awaited slaveholders at the end of time.

Many enslaved Africans and African Americans arrived in Indian country conversant in the precepts of evangelical Christianity and turned to missionaries not as much for religious training, or even for momentary authority over their masters, as for opportunities that might temporarily curb the reach of their masters' control. No matter how grateful the enslaved were for the chance to learn and pray at the missions, they were never wholly reliant on the missionaries for religious and secular instruction.

It is evident in mission records that generations of enslaved men and women organized their own spiritual gatherings apart from the direction and supervision of both missionaries and masters.[35] In the summer of 1822, enslaved people in the Choctaw Nation's Western District attended services at Newell, a newly established mission in the area, but "nearly every evening the blacks in different places meet for prayer among themselves." Among the enslaved people in that area, a man named Peter, the son of a black Baptist preacher from the states, distinguished himself in their "social meetings [as] the principal leader." Despite their inability to read, Peter's group was able to "exhort with much feeling & propriety and sing several hymns very well." Another enslaved man named Solomon, whose literacy predated the missionaries' arrival, also preached and sang to gatherings of his fellow slaves.

Establishing ties with the local missions may very well have provided enslaved men and women with precisely the opportunities they needed to build and maintain their own religious gatherings. In the 1820s, more enslaved people than Indian slaveholders attended mission services. Though some slaveholders joined the church, there is little indication that Choctaw and Chickasaw slaveholders relied on proslavery interpretations of the Bible when directing and disciplining their slaves. Slaveholders, as missionaries complained, invested little energy in propagating the Gospel in slave quarters.[36]

Given masters' general lack of interest in their slaves' religiosity, enslaved people had the opportunity to organize their own meetings without arousing their masters' suspicion or intrusion. In the Chickasaw Nation, an enslaved man living only ten miles from the Monroe mission church held weekly prayer meetings in his cabin every Wednesday morning. Initially, his gatherings numbered only six participants, but over time, he attracted crowds of just over fifty people that included mostly slaves but also many Chickasaws. The group prayed in "the Chickasaw language" and was taught by at least one enslaved person who could "read some."[37] Likely drawing on earlier experiences of autonomy in black churches and other settings, enslaved men and women in the Choctaw and Chickasaw Nations developed and sustained their own religious institutions even as they formed close relationships with missionaries.[38] Among enslaved people in the Low Country, Margaret Washington Creel explains, formal membership in Baptist and Methodist churches diverted slaveholders' attention from slaves' secret and autonomous social and religious societies.[39] In a similar fashion, joining mission churches in Indian country likely provided enslaved people with the cover they needed to gather on their own for religious and secular reasons.

In addition to holding their own prayer meetings, individual enslaved men and women also seized the time and space to pray spontaneously and privately. One elderly woman, for example, testified at a mission meeting that when she felt the power of the Holy Spirit move her, she would "go in de bush" near her master's farm and pray. It should be noted that this woman felt "so heavy burden wid sin" when she was working in her master's fields. "I pray & pray and pray all de time when I go work in de field," she said. Stealing away to pray at such moments relieved her of the weight of a hoe or a plow, along with the load of her sin. Other women and men spoke of receiving spiritual inspiration and praying fervently in secluded spots away from their masters' homes and fields.[40] Large gatherings in each other's cabins and individual prayer sessions in hush arbors are best understood in the context of what historian Stephanie Camp terms a "rival geography," the ways enslaved people used and moved through time and space on their masters' plantations to serve their own needs and interests. In the Choctaw and Chickasaw Nations, as in other parts of the

Deep South, enslaved people's rival geography created opportunities for private reflection, communal exchanges, and respite from work but did not secure their unmitigated autonomy or threaten to destroy the institution of slavery.[41]

The religious gatherings and prayerful moments orchestrated by enslaved men and women in the Choctaw and Chickasaw Nations afforded them distance but never complete independence from either their masters or missionaries. Missionaries kept a close watch on enslaved worshippers, determined to stamp out the last vestiges of heathenism among them. Believing that the path to salvation lay in the opening of one's heart and soul to the workings of the Holy Spirit, missionaries watched slaves closely for the outward signs of their inner conversion. Missionaries were also on the lookout for insincerity, scrutinizing enslaved people's words and actions in religious settings to determine if they were sufficiently serious and pious. In the Chickasaw Nation, for example, one missionary clamped down on enslaved people's meetings, explaining: "I have thought it expedient to discourage lay preaching among the slaves, on account of their ignorance, and for other reasons."[42] When an enslaved woman named Kate felt called to testify to other slaves about her religious rebirth, it was noted in a mission journal: "She has always been considered a very ignorant woman."[43] Missionaries in the Choctaw Nation had few kind words for the enslaved man Solomon who preached to other slaves. Though he regularly attended services at the Bethel mission, the missionaries objected to his insistence upon preaching and reading the Bible to his fellow slaves because he lacked the "self-abasement and lowliness of mind" that the missionaries preferred among enslaved congregants.[44] Missionaries were pleased to welcome enslaved people into their prayer meetings and congregations, but they were less gratified to see the enslaved organizing their own gatherings and nominating teachers and preachers from within their ranks.

Choctaw and Chickasaw slaveholders may have found themselves at odds with missionaries over the desirability of extending American "civilization" into Indian country, but they shared a firm belief in the need to monitor and contain black mobility and autonomy, especially when it came to visiting and praying at the missions. Though slaves often received permission to attend church meetings at the missions, they did not have free rein to travel and worship at will. In the early 1820s, few enslaved people in the Choctaw Nation went to the church at the recently established Bethel mission because many masters looked askance at "any private attempt to instruct or converse with them," convinced that religious education, including learning to read the Bible, would "spoil" slaves.[45] When Harry, an enslaved man, professed his faith, he was "treated poorly and whipped without cause" by his mistress. A Choctaw slaveholding woman forbade her slave Hannah from attending services at the Elliot mission in the winter of 1822.[46] Choctaw and Chickasaw slaveholders harbored a persistent distrust of the missionaries, especially because of their antislavery stance, and never ignored the issues of time, mobility, and independence that arose when enslaved people went to mission churches.

Certainly the issue of slavery strained Indian slaveholders' relations with missionaries, but it is not clear how deeply antebellum political and moral debates over slavery permeated and divided Choctaws and Chickasaws before the advent of the Civil War. In the Cherokee Nation, Christian Cherokees and Cherokee traditionalists joined together to form the Keetowah secret society, a group dedicated to returning control of the nation's government to Cherokee traditionalists who opposed assimilation. Not an abolitionist organization, the Keetowah society nonetheless rejected the concept of chattel slavery as antithetical to traditional Cherokee values and practices.[47] If Choctaw and Chickasaw adversaries of assimilation and slavery formed a society similar to the Keetowahs, it remains a secret.

Defenders of slavery, by contrast, did not hesitate to share their views with their fellow slaveholders and also with missionaries. The *Choctaw Telegraph*, published through much of 1849, reprinted critiques of abolitionists drawn from other southern newspapers and also included local reports on the perceived threat missionaries posed to slavery in Indian Territory. In public venues and private exchanges, the refrain was the same: Indian slaveholders suspected missionaries of working to disrupt if not destroy slavery.[48] George Harkins denounced "those stinking abolitionist[s]," and Robert Jones, likewise, complained that the missionaries were hardly reluctant to "preach abolitionism."[49] In the winter of 1847, Choctaw slaveholder Israel Folsom informed Cyrus Kingsbury that the Folsom family would no longer attend Kingsbury's church because of its antislavery position. There is considerable irony in Folsom's move because Kingsbury's continued insistence upon admitting slaveholders like Folsom to mission churches ultimately resulted in the American Board severing ties with the Choctaw missions in 1859.[50] Indian slaveholders, however, did not see their church admission as a sufficient bulwark against the threat of abolitionism.

Suspicious of northern missionaries' antislavery leanings, as well as their colonial intentions toward Indians, slaveholders struck a double blow when they prevented enslaved people from attending the mission churches. By prohibiting their slaves from worshipping at the missions, slaveholders used them to strike back against the religious branch of the larger federal project of cultural assimilation and land appropriation. When leading Choctaws and Chickasaws grew tired of the missionaries' condescending attitudes or questioned their pedagogical approach toward both Indian pupils and black worshippers, they withdrew their children, slaves, and financial support from mission schools and churches. In 1824, for example, Louis Leflore objected to the course of education and discipline imposed on his son and other Indian boys at the Bethel mission school and withdrew eight Indian children from the school; he also barred his fifty slaves from attending prayer services at the mission.[51] Withdrawing students, as well as funds, rendered the federal government's and missionaries' investments of time and resources in the schools and churches virtually worthless. In the wake of Leflore's removal of the Indian pupils and black congregants from Bethel, missionary Loring Williams lamented: "The vast expense incurred—for what?"[52]

Barring slaves from traveling to the missions for worship and education was much more than an attempt to disrupt the missions' viability. It was also a clear expression of slaveholders' power to control the lives and bodies of the people they owned. Slaveholders exercised their mastery over slaves by dictating when, where, and with whom they could move, gather, and pray. Choctaw and Chickasaw masters, whether they converted to Christianity or not, did not rely on religion as a weapon of control in their interactions with their slaves. Christian masters did not preach to their slaves, nor did they solicit proslavery ministers to preach from the Pauline epistles and other New Testament chapters that advocated servility. Slaveholders did not seek to dictate the content or even the form of slaves' prayers, but they did create a "geography of containment" regulating enslaved people's mobility and use of space, and in this case, ruling over the time and location of enslaved people's religious gatherings.[53]

Eventually, slaveholders' determination to limit slaves' contact with missionaries and thus to exert greater control over enslaved people's time and movement found clear expression in the legal code. In 1836, shortly after the Choctaws and Chickasaws had left Mississippi for Indian Territory, Choctaw lawmakers governing both the Choctaw and Chickasaw people prohibited teaching slaves "to read, to write, or to sing in meeting-houses or schools or in any open place" without their master's permission. Subsequent laws restricted enslaved people's possession of horses in an effort to hinder them from attending mission church services.[54] Cherokee and Creek lawmakers enacted similar legislation around the same time, ostensibly reining in missionaries but really clamping down on slaves.[55]

Slaveholders exaggerated the threat that missionaries might launch an abolitionist assault in Indian country and often missed the ways in which enslaved people directed missionaries' antislavery sentiment to their own benefit. Over the years, a number of enslaved people owned by Indians were hired to work at the missions, and some of them successfully liberated themselves by convincing the missionaries to purchase their freedom. Ironically, enslaved people came to work at the missions not because missionaries set out to rescue them from bondage but because missionary men and women sought laborers.

Missionaries hired slaves to construct and maintain buildings, grow food crops, handle livestock, and tend to domestic labor such as laundry and cooking. When it came to hiring out their slaves, Choctaw and Chickasaw slaveholders were not so troubled by slaves' mobility or sustained contact with missionaries. Having devoted themselves to preaching and teaching and also lacking skills and stamina, the missionaries relied on the labor of enslaved carpenters, blacksmiths, farmers, cooks, and laundresses to ensure the smooth functioning of the mission stations.[56] The American Board could not afford to hire enough skilled white workers to staff the mission stations. Missionaries quickly decided to meet their labor needs by renting slaves from the Indian slaveholders who lived near the missions. They justified the decision to hire slaves on financial and racial grounds. It cost less to hire enslaved workers than free white laborers, missionaries stated, and black people could "endure the summer better than whites, too."[57]

Meeting their labor demands by hiring enslaved workers was an issue that troubled a number of missionaries and sparked some three decades of ongoing and often heated debate in religious antislavery circles in the United States. Not long after their arrival in Indian country, missionaries wrote to the Prudential Committee, the American Board's governing body, for guidance on the subject of hiring slaves. Missionaries presented their reasons for hiring slaves—their need for labor and lack of money to pay free white workers—but acknowledged that the prospect of using enslaved workers pained them. Still, missionaries managed to overcome their shame and despair, and by the spring of 1822, enslaved men and women owned by Anthony Turnbull, a Choctaw living near the Elliot mission, had been hired to work in the mission's fields and kitchen.

After touring the Choctaw missions in the spring of 1824, Jeremiah Evarts, the secretary of the American Board and a nationally known antiremoval activist, concluded that it was appropriate for missionaries to hire enslaved laborers. Some missionaries balked at his position. Loring Williams suggested that hiring slaves not only appeared to condone slavery but possibly "encouraged slaveholders to buy slaves that we might have their services." Cyrus Byington lamented his role in an organization that "could require me to sanction slavery."[58] As the American abolitionist movement gained momentum through the 1830s, questions about the missionaries' stance toward slavery, slaveholders, and slaves plagued the American Board, drawing criticism from within its ranks and from a wide range of white and black Christian reformers and abolitionists.

At the American Board's 1844 annual meeting, the subject arose in the presentation of memorials that expressed grave concerns that "slavery is actually tolerated in the churches under the patronage of the Board among the Choctaws, and other Indian tribes." Outraged reformers defected from the American Board and withdrew their financial support for its missionary projects. The American Board, along with some of its constituent denominations, remained hesitant about taking an unequivocal position on the subject of slavery.

Missionaries continued to defend their actions, insisting that although they abhorred slavery, they could not impose their belief on Indian slaveholders or use it as the shibboleth for church admission. Hiring and even purchasing slaves, they argued, ultimately served the greater good: not only did the practice ensure the missions' continued operation, but also slaves received religious education. When the American Board had ruled in 1836 that its funds could not be used to hire or purchase slaves, missionaries responded by using their own money instead.

Toward the end of 1847, the American Board directed its secretary, the Reverend Selah Treat, to visit the Choctaw and Cherokee Nations with the aim of investigating and reporting on the issue of slavery. Treat presented his report at the 1848 annual meeting in Boston, and his findings mainly echoed the missionaries' voices: slavery was deplorable, but both slaves and slaveholders were well served by the missionaries.[59] At this and subsequent meetings, the American Board's apparent tolerance of slavery generated widespread public discussion in print and at the meetings of abolitionist societies.[60]

Antislavery newspapers in the United States, Canada, and England brought the plight of enslaved people in the Indian nations to the attention of their black and white readers by carrying the proceedings of American Board meetings and printing editorials and other items on the subject. According to the editors of the assertively antislavery *National Era*, the American Board had all but lost the confidence of Christian abolitionists by admitting slaveholding Indians to mission churches and allowing the hiring of slaves at the missions.[61] Frederick Douglass's *North Star* covered the proceedings of American Board meetings and denounced the missionaries for accepting slaveholders into their churches and failing to preach an explicitly antislavery message to both the enslaved and slaveholders in the Indian nations. In the autumn of 1848, an item in the *North Star* summarized the American Board's recent meeting and characterized the organization as "lamentably pro-slavery."[62] A few years later, the black editors of

Canada's *Provincial Freeman* indicted the American Board for its "pro-slavery sins" in Indian country and presented recent debates among British abolitionists over whether to continue supporting the American Board.[63]

Over the years, missionaries remained largely impervious to such criticism and persisted in hiring slaves. Though they opposed slavery, few missionary men and women openly rejected the racial hierarchy that justified the subordination of black laborers, and they hired enslaved people to perform work they deemed socially and physically inappropriate for educated and respectable white people. In 1822 the Elliot mission hired two enslaved women from nearby slaveholders who each received ten dollars a month for the women's labor. The women, Elsy and Violet, were hired to work in the kitchen and washhouse because the missionary women "cannot do this kind of heavy & hard work."[64]

The conceptions of race that informed missionaries' use of enslaved laborers and also their training of Indian students were informed by and inseparable from their understandings of gender. In the context of preaching and proselytizing, they viewed black Christian men and women as more advanced than Indians in terms of their religious convictions. Black male and female workers, however, were seen as inappropriate models of gender and labor for Indian boys and girls on the path toward assimilation. For example, missionaries at Wheelock requested that American Board officials send funds for the hiring of white women to work in the kitchen. The teachers wanted to train Indian girls in "domestic labor" but could not do so "if we had a black woman in the kitchen."[65] The missions hired black men to work in the fields but were careful to keep them apart from the Indian boys who were also expected to do fieldwork. Indian boys, missionaries reasoned, should work in the fields to gain technical knowledge and develops traits associated with civilized masculinity, such as industry and independence. Despite having a shortage of teachers at Elliot, missionaries did not hire a white man to help teach Indian boys about agriculture because placing them under the supervision of a hired white man seemed perilously close to putting them to work under a paid overseer, which would make the boys "too much like negroes."

Though they clearly did not embrace racial egalitarianism, the missionaries were nonetheless averse to slavery and squeamish about their own reliance on enslaved people's labor. They partially justified hiring slaves by pointing to Indians' shortcomings as masters and identified their flaws as racial characteristics, such as indolence and cruelty. Even Indians with Euro-American ancestry were seen as only "half-enlightened, half-civilized," and unlikely to embrace Christianity and reject slavery on their own and before their white neighbors did so.[66] When defending their decision to hire slaves, missionaries cited not only Indians' limitations as masters but also the intangible benefits enslaved workers received at the missions. Almost no hired slaves received cash wages, but from the outset, missionaries convinced themselves that enslaved workers were grateful for the opportunity to work at the missions because "they may at least be better treated here than at home & will receive religious instruction." As late as 1857, the Reverend Greene highlighted the "humane and Christian treatment" given to enslaved workers at the missions.[67]

Claims of kind treatment notwithstanding, enslaved workers bore the responsibility for a number of jobs and much of the labor critical to the missions' smooth and continuous operations. Enslaved carpenters and blacksmiths worked at the mission, along with men who grew food crops and raised livestock; enslaved women worked as domestic servants, cooking, cleaning, and doing the laundry.[68] They performed strenuous labor and worked to sustain not only the missionary men and women who hired them but also the Indian students at the schools, whose populations numbered anywhere from a dozen to over fifty.[69] Missionaries fancied themselves kind and gentle employers because they did not hire overseers or rely on physical violence and coercion to drive their workers. They did, however, demand considerable time and output from the men and women they hired. Henry Copeland, for instance, wrote in 1852 that he hoped to employ "a good strong colored woman, one who would be able to perform the greater part of the kitchen work" at the Wheelock mission in Indian Territory.[70] Whether or not enslaved people preferred the working conditions, including access to church and education, at the missions to their masters' farms or plantations, they readily perceived the tremendous possibility for freedom that lay exclusively in working for the missionaries.

That enslaved people regarded the missions as potential sites of liberation almost as soon as they were established adds another dimension to their interest in joining mission churches. Missionaries in the Indian nations and their superiors in New England agreed that the missions should hire only those enslaved people who knew in advance both the work that would be expected of them and the "advantages" they would enjoy.[71] Given the number of enslaved people who gathered at mission prayer meetings and this open communication about the terms of mission employment, information about the immediate and potential future benefits of working at the missions was surely commonplace. Enslaved participants in religious meetings knew that conversion and prayer relieved the burdens of sin, and building personal connections with missionaries could free their living bodies from the chains of bondage. This is not to suggest that enslaved people only made calculated decisions to attend mission churches with the aim of gaining their freedom but that

Wood fence rails made by Chief Leflore's slaves near Wheelock Church. (W. B. Morrison Collection; courtesy of the Oklahoma Historical Society)

spiritual and secular objectives could overlap to such a degree that they became indistinguishable.

In the early to mid-1820s, an enslaved woman was hired to work at the boarding school at the newly established Mayhew mission, and within two years of arriving at Mayhew, she approached Kingsbury about obtaining her freedom. Appealing to both Kingsbury's humanitarian concern for slaves and paternalist disapproval of Indian slaveholders, the woman, whose name was not recorded, succeeded in convincing Kingsbury to buy her and agree to her future liberation.[72] Gaining her freedom through purchase was surely a bittersweet victory for this woman. Here, the autobiography of Harriet Jacobs, who escaped from her master in North Carolina and ultimately found freedom in New York, is instructive. In her narrative, Jacobs describes the mix of anger and joy she felt when a benefactor purchased and freed her: "I am deeply grate-ful to the friend who purchased it, but I despise the miscreant who demanded payment for what never rightfully belonged to him or his."[73] Unlike Jacobs, however, the unnamed woman at Mayhew was not immediately liberated by her intercessor. She owed Kingsbury and had to work at the mission until she repaid "her price plus expenses."

Over the years, a small number of enslaved women and men called on the missionaries to help secure their freedom. At the short-lived Monroe mission in the Chickasaw Nation, Dinah earned enough money working as Reverend Stuart's translator that she was able to buy her own and her husband's free-dom. Most cases, however, occurred at the Choctaw missions. Missionaries purchased slaves from Choctaw masters and then required the enslaved people to repay the cost of their purchase before manumitting them. In 1830 an en-slaved man named George who worked at Mayhew asked that Kingsbury buy and eventually liberate him, and Kingsbury complied. This man, who would forever proclaim his liberation by taking the surname Freeman, took four years to work off his purchase price and then went to work for wages at the Dwight mission in the Cherokee Nation. Kingsbury reported that by 1840, he had pur-chased three enslaved people with the intention of freeing them. Missionaries were not impeded by an 1846 Choctaw law that required Indian slaveholders to obtain the permission of the Choctaw General Council before manumitting a slave. By 1857 approximately one dozen more enslaved men and women had entered similar arrangements with missionaries to secure their freedom.[74]

Liberation did not come swiftly or painlessly to those who succeeded in arranging for their purchase and eventual manumission. Missionary men and women bought slaves with the understanding that they would remain in bond-age and be expected to work until they had repaid their purchase price, the cost of their food and clothes, and, in some cases, "moderate interest." The terms of the agreements rarely favored the enslaved. Like later generations of freedpeople who worked as sharecroppers, the enslaved people purchased by missionaries had virtually no control over the expenses levied against them and could not ensure that they were properly credited for the payments they made in kind and cash against their debts.

Allegations of fiscal impropriety regarding hiring slaves dogged missionar-ies. In 1840 or 1841, an elderly man named Bartley approached Kingsbury with the request that the missionary purchase him. Bartley took four years to work off his purchase price plus interest, a debt totaling $175, and was freed in 1845. Two years later, American Board officers were still incredulous that Kings-bury had taken so long to clear Bartley's debt.[75] In January 1850 Mrs. Wright, a missionary at Wheelock, purchased a young woman named Phillis for approximately $500 or $600 dollars. Mrs. Wright then hired Phillis to someone else, and she worked for four years without receiving either the cash wages she was promised or any work credits against her debt, which included her purchase price plus interest and the cost of her clothes. Mrs. Wright also intimated to Phillis that even after her manumission, she would be obligated to remain as Wright's servant. Ultimately, Phillis gained her freedom when another missionary, Henry Copeland, paid off her debt and drew up papers attesting to her free status.[76] Enslaved people endured considerable obstacles and indignities on the path to freedom, but they did not shy away from pursuing arrangements with missionaries that would lead to their manumission.

Many of the men and women who were purchased and manumitted by missionaries remained connected to them but did not orient themselves exclusively toward mission life. Free people did not feel the calling to join missionaries in their campaign to evangelize and assimilate Indians, nor did their faith inspire them to remain at the missions. Once freed, men and women directed their energies toward building families, controlling their labor, and safeguarding their hard-won freedom. In all of the discussions about Phillis's debt and future employment, she made clear to Mrs. Wright and the other missionaries at Wheelock that she was unwilling to move or be moved away from her husband. A year after her debt was finally cleared, Phillis and Andrew, her husband, moved together to Ohio, possibly joining the Copelands, who had by then retired from missionary work. Bartley, likewise, moved away from Kingsbury and the mission. He found wage work closer to where his enslaved wife and children lived. Unhappy with his employer, however, Bartley eventually returned to work for Kingsbury, but he negotiated for compensation that included a horse so he could easily visit his family and friends. Given his failing health, Bartley also arranged to do minimal work during the winter in exchange for room and board for himself and his horse; during the summers, Bartley worked more and received cash wages. Freed black men and women did not find the lives or labor they desired at the mission stations. Their family and community ties beckoned, and a desire to safeguard their freedom would eventually lead a small contingent of free black people away from the missions and well beyond the limits of Indian country.

Life for free black people in the Choctaw and Chickasaw Nations was never easy, especially in the years leading up to the Civil War. The change in their legal status from slave to free by no means ensured them a peaceful or prosperous life, and some people renewed their ties to missionaries and the church to preserve their safety and freedom. By the 1840s, proslavery ideology hardened in the Indian nations, creating a climate of animosity toward all black people, especially those who were free. Indian law and custom unequivocally linked blackness with servitude and defined citizenship in terms of race, effectively making free black people social and civic anomalies. In the 1840s, the slave code expanded well beyond earlier laws that aimed to constrain the enslaved by regulating their contact with missionaries. The Choctaw General Council enacted legislation in October 1840 that mandated the expulsion of all free black people "unconnected with the Choctaw & Chickasaw blood" by March 1841; those who remained in the nation risked being sold at auction and enslaved for life. The law also criminalized the hiring or harboring of free black people and barred free black people from the United States from entering the nation, imposing fines ranging from $250 to $500 or fifty lashes on the bare back. Finally, the law included a provision that called for the arrest of black people who were merely suspected of being free and imposed on them (or their masters) the burden of proving their slave status. This provision empowered lighthorsemen (police) and citizens to use violence and even deadly force, if necessary, when taking a suspected free black person into custody. An 1846 law forbade masters from manumitting their slaves without presenting the case to the General Council for approval. Manumitted slaves were given thirty days to leave the nations and risked arrest and five years enslavement if they returned.[77]

Indian lawmakers took an unabashedly proslavery stance in the 1840s, and their language and objectives were in step with, and even predated, similar laws in the United States. In 1850 the U.S. Congress made its most dramatic legislative move against free black people in the United States with its approval of the Fugitive Slave Act. The law expanded the rights of slaveholders, requiring minimal proof of ownership and allowing them to enlist federal marshals and use force when pursuing and capturing alleged fugitives. Slaveholders were no longer constrained by state due process requirements, and marshals faced severe financial penalties for failing to imprison and return accused fugitives. The accused and their advocates, in turn, were stripped of opportunities to offer a defense, placing free black people in jeopardy of being kidnapped or reenslaved. Across the country, the law created a climate of profound fear among free African Americans, immediately prompting hundreds of people in northern cities to dispose of their property quickly and flee to Canada rather than risk reenslavement. By 1860 an estimated 20,000 people had fled to Canada.[78] In both the Indian nations and the United States, lawmakers strengthened the institution of slavery by intensifying the association of blackness and servitude and severely constraining the rights and protections extended to free black people.

Despite Indian lawmakers' determined measures to rid Choctaw and Chickasaw territory of free black people, laws were applied unevenly, and some free black people remained in the nations apparently undisturbed. When the 1840 expulsion law was approved, in fact, lawmakers immediately exempted two men, William Black and Lewis Durant, from its provisions. In 1860 census takers from Arkansas crossed into Indian Territory and enumerated the non-Native inhabitants in the Indian nations. Of the fifty-seven non-Native households identified in the Chickasaw Nation, three were composed of free black people. In the Choctaw Nation, free black men and women headed just thirteen of the 270 non-Native households and were also included in four additional households headed by white residents. The seventy-six free people of color in the Choctaw and Chickasaw Nations in the 1860 census made up slightly less than 10 percent of the free non-Native population. Identified in the census as "black" or "mulatto," at least twenty of these free people shared surnames with prominent Choctaws and Chickasaws, mostly slaveholders, such as Folsom, Colbert, Batiest, Brashears, and Ischomer. These names and the presence of the free black people who bore them hint at earlier relations of enslavement, consanguinity, and manumission and also suggest that the patronage of prominent Indian slaveholders shielded some free black people from kidnapping, arrest, or reenslavement.[79] Despite the paternalist protections some people received, the mounting national crisis over slavery in the states and the increasingly hard-line stance of Indian slaveholders made Indian Territory a dangerous place for most free black people.

Living in a slave country bordered by the slave states Texas and Arkansas, free black people in the Choctaw and Chickasaw Nations faced the very real threat of kidnapping and sale by both Indians and white Americans. In one widely known case that dragged on from the 1830s to 1856, white slaveholders and speculators conspired to seize and sell members of the free black Beams family. In another case from the mid-1840s, Choctaw lighthorsemen arrested a free black woman and her children at the urging of a Chickasaw woman and her white husband, who hoped to enslave them. The court ruled that the family was free, and the chief of the district where they lived ordered them to comply with the law and leave the nation.[80]

Though paternalism sometimes motivated prominent Indians to protect free black people, political leaders and slaveholders generally viewed free black people as magnets for white thieves and thus a menace to slaveholders and national security. In an 1842 letter to the U.S. secretary of war, Choctaw Peter Pitchlynn complained about the "armed Texans" who charged into Choctaw country and kidnapped the Beams family. Citing this as evidence of white Americans' disregard for Indian sovereignty, Pitchlynn insisted that the United States enforce the laws prohibiting unauthorized border crossings and thus protect Choctaw lives, homes, and property from U.S. assailants, but he did not mention the issue of defending the lives or legal status of the free black people in the Choctaw Nation.[81]

As word of the 1840 expulsion law spread among free black people and missionaries, concern about their safety became paramount. In Indian country, as in the United States, a change in legal status from slave to free did not offer a lifetime protection from reenslavement, nor did it indemnify free black people from violence, harassment, and continued exploitation. The law promised to disrupt black people's family and community relations with the expulsion of free relatives and loved ones. The bitter irony for those who had secured their manumission through protracted labor and payment plans with missionaries was that their hard-won freedom made them vulnerable to reenslavement. Facing these dismal options, some free black people considered leaving Indian country for Liberia. Just a few months after the law's passage, a letter attributed to an unnamed missionary in the Choctaw Nation stated that this "trying exigency" had motivated "several" free black people to view Liberia "as presenting the only safe asylum for the oppressed of their race."[82]

From the 1820s, when missionary activity first got under way in the Choctaw and Cherokee Nations, African Americans and Indians became acquainted with the American Colonization Society (ACS) and its twin goals of deporting free African Americans and exporting Christianity to Africa. Kingsbury was a leading proponent of the ACS. Before the Choctaw removal, he persuaded one slaveholder to manumit over twenty people and send them to Liberia.[83] When he first entertained the notion of purchasing enslaved laborers, he imagined they might work to buy their freedom and continue working until they saved enough money to "remov[e] themselves to Hayti or Liberia."[84] Kingsbury made regular donations to the ACS through the 1840s and 1850s and encouraged both fellow missionaries and Indian slaveholders to make contributions, as well. He also solicited funds from white supporters of colonization in the states to underwrite the purchase, manumission, and emigration of enslaved people in the Choctaw Nation. In the 1820s, Kingsbury and his colleagues were not alone among a large contingent of white reformers who simultaneously opposed Indian removal and endorsed African colonization.[85]

Barely a decade later, however, missionaries' continued support of the ACS set them apart from white advocates of colonization who had reconsidered their position after the publication of William Lloyd Garrison's powerful 1832 pamphlet *Thoughts on Colonization*. In it, Garrison set forth a vigorous denunciation of the ACS and colonization as unjust and antiblack. His fiery treatise inspired white antislavery reformers to abandon colonization and join northern black activists in creating interracial antislavery organizations and calling for the immediate abolition of slavery. Kingsbury, by contrast, apparently remained skeptical of immediate abolition, writing in 1847 that emancipation would be "a misfortune and not a blessing" to enslaved people in Choctaw country and staying true to the ACS for the duration of his career in Indian country.[86]

Though the role of missionaries in promoting Liberia cannot be discounted, attributing free and enslaved people's interest in emigration exclusively to their influence would be a mistake. Black people in the Choctaw Nation had to look (or listen) no farther than the newspaper printed in the Choctaw Nation for favorable news and editorials about the ACS, as well as information about the Fugitive Slave Law and the kidnapping of free black people in the states.[87] News from emigrants to Liberia arrived in the *Liberia Herald*, which missionaries requested from the ACS when they sent in their donations. Under the stewardship of African American newspapermen John Russwurm, once a vocal critic of the ACS, and Hilary Teague, a Virginia-born Baptist minister and merchant, the *Herald* reported on Liberian politics and business, carried items from American newspapers, and ran editorials counseling black people's self-improvement through education.[88]

While enthusiastic endorsements of emigration could be found in newspapers and conversations with missionaries, free and enslaved black people likely had the opportunity to consider alternative viewpoints, including their own. Because the ACS and the issue of emigration had been widely debated in black newspapers, public lectures, and private organizations for decades, they were subjects well known to many free and enslaved black people throughout the states. Enslaved people who arrived in Indian country via cities such as Charleston or Savannah may very well have heard or participated in discussions about African colonization. In conversations, arguments, or idle musings lost to the written historical record, information and ideas about the ACS, Liberia, and colonization flowed across the borders between Indian country and the states with the sale, travel, and escape of free and enslaved people. Since the 1820s, free and enslaved people in the Choctaw, Chickasaw, and Cherokee Indian nations had contemplated the possibility and consequences of emigration. By the 1840s, a small number of black people decided to leave Indian country for Africa.[89]

Viewed from Indian Territory in the early 1840s, Liberia appealed to free black people with promises of safety and prosperity, just as Indian country (and Canada) beckoned African Americans from the states in the years immediately following the 1850 Fugitive Slave Law. In one case, a nineteen-year former slave named Israel Mills escaped from the Choctaw Nation to Liberia when his former master destroyed his manumission papers and tried to reenslave him.[90] Once George Freeman purchased his freedom from Kingsbury, he joined the church and began making donations to the ACS in 1842 in preparation for his eventual departure in 1852. Before Phillis finally secured her freedom from Mrs. Wright, she and her husband, Andrew, expressed their eagerness to settle their debts and "go to Liberia."[91] Phillis and Andrew never made it to Africa but instead moved to Ohio. George Freeman, however, left the Choctaw Nation with his wife and two young daughters in 1852, and they sailed from New Orleans on the *Zebra* on December 31, 1852. It is hard to know for certain how many emigrants left the Choctaw Nation, or the other Indian nations, for Liberia. Total numbers of emigrants from Indian country only appear in the ACS annual reports for 1853 (five people from the Choctaw Nation) and 1856 (seven people from the Choctaw Nation), but published passenger manifests indicate the departure of some more emigrants from Indian country in the 1850s.[92]

Emigrants made the decision to leave behind family, friends, and familiar places and sail across the Atlantic for Liberia, and missionaries provided financial and spiritual support. On November 25, 1852, George Freeman and a small contingent of emigrants began their journey by praying and singing hymns with the missionaries at Mayhew. If Freeman and his family envisioned a brighter and blessed future in Liberia, those dreams proved ephemeral. The brig *Zebra* set sail from New Orleans on December 31, 1852, with twenty-three free-born black people, ninety-seven people who had been manumitted, and another fifteen who had purchased their freedom directly from their masters. Interestingly, George Freeman was identified as a "slave" who had been emancipated by his master (Reverend Kingsbury), not as a man who had purchased his freedom. Only a few days into the journey, improperly cured water barrels unleashed an outbreak of cholera on the ship, and thirty-five emigrants, along with the captain, the first mate, and three crewmen, died. The disease struck Freeman and his wife, Mary, orphaning their young daughters, Rachel and Elsie. A formerly enslaved family from the Cherokee Nation also perished on the ship. Abraham and Nancy Moore had purchased themselves and their son, Charles; their adult daughter, Violet, had purchased herself. They all succumbed to the cholera. The only surviving member of the Moore family was eighteen-year-old John.[93] The Freeman and Moore families met with a tragic end only a few miles from the American coast, but even those who made it to

Liberia struggled to discern the glorious landscape of black prosperity trumpeted by white and black advocates of colonization.[94]

The only emigrant from the Choctaw Nation to leave behind written records of his Liberian life was the Reverend Simon Harrison, a licentiate minister who left Indian Territory for the African colony in the spring of 1853. Though other emigrants from the Indian nations shared Harrison's religious convictions, only he embarked for Liberia with an explicitly religious agenda: to work for the ACS as a teacher and a minister. Like George Freeman, Harrison was a slave owned by a Choctaw master, and Kingsbury had intervened to obtain his freedom. In Harrison's case, Kingsbury appealed widely to white supporters of colonization to raise the money for Harrison's purchase. White and black donors from the states, along with missionaries, Choctaws, and free black people in the Choctaw Nation, raised $2,000 for the "redemption" of Simon Harrison; his wife, Nice; and their three children, Daniel, Matthew, and Martha.[95]

A few months after he and his family arrived in Liberia, Harrison wrote to ACS leadership and Kingsbury, informing them of his safe arrival. Like many other emigrants, Harrison was sorely disappointed by the climate and material conditions of his newly adopted homeland. Malaria, food shortages, and limited economic opportunities drove a large percentage of emigrants back to the United States within a year of their arrival in Liberia. Though Harrison's letters do not betray a wavering commitment to emigration, they do hint at the deep sorrows and pain that accompanied him to Liberia. When Harrison first disembarked in Monrovia, he learned that he had to travel farther to get to his destination in Bassa Cove. Dismayed that he "could not yet be released from another water passage," Harrison hardly felt like a free man. To the contrary, having "long since learned the lesson of obedience, I was willing to submit."[96] Manumission had not liberated Harrison from the psychic and bodily memories of bondage, and no amount of hope for his future in Liberia could fully erase or soothe the agonies of his past in Indian Territory.

3

Slave Resistance, Sectional Crisis, and Political Factionalism in Antebellum Indian Territory

Enslaved people in the Choctaw and Chickasaw Nations had no illusions about what it meant to be owned and exploited as chattel, and they engaged in a wide range of resistance strategies to ease the burdens of enslavement. Whether they settled on everyday acts of defiance or more dramatic moments of violence and insurrection, enslaved people understood the complicated ways that the institution of slavery shaped political, social, and economic life in the Choctaw and Chickasaw Nations. So, too, did they grasp the ways slavery in Indian Territory was inextricably linked to slavery in the United States. Enslaved people's wide-ranging acts of opposition and resistance usually aimed to test the limits of slaveholders' control over black bodies, time, and resources in the context of daily practices and interactions. Enslaved people, for example, disrupted work routines, talked back to their masters, spoke too loudly, got drunk and fought with each other, and sometimes used deadly force against their masters. Slaves' defiant and unruly behavior occurred in various sites: slaves' cabins, country roads, cotton fields, forests, town centers, and mission stations.

Enslaved people knew a great deal about the physical world around them and also about the political and social climate in Indian Territory and beyond. Networks of communication linked enslaved people across the nations in Indian Territory and reached into the surrounding slave states, especially Texas and Arkansas. The lines of communication and collaboration linking the enslaved become most visible in instances of slaves' escapes, especially when slaves crossed the boundaries that divided Indian Territory and the borders between Indian Territory and the United States.

When slaves on either side of the Indian Territory–U.S. border fled into the neighboring territory, their movement usually triggered conflicts between Indian and white slaveholders. These disputes were never simply local or isolated interactions but frequently became matters that engaged federal authorities, as they so often hinged on broader questions of jurisdiction and the respective property rights of Indians and white people.

By the 1850s, enslaved people's resistance in the Choctaw and Chickasaw Nations played out in the context of the sectional crisis roiling the United States. The sectional crisis arrived at Indian Territory's doorstep with the 1854 Kansas-Nebraska Act, which created the Kansas Territory just north of Indian Territory. Native peoples in Kansas were stripped of their land and relocated to open the way for white settlement. The creation of Kansas and the ensuing bloodshed over whether Kansas would become a slave or free state greatly alarmed Choctaw and Chickasaw slaveholders and lawmakers and amplified existing tensions among them. Indian leaders debated and disagreed over how to protect their land and slaves from being overtaken by either lawless white mercenaries or the federal government. Enslaved people's resistance exacerbated the slavery-related disputes among Indian leaders and fueled their conflicts with federal authorities.

Indian Territory rarely, if ever, appears in studies of the U.S. sectional crisis and the fights over slavery's westward expansion. Yet it is clear that enslaved people's resistance efforts in the 1850s and Indian slaveholders' responses were bound up in the mounting crisis over slavery. Slaves and slaveholders in the Choctaw and Chickasaw Nations understood the ways their lives could be changed by events in the states, and they also recognized the moments when they might alter the course of things through their own actions.

IN THE YEARS AFTER their deportation from Mississippi to Indian Territory, many Choctaw and Chickasaw slaveholders sought to reestablish their wealth and prestige and deployed their slaves to build up extensive and profitable farms and plantations. Though both free and enslaved emigrants were buffeted by the hunger and disease that plagued removal, slaveholders in Indian Territory looked forward to better days. Toward the end of 1832, Choctaw slaveholder David Folsom led a removal party of nearly 1,000 people, including slaves, to an area near the Red River. By the spring of 1833, Folsom had already written back to John Pitchlynn in Mississippi, assuring him that the region was "cotton country."[1] U.S. Indian agents, too, were equally optimistic about Choctaw and Chickasaw slaveholders' prospects for the future. In his 1836 report, one agent predicted that "the Red River part is destined soon to be a fine cotton-growing country" and expected a yield of some 500 bales of cotton that year. The following year's report praised the "large quantities of cotton" grown on Red River plantations. Even when smallpox killed between 500 and 600 Chickasaw emigrants in 1838, the U.S. agent focused his attention on the likely economic success of Chickasaw and Choctaw cotton planters in the coming years.[2]

Ed Bailey, formerly a slave of Robert M. Jones, Choctaw Nation. (Robert L. Williams Collection; courtesy of the Oklahoma Historical Society)

It was, of course, enslaved people's labor—draining swamps, cutting trees, hauling logs, and building fences—that transformed the land into "cotton country." In the summer of 1834, Peter Pitchlynn moved his family and slaves out of the flood-damaged Mushulatubbee District and settled near the Mount Fork River in the Apukshunnubbee District. There, his slaves were put to work, clearing the land, constructing their own cabins, and also building a large home for the Pitchlynn family. A few years later, Pitchlynn claimed another tract of land not far from the Wheelock Mission and even closer to the Red River.[3] Polly Colbert, a former slave of the Chickasaw Colbert family, said of the early days in Indian Territory: "The land was first cleared up and worked by . . . slaves." Chickasaw planters and farmers, too, settled close to the Red River, the southern boundary of Indian Territory that separated the Indian nations from Texas. Chickasaw George Colbert operated a plantation where his 150 slaves were expected to "cultivate, [in 1838], from three to five hundred acres in cotton, besides making corn sufficient for his hands."[4]

Over half of the enslaved population was concentrated on farms and plantations in the southern counties close to the Red River. Polly Colbert recalled: "I was born at Tishomingo and we moved to de farm on Red River soon after." On the eve of the Civil War, Choctaw Robert Jones owned at least 227 slaves and operated four plantations that stretched across this region.[5] Some estimates put the number of slaves owned by Jones closer to 500, which would have made him one of the largest slaveholders in Indian Territory *and* the United States.[6] By the 1850s, a growing number of slaves could also be found on newly established plantations farther north, close to the Arkansas River in Skullyville County. In 1846 the U.S. Indian Agent found that the more prosperous Choctaw and Chickasaw planters had "most excellent cotton gins" and had little difficulty selling "their produce" in the neighboring states.[7]

Indian planters found ready markets for their slave-grown corn, cotton, and cattle in the surrounding states and closer to home at the U.S. military posts in Indian Territory.[8] The town of Doaksville, in Towson County, developed as a principal hub of commerce in the nation, with boats collecting and delivering merchandise and mail at Fort Towson landing, close to the mouth of the Kiamichi River. Steamboats plied the Red River and its tributaries, picking up bales of cotton at Fort Towson and linking Indian planters to markets and merchants in Shreveport and New Orleans. Newspapers in Texas and Indian Territory routinely advertised the packets running on the Red River between Indian country and Louisiana. For example, a boat went up the Boggy River to one of Robert Jones's plantations to collect his bales of cotton. Like Jones, other wealthy planters expanded their investments in the slave-based cotton economy by establishing trading firms and acquiring steamships. Chickasaw planter Benjamin Franklin Colbert, for example, operated a ferry across the Red River to facilitate travel and commerce between Indian Territory and Texas.[9] So thoroughly had slavery and cotton infused the society that Chickasaws named their county with the largest number of plantations, cotton gins, and steamboat landings "Panola," a variant of "ponola," the Chickasaw word for "thread" and Choctaw word for "cotton."[10]

The development of cotton plantations and other commercial agricultural and livestock enterprises in the unified Choctaw/Chickasaw Nation paralleled the growth of cotton agriculture in the Creek and Cherokee Nations. Historian David Chang explains that the proliferation of individually operated farms and plantations in the Creek Nation rested squarely on a widening notion of "private ownership of land-use rights." Among Cherokees, likewise, daily practices and legal definitions of land use shifted to permit and protect the ability of individuals and families to acquire and claim land for their personal

Riverside, the home of Benjamin Franklin Colbert at Colbert's Ferry, south of Colbert on the Red River. (Robert L. Williams Collection; courtesy of the Oklahoma Historical Society)

benefit. Similar changes were also under way among Choctaws and Chickasaws. The privatization of land use among Indians expanded and became increasingly profitable after removal as slaveholders heightened their demands and control of slaves' productive and reproductive labor.

In just under three decades, from the era of removal to the eve of the Civil War, the enslaved population grew considerably. The birth of enslaved babies and the importation of enslaved people purchased from the United States combined to increase the enslaved population of the Choctaw/Chickasaw Nation.[11] To characterize the growth of the enslaved population as "natural increase" is to miss the commodification, if not coercion, underlying enslaved women's reproduction. "The stock and negroes are doing and increasing finely . . . our horses, hogs and negroes look the fattest and sleakest [*sic*] of all the horses and negroes in the country," wrote Lycurgus Pitchlynn to his father. As legal-studies scholar Margaret Burnham has written, slaveholders appropriated the most intimate and important social events in enslaved people's lives and transformed them into economic moments of property and profit.[12] Slaveholders' claims to enslaved women's reproductive capacity extended beyond pregnancy when they insisted that new mothers breastfeed their owners' babies. Enslaved women resisted their owners' efforts to control their reproductive bodies in many ways, including opposing the role of wet nurse. Ex-slave Kiziah Love, for example, reported that she "begged so hard" not to be the nurse for her master's baby. Another enslaved woman was then directed to nurse the baby, but she moved so slowly when called to care for the baby at night that her master whipped her.[13]

Slaveholders aimed to control slaves' labor, as well as their reproduction, for economic gain. At least a decade before removal, Choctaw and Chickasaw slaveholders formulated and imposed regulations on slaves' labor, time, and movement that closely follow the model drawn by historian Stephanie Camp in her study of southern plantations.[14] By controlling enslaved people's bodies, slaveholders sought not only to derive profits but also to demonstrate their mastery. "The slaves did all the work," recalled ex-slave Ed Butler, while owners "guided the work done by the slaves."[15] Solomon Pitchlynn said of his owner's son Peter Pitchlynn Jr.: "He stands at my back."[16] Kiziah Love recalled: "I worked ever day." Enslaved children, too, were expected to work. They gathered firewood, milked cows, carried water, took care of younger children, and performed other indoor and outdoor chores. Matilda Poe, who had been owned by Chickasaw Isaac Love, explained how he orchestrated slaves' movement through the day and night. Enslaved men rose at dawn to feed the horses, and then the plantation bell summoned everyone to breakfast. After eating, enslaved workers went into the fields until the next bell signaled a midday break. The workday then continued until sunset, when enslaved people returned to their cabins for the night.[17]

When enslaved people challenged or circumvented the spatial and social boundaries imposed by their owners, their actions were deemed "unruly." Slaveholders, moreover, responded decisively to these perceived challenges. During an absence from his plantation, Peter Pitchlynn directed his wife to call upon his brother "should any of the blacks get unruly" and ask him "to whip them."[18] A few years later, Israel Folsom wrote to Pitchlynn about an outburst on his plantation: "[T]hings do not go altogether right with some of your slaves—perhaps you have heard [of] Wash's capers."[19] No matter the impetus and aim underlying everyday acts of opposition, enslaved people routinely tested the limits of their owners' control. Slaveholders, in turn, moved quickly to reassert their dominance. For much of the antebellum period, plantation governance was largely a private affair, with individual slaveholders rather than lawmakers setting forth the rules and ensuring compliance through coercion and violence.

Enslaved people's independent gatherings proved especially nettlesome to slaveholders in the Red River region. While many owners permitted slaves to hold prayer meetings or social gatherings at appointed hours and places on their land, enslaved people also assembled at times and sites of their own choosing. The September 6, 1849, issue of the *Choctaw Intelligencer*, a short-lived English- and Choctaw-language newspaper, included an item about the enslaved people around Doaksville who "congregate in riotous groups on the Sabbath, and at all times of night." These noisy conclaves constituted a "perfect nuisance to good order and society . . . and peace." Worse yet, the author complained, slaves' late-night affairs threatened to decrease their daytime productivity.[20] Public and private discussions about slaves' disruptive behavior sounded the call for slaveholders to impose stricter controls on their slaves. "Something ought to be done," Thomas Pitchlynn complained about a man whose farm was "a great place for the negrows to meet on Sundays."[21]

By the 1850s, Choctaw and Chickasaw slaveholders shifted some of their individual authority over their slaves, especially over slaves' mobility, to their national government.[22] Adding to the existing body of laws governing slavery, lawmakers expanded the right to control slaves' movement beyond individual slaveholders by creating patrols and requiring slaves to carry written passes.[23] An 1848 law punished slaves "found at such assemblies or strolling about from one plantation to another without a pass from his master mistress or overseer" with up to ten lashes on the bare back. The punishment could be inflicted either by the lighthorsemen or any citizen of the nation.[24]

A few years later, after the Chickasaws reestablished their independent government, Chickasaw legislators enacted their own legal code that directly addressed a number of issues related to slavery. One law made it illegal to harbor or "clandestinely support" runaway slaves and appropriated funds to pay a jailor, who would be responsible for keeping captured runaways or other disorderly slaves in custody. During the Chickasaw legislature's October 1857 session, payments were authorized to Sheriff Ad-koutch-an Tubby and S. Colbert for holding slaves under arrest. Slaveholders were required to give slaves written passes to travel. County judges were directed to assemble patrols in the areas where such a policing mechanism would be most "useful." It was expected that the patrol would ride three nights per week, and patrollers had the authority to establish their own rules, such as determining how long a pass was valid. Slaves caught without a pass would be punished with thirty-nine lashes on the bare back.[25] According to ex-slaves, such measures proved effective. Matilda Poe indicated that few slaves left Isaac Love's plantation because of the "patrollers." Polly Colbert said that "patrollers" basically functioned as policemen, and that she was afraid of them. Kiziah Love remembered that slaveholder Buck Colbert rode with patrols who regularly stopped black people on the road and demanded to see their passes, telling them "they had stayed over time" and "didn't have any business off the farm and to git back there and stay there."[26]

Enslaved people also ran afoul of slavery's social order when they spoke up or talked back. Even when their bodies were in the proper location, their insolent speech defied the social limits of subordination and was no less a violation than defying work orders. Matilda Poe, for example, recalled that her owner punished slaves who were "sassy or lazy."[27] Unlike legislators in the southern states, Choctaw and Chickasaw lawmakers did not enact legislation governing enslaved people's speech, but slaveholders were certainly sensitive to the content and tone of their slaves' speech.[28] Whether complaining and grumbling about working conditions, exhorting people to prayer, or reproaching their owners, enslaved people could not speak any more freely than they could move. Malvina Pitchlynn, one of Peter Pitchlynn's daughters, went to visit her sister at Wheelock mission, and she brought along an enslaved girl to care for her child. At Wheelock, this girl met Phillis, the enslaved woman who had negotiated with missionaries for her purchase and eventual liberation. When Phillis spoke to the visiting slave girl, her mistress interpreted their conversation as "impudent language directed to herself . . . and threatened to beat Phillis, but did not." Within a day or two, Loring Folsom, Malvina's husband, returned to the mission, restrained Phillis, and punched her head and face, "which made the blood to flow."[29] The Reverend Copeland intervened to protect Phillis, and Folsom replied with a racial epithet directed toward Phillis and threats that he would whip her for her insolence. The racial hierarchy that shaped slavery's social order encompassed not only enslaved people but also free or quasi-free black people such as Phillis.

This incident also reveals the ways in which Choctaw women wielded power over their slaves' movement and speech. Like other references to slaveholding women's domination, it reminds us that Choctaw and Chickasaw women played important roles in maintaining the brutal hierarchies of race and slavery.[30] Regardless of what Phillis said and how she said it, her conversation exceeded the limits of subservience, if not silence, expected from black people.

Slaveholders monitored the way slaves spoke to them but also the ways they interacted with each other. Enslaved people's disorderly conduct or speech did not always manifest as blows against their owners but sometimes emerged in conflicts with other slaves. Disputes among enslaved people engaged their owners when they became loud, violent, or deadly, upending the spatial, social, and economic order slaveholders sought to maintain. In 1832, for example, an enslaved man owned by John Pitchlynn killed his wife and then shot himself. Pitchlynn had little to say about the couple other than identifying the woman in terms of her monetary value: "I give 500 dollars for her."[31] In the summer of 1834, a number of the enslaved men on Peter Pitchlynn's plantation became "quite unruly." One man, Battice, proved especially unmanageable. "Drunk on all occasions," he was quarrelsome and threatening toward everyone and tried to kill an enslaved woman. While Pitchlynn's uncle Edmond Folsom did not feel at liberty to punish Battice without first receiving direct approval from his nephew, issues of ownership apparently did not deter the unnamed Choctaw woman who "downed" Battice during one of his outbursts.[32]

Through much of the early nineteenth century, concerns about excessive alcohol consumption were nearly ubiquitous among Choctaws and Chickasaws, including those who owned slaves. The earliest iterations of the Choctaw written legal code, for instance, prohibited bringing "whiskey or other ardent spirits" into the nation and called for the destruction of any alcohol found in the nation. In later decades, lawmakers refined the law, explicitly barring slaves' possession of alcohol.[33] When relationships among enslaved people unraveled, the situation strained slaveholders' control and occasioned even greater efforts at domination.

Whether on a single plantation, across the Choctaw/Chickasaw Nation, or across the Deep South, enslaved people did not conceive of themselves as a single, unified community. Historians such as Stephanie Camp, Anthony Kaye, and Dylan Penningroth have highlighted the many fault lines that divided enslaved people and precipitated disputes among them. Arguments over the possession of goods, disagreements over aiding fugitive slaves, quarrels between lovers, and general animosity shatter the mythical image of unwavering solidarity and a singular community.[34] Conflicts among enslaved people, however, did not mitigate their opposition to enslavement and their owners' control. Indeed, in some instances, disputes among slaves were inextricably linked to their acts of resistance, as in the following case.

Just after Christmas in 1858, an enslaved man named Prince confessed to murdering Richard Harkins, his master. Harkins was married to Lavinia Pitchlynn, one of Peter Pitchlynn's daughters, and was the brother of George Harkins, a prominent political figure and district chief in the Choctaw Nation. Like the Pitchlynns, members of the Harkins family were slaveholders.[35] On the morning of December 28, 1858, Prince was splitting and hauling fence rails down the road from the Harkins house. Richard Harkins left his house after breakfast to go hunting but first stopped to check on Prince. Though

Prince was expected to work on his own, he remained under the intermittent surveillance of his master. Harkins dismounted his horse to help Prince roll a log, and Prince struck him with his axe, breaking Harkins's skull and severing part of his right ear. Prince concealed the body in some tree branches he had cut down and then rode Harkins's horse to a spot called Ashley's Ford, a deep crossing on the Little River. Prince was careful to lead the horse into and out of the river before setting it loose in the woods, making it seem as though Harkins had fallen off the horse and drowned while trying to cross the river. He then went back for Harkins's body and took it to the river. Prince used a rope to tie a twenty-five-pound rock to the corpse and sunk it in a deep section of the river. At some point along the way, Prince slit Harkins's throat and stuffed leaves and mud into his mouth. When Harkins failed to return home that evening, his wife immediately suspected her slaves of foul play, refusing to believe that her husband had gotten lost in the woods or drowned.[36]

For five days, men connected to the Harkins and Pitchlynn families investigated the case. With the assistance of Solomon and Adam, two enslaved men owned by the Pitchlynns, the search party crossed the river, spoke with neighbors, tracked the horse, and looked for clues to Harkins's disappearance.[37] By January 2, 1859, all signs pointed to Prince, who was confronted and tied up. When threatened with a "severe whipping," Prince confessed to the murder. Harkins had not provided a Christmas celebration for the slaves, and Prince supposedly killed him in retaliation for withholding this customary celebration and respite from work.[38] The day after making his confession, Prince led the men to the spot where he had submerged Harkins's corpse. Screaming that his master's ghost was tormenting him, Prince slipped his chains, plunged into the river, and drowned.[39]

When Prince confessed, he initially named two other slaves as his accomplices but then changed his story to implicate only one other person. He first claimed that his uncle Adam had helped him kill Harkins and hide his body in the tree, but later Prince said that Adam did not know anything about the murder. Lycurgus Pitchlynn, Lavinia Pitchlynn Harkins's brother, believed that Adam had not been involved and that Prince had taken the name of the second accomplice to his grave. Prince also named his aunt Lucy as the principal agent behind the crime, saying that she had been urging him to kill Harkins for some time. Lucy had promised to take good care of Prince and assured him that if Harkins were dead, Lavinia would move the slaves back to the Pitchlynn's Mountain Fork estate. Even after Prince retracted his claim that Adam had assisted him, he continued to implicate Lucy. He maintained that it was Lucy who had spent months planning the murder. She had given Prince her rope and shown him how to secure the rock and sink Harkins's dead body. From the time of Harkins's disappearance to Prince's suicide, however, Lucy never confessed.[40]

After Harkins's family dragged his waterlogged corpse from the river at the exact spot Prince had shown them, they pulled Prince's lifeless body from the water. The events that followed soon caused a local and then international sensation. Lavinia Pitchlynn Harkins demanded that Lucy, who never admitted having a role in the murder, be put to death immediately. According to Loring Folsom, the dead Prince and living Lucy were "placed upon a log heap and burnt up." Choctaw murder statutes required a trial and conviction before the execution of a murderer. The law did not specifically address slaves murdering their masters; such cases perhaps fell under the general body of laws governing murder. The law did, however, define "willfully murdering a negro" as a capital crime.[41] If Lavinia believed her actions were in line with older traditions of Choctaw female authority in matters of vengeance and thus not governed by the nation's legal code, her family thought otherwise. Her brother described her at this time as "a raving maniac" and "deranged," and her brother-in-law called her actions "half crazy."[42]

News of Harkins's death and Lucy's execution must have traveled quickly and widely, because later accounts indicated that "many persons" who may have assisted with the search witnessed the burning.[43] Not everyone flocked to watch Lucy die. "I did not see the negroes burnt," Lycurgus Pitchlynn wrote to his father. "I did not want to see it."[44]

Among some local slaveholders, the incident prompted an outcry against Peter Pitchlynn for failing to keep his slaves under control.[45] According to his son Lycurgus, there were rumors that the elder Pitchlynn harbored free black people on his plantation in violation of the nation's laws. Nothing in Pitchlynn's correspondence suggests that he knowingly offered refuge to fugitive slaves or permitted free black people to stay on his property. Lycurgus Pitchlynn also complained to his father that their slaves had not been working sufficiently since their overseer left, suggesting that the concern may not have been so much about "free" black people but about the absence of strict control of slaves. Even Lavinia blamed her father for his slaves' actions. In a moment of pique, Lycurgus Pitchlynn suggested that his father either "sell every cursed negro" or send them to Liberia to preclude his children's "fighting over a little negro property" after his death.[46]

The tragic events gained a wider audience in 1860, when missionaries' accounts of Lucy's gruesome execution at the hands of a church member— Lavinia Pitchlynn Harkins—came to the attention of the American Board of

Commissioners, the Presbyterian Board of Foreign Missions, and the general public in the states. Richard and Lavinia Harkins were members of the Reverend Cyrus Byington's church at Stockbridge Mission. Reports indicated that someone else in the mob that had killed Lucy also belonged to the church but was not in good standing at that time. Lucy, too, had belonged to Byington's Stockbridge church, which was about ten miles from the Harkins's home. When the story became widely known in religious and abolitionist circles in the states, the central point of contention was whether Reverend Byington, who had known about Lucy's execution, should have reported the events to his superiors and allowed Lavinia Harkins to remain in good standing in his church.[47] Byington explained to the secretary of the Presbyterian Board that in the months after Richard Harkins and Lucy were killed, he often visited, read the Bible with, and prayed with the widow Harkins and her family. He did not mention whether he also ministered to Lucy's survivors.[48]

Historians have written about this episode almost exclusively in terms of the heightened state of conflict between Choctaw slaveholders, missionaries, and abolitionist clergy in the states in the 1850s. As discussed in the previous chapter, many Choctaw and Chickasaw slaveholders worried about missionaries' antislavery leanings, while abolitionist clergy in the states accused missionaries of sanctioning slavery in the Indian nations. With the principal scholarly focus on missionaries' efforts to fend off all their critics, the issue of slave resistance has received very little attention.[49]

The accounts of Prince's actions, confession, and suicide point to the dense web of relationships that bound enslaved people together. There are too many silences in the records to know for sure who instructed Prince to kill Harkins and what inspired that plan. At the same time, the gaps call attention to the alliances, antagonisms, or indifference that shaped enslaved people's interactions with each other and their plans for opposing their masters. What drove Prince either to name his accomplices or to falsely accuse the people around him? Who and what beckoned Lucy back to Mountain Fork, a place where Pitchlynn's enslaved women and men were driven hard in the cotton fields and lived in cramped and filthy quarters, where women were expected to breed and everyone routinely suffered from "sickness"?[50] How did Lucy's loved ones and fellow churchgoers react to the news of Prince's accusation and her execution? Prince said he used Lucy's rope: "the rope came around aunt Lucy's basket when she come from Mountain Fork." Was it a basket for work, or did it carry personal belongings? What happened to Lucy and Prince at Christmastime that set these events in motion? When Prince brought his axe down on Harkins's head, he transformed the tool of his forced labor into a weapon of willful opposition. The grisly outcomes in this case were extreme but hardly unique.

As other accounts of violent resistance reveal, enslaved people lashed out against their owners with fatal consequences. An African Cherokee slave called Smoot attacked his master and mistress with an axe, killing them while they slept. Peter Pitchlynn's chronically drunk slave Battice repeatedly brandished weapons and threatened to kill the overseer. The fact that few Choctaw and Chickasaw slaveholders hired overseers did not alter the power dynamics between overseers and slaves or lessen slaves' anger toward them. A slave sniper shot and killed the overseer hired by Chickasaw Jackson Kemp while he dispensed the weekly rations on Kemp's plantation. Whether carrying out a well-devised plan or acting in the heat of the moment, slaves in Indian Territory sometimes opposed their owners and overseers in the deadliest manner.[51]

Enslaved people who ran away from their owners took a less-confrontational but no-less-violent path than those who killed their masters. Runaways directly challenged slaveholders' authority and the fundamental premise of chattel slavery by taking full possession of their bodies and lives. Slaveholders, in turn, met these defiant acts of self-liberation with brutal retribution. Contrary to contemporary depictions of Indian slaveholders as lax about preventing slaves from escaping, Choctaw and Chickasaw slaveholders had little tolerance for runaways and showed faint mercy for those who were captured and returned to bondage.[52] In 1851 a man named Aleck ran away from Choctaw Henry Folsom, taking with him a horse, a new saddle and bridle, and a double-barreled shotgun. Casting a wide net in his efforts to retrieve Aleck, Folsom placed notices about Aleck's disappearance in Choctaw, Cherokee, and Arkansas newspapers. Determined to wield the ultimate authority over Aleck, Folsom offered a reward for the return of his slave and other property but also promised to pay "for his scalp" if Aleck could not be captured alive.[53] A few years later, Len and John ran away from Loring Folsom, taking his "best horses," clothes, and guns. In this case, slaves' efforts to escape again were met with violent reprisals. Folsom caught up with Len a week after his escape and ordered a companion to "pepper" Len's leg with buckshot to stop him in his tracks. John was eventually caught in Texas. Folsom knew that the men wanted to be sold to another owner but preferred to keep and "brake [sic] them" instead of yielding to their preferences.[54] The loss of property—inanimate objects and chattel—rankled slaveholders, but so did losing control over slaves.

Enslaved women, like men, sought to free themselves from slavery by running away. Because of the fragmented nature of the extant sources, it is difficult to estimate the number of runaway women and men. The available documentation, however, firmly supports the conclusions that enslaved women ran away from their owners with the goal of liberation and that runaway adults sometimes took children with them. The networks and alliances among enslaved women and men that transformed dreams of freedom into the reality of escape stretched across plantations and even across Indian Territory. In one dramatic case from the winter of 1842, a group of eight fugitives from Choctaw masters—one man, two women, and five children—ran away and headed west but were captured by a white man named James Edwards and a Delaware Indian man named Billy Wilson. By chance, the group encountered a large party of runaway slaves who had escaped from their Cherokee and Creek owners. These escapees killed Edwards and Wilson, liberating the other runaways (those with Choctaw masters). The two parties of fugitives merged, and eventually the group was captured. Some were jailed at Fort Gibson, the U.S. installation in the Cherokee Nation, while others were returned to their owners.[55] Choctaw and Chickasaw lawmakers confronted this problem head-on by declaring it the "duty" of members of the nation to seize suspected runaway slaves and deliver fugitives to district authorities. Local authorities were supposed to locate a runaway slave's master or, after six months, have the lighthorsemen sell the fugitive at a public auction.[56]

Runaway slaves from Indian Territory often set out for Texas, possibly en route to Mexico, where slavery had been abolished; but fugitives from bondage in Arkansas and Texas took the reverse course, heading into Indian Territory.[57] It was this multidirectional flow of fugitives that drew Indian and white slaveholders into ongoing conflicts and also generated considerable political discord for both Indian and American lawmakers. Runaways who made it from the states into Indian Territory hid out in the woods and sometimes received assistance from nearby enslaved communities. Incoming fugitives could not be certain they would find safe haven in the Choctaw/Chickasaw Nation. Slaveholders in Texas and Arkansas placed notices in the *Choctaw Intelligencer* announcing slaves' escapes and offering rewards for their capture and return. Choctaw and Chickasaw slaveholders and patrollers kept watch over the roads and woods, warning off potential escapees within the nation and tracking fugitives from the states. An article in the *Choctaw Intelligencer*, for example, described one instance when "one of our citizens" captured a runaway slave from Texas. In another case, the U.S. Indian agent to the Chickasaws sent a notice to the *Northern Standard* (Clarksville, Texas) that he had taken custody of a runaway man owned by a Texan.[58]

The presence of African American fugitives from the states alarmed the free residents of the Choctaw/Chickasaw Nation for a number of reasons. Fugitives hiding out in remote encampments might spur enslaved people to run away from their owners or at least steal food and supplies to assist them. The presence of fugitives from the states within the limits of the Choctaw/Chickasaw Nation also threatened to draw white slaveholders and trackers from the United States into the nation. Citizens of the Choctaw/Chickasaw Nation had never looked kindly upon their neighbors in Texas and Arkansas who entered Indian Territory illegally. As much as Indians, especially slaveholders, objected to the presence of fugitive slaves in their midst, they bristled even more at the prospect of white intruders, including slave hunters, trespassing through their nation.[59]

Joined by their ideological and economic investments in slavery, white and Indian slaveholders parted ways over issues of Indians' territorial and political autonomy, even in the context of tracking runaway slaves. Through the antebellum period, white slaveholders and speculators pressed for greater access to Indian Territory, arguing for the extension of U.S. laws regarding the capture and return of fugitive slaves. In 1838 the U.S. attorney general B. F. Butler had determined that Article IV of the U.S. Constitution, which provided for the return of runaway slaves, did not apply to Indian Territory. In the summer of 1850, the editors of the *Northern Standard*, a proslavery Texas newspaper, weighed in on the subject of fugitive slave laws. They called on Congress to pass a law that would enable Texas slaveholders to retrieve runaway slaves from Indian Territory and hold missionaries accountable for abetting fugitives. Members of the U.S. Congress spent the better part of that year hashing out the provisions of the Compromise of 1850, including the Fugitive Slave Act of 1850.[60] Reinvigorating both the fourth article of the U.S. Constitution and a 1793 law governing the return of fugitive slaves, this new act held state and national governments responsible for restoring runaway slaves to their owners. The 1850 law also criminalized and imposed stiff penalties for assisting fugitives or impeding their capture and arrest.[61] By February 1854, Attorney General Caleb Cushing overruled Butler's 1838 position and held that the Fugitive Slave Act of 1850 did in fact extend over Indian Territory. Citizens of the United States, he indicated, could lawfully enter Indian nations to retrieve fugitive slaves and could call on federal authorities for assistance if necessary.[62] The intensifying national crisis over slavery in the United States that produced the 1850 Fugitive Slave Act also entailed bitter debates over the westward expansion of slavery. The westward migration of both U.S. citizens and governmental authority immediately raised questions about the territorial and political future of Indian Territory that Choctaws and Chickasaws found most unsettling. Texas statehood (1845) and the transfer of land from Mexico to the United States under the 1848 Treaty of Guadalupe Hidalgo put the issue of slavery's westward expansion on center stage in U.S. national politics.[63]

The passage of the Kansas-Nebraska Act in 1854 brought the matter even closer to home for Choctaws and Chickasaws, who paid careful attention to the debates and events unfolding to their immediate north, where Native peoples of the Central Plains had just been dispossessed of their land. The Kansas-Nebraska Act left the decision of whether or not to allow slavery in Kansas and Nebraska in the hands of each territory's white male electorate. Consequently, white settlers from northern and southern states poured into Kansas over the next two years, hoping not just to acquire land but also to influence election outcomes and thus decide the status of slavery.[64] Contested elections and the creation of parallel proslavery and free-state governments quickly led to violent clashes in Kansas that gained widespread national attention. In the spring of 1854, writing from Union Theological Seminary in New York City, Choctaw Allen Wright said of the Kansas-Nebraska issue: "I am perfectly indifferent how much the white people quarrel over it among themselves—if they do not trouble the Indians."[65]

Yet leading Choctaws and Chickasaws, including Wright, did follow the events that unfolded in "Bleeding Kansas" and found them worrisome because they anticipated the possibility that Americans' desire for land and battles over slavery would spill over into Indian Territory. Their apprehensions about U.S. designs on Indian Territory were not unfounded. As historian Clara Sue Kidwell explains, Congress had proceeded with the creation of the Kansas Territory despite the presence of many Indian reservations in Kansas. Choctaw leaders, furthermore, were well aware of federal and state lawmakers' growing interest in transforming Indian Territory into a formal territory of the United States, which would, of course, entail stripping the Choctaw people of their government and land. According to the U.S. Indian agent, Indians were "fully alive to the fact that no mere parchment barriers" would protect them against the "expansive force" of white Americans.[66]

Whether Kansas wound up a slave or free state, prominent Choctaws worried that their territory would become the next battleground in the fight over expanding slavery. In 1856 George Harkins feared that if Kansas became a free state, proslavery southerners would then set their sights on Choctaw country. The following year, Sampson Folsom indicated that the Choctaws and their land would not be safe from either advocates or opponents of slavery's geographic expansion: "[I]f the North or South are anxious for us to come in as a state or territorial, they must not make our country another Kansas lobby of it. For *we* the Indians, have but little confidence to spare for either Northern or Southern policy when the question of African *slavery* and Indian title to land are in vogue. North or South wants land bad."[67] Choctaw leaders were as concerned about grassroots campaigns to overtake their country as they were about federal plans to absorb Indian Territory.[68] An 1859 report from a South Carolinian in Kansas, which was reproduced in abolitionist and proslavery newspapers in the states, lent credence to their fears with its prediction, or threat: "The next theatre for action *will be the Indian territory south of Kansas,* including Cherokee, Creek and Choctaw nations."[69]

At the same time that Choctaws and Chickasaws watched civil strife break out among white people in Kansas, they faced the very real possibility of hostilities erupting among themselves through the 1850s. Though Choctaw and Chickasaw slaveholders shared an interest in maintaining the stability of slavery, an array of other domestic issues fractured the ties between their nations. Chickasaws' increasing dissatisfaction with the limited strength of their representatives in the National Council and ongoing disputes over the boundaries of the Chickasaw district threatened to spark hostilities between the two peoples. Despite their grave concerns about the expansion of white settlement closer to their territory, Choctaw and Chickasaw leaders capitalized on the federal government's pressing need to obtain land for resettling Indians from Kansas and Nebraska. Choctaw leadership successfully leveraged both an ongoing dispute with the federal government over payment for Mississippi land claims and the worsening political tensions between the Choctaws and Chickasaws to negotiate a new treaty with the United States. The Treaty of 1855 ceded and leased portions of the Choctaw Nation's westernmost land to the United States and also reestablished the Chickasaw Nation's political autonomy.[70]

The nations' 1855 split had little immediate consequence for enslaved people's daily lives, but continued conflicts among the Choctaws through the late 1850s ultimately opened new avenues for slave resistance and unrest.[71] After the Chickasaw Nation reestablished its government, its legislature enacted a fairly extensive slave code that regulated enslaved people's movement and actions and also denied the national government the power to emancipate slaves without compensating slaveholders. By contrast, factionalism destabilized the Choctaw national government when it attempted to write a new constitution after the 1855 split from the Chickasaws.[72] The political conflict erupted in the autumn of 1856 when the National Council called a constitutional convention in Skullyville. The convention generated a new constitution in January 1857 that dramatically altered the structure of the national government by centralizing and concentrating power in the hands of a single national governor. A constitutional crisis ensued when a majority of the citizens refused

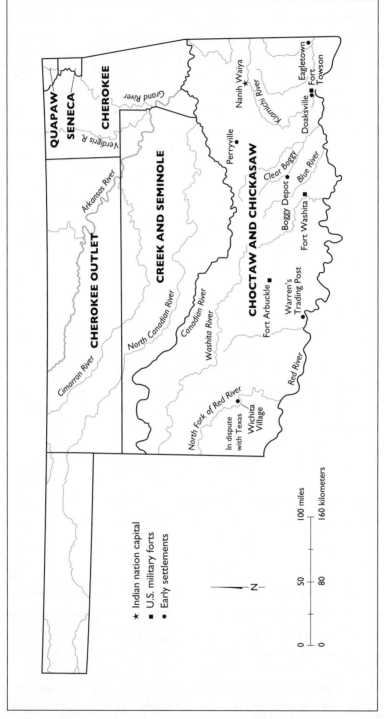

Map of Choctaw and Chickasaw territory in Indian Territory, 1855. (In Clara Sue Kidwell, The Choctaws in Oklahoma: From Tribe to Nation, 1855–1970 [Norman: University of Oklahoma Press, 2007])

to acknowledge this new constitution and its government. Factionalism then roiled the nation for three years. Though people clashed over the structure and power of the national government, this was not the only issue at the heart of the turmoil. Slavery emerged as a key point in the conflicts over the strength and direction of the national government. Some participants in the political struggles referenced "free soil" sentiment in the nation, but Choctaw leaders' willingness to protect slavery was not the contested issue. Rather, men on all sides of the conflict worried about forestalling an onslaught of antislavery and proslavery white settlers from the states. The question of slavery in the Choctaw Nation thus came to the fore, as Choctaw leaders assessed the likelihood of white Americans making Indian Territory their next battleground over slavery.

The 1857 Skullyville Constitution, for example, directly addressed the national government's power to regulate slavery. The first provision barred the General Council from passing "laws for the emancipation of slaves, without the consent of their owners." It also denied the council the power to block emigrants from the United States from bringing slaves into the nation. Yet the next paragraph seems to reverse course, vesting the council with the power "to pass such laws, regulating or prohibiting the introduction of slaves, into the Nation, as may be deemed proper and expedient."[73] Tandy Walker, who headed the Skullyville convention, predicted that these measures would surely make the Choctaw Nation vulnerable to invasion from white slaveholders in neighboring states. Texas and Arkansas, Walker wrote, would not tolerate Choctaw country becoming "another Canada" and would "overrun [us] and our Nationality [would be] destroyed and our country taken away from us." Slaveholder George Harkins, by contrast, feared the Skullyville Constitution's second provision "was all that a free-soiler could desire to see incorporated into [a] Southern Constitution."[74]

During the following year, another contingent of Choctaw leaders organized their supporters in opposition to the Skullyville constitution and drafted an alternative document: the Doaksville Constitution. Though slaveholder George Harkins led this faction, the Doaksville Constitution (May 1858) was met with accusations of abolitionism.[75] "We have now a regular abolition constitution," Lycurgus Pitchlynn wrote to his father.[76] Charges of abolitionism clouded the entire constitutional crisis. Slaveholding men in both the Skullyville and Doaksville factions accused each other of "abolitionism," though there is virtually nothing to suggest that any political leader advocated abolishing or even curbing slavery. Used as an epithet, "abolitionist" had the same rhetorical force as the term "Black Republican" in the states. Both aimed to consolidate political support by exploiting racist fears of black people's freedom and equality. The term also invoked the specter of meddlesome antislavery U.S. citizens, which also worked to unify Choctaw voters.[77] The political unrest of the late 1850s came to an end in 1860 with the creation of a revised constitution that was widely accepted by voters. The restoration of the national government, however, did little to quell Choctaw concerns about the stability of slavery.

By 1860, however, Choctaws increasingly identified enslaved people within the nation rather than white outsiders from the states as the principal threat to slavery. For much of that year, accounts of enslaved people's resistance and plans for violent rebellion engulfed the Choctaw Nation. In the summer of 1860, news of suspicious fires sweeping through stores and warehouses in Texas reached the Choctaw territory. Texas newspapers attributed the arson to enslaved men and women but, unwilling to give sole credit to the enslaved, the papers also accused white abolitionists of encouraging them. Though Choctaw slaveholders were not immediately inclined to suspect their own slaves of similar insurrectionary inclinations, they certainly remained alert for signs of rebellion. In July 1860, for example, Israel Folsom did not believe there were plots under way in the Choctaw Nation but conceded: "Still danger may be nearby."[78] Barely a month later, men like Folsom came to realize that the danger was indeed inching closer to home.

By August 1860 enslaved people from Texas, Arkansas, and Louisiana fled their owners and arrived in the Choctaw Nation. Suggesting the expansive networks of communication that linked slaves in Indian Territory to their fellow slaves in the neighboring states, word had spread outward from the Choctaw Nation that it would soon be free territory. Joseph Dukes, one of the candidates for the office of principal chief, was reported to be an abolitionist. Slaves from the surrounding area believed that he would pave the way for black freedom in the Choctaw Nation. The enslaved were not the only ones who suspected Dukes of antislavery sentiment. That summer, Israel Folsom assured his good friend Peter Pitchlynn that they should support Dukes's candidacy and not worry about his alleged abolitionist sympathies because, unlike the other candidates, "we control [Dukes] so easy."[79] Dukes lost the 1860 election, but that did not deter black people in the Choctaw Nation or in the states from pushing ahead with their plans for self-liberation.

In the early fall of 1860, there was "a good deal of excitement" in the Pitchlynns' neighborhood. Slaves in the area were suspected of organizing an insurrection and having collaborators in Arkansas. It seemed their leader was "*old 'free Dick,'*" who had been spotted on Pitchlynn's plantation and was later seized in Paraclifta, Arkansas, where he was found with a group of slaves that were "in the possession of armes."[80] Such insurrectionary impulses were hardly

unique to the Choctaw Nation or Indian Territory. A group of African Cherokees was suspected of plotting to poison their owners around the time of the
Texas fires. In the southern states, the months leading up to the 1860 presidential election were a tumultuous time in which many enslaved people believed
the moment had arrived to seize their freedom one way or another. Like the
accounts of runaway slaves arriving in the Choctaw Nation from Arkansas and
Texas with the hope that Joseph Dukes would inaugurate an era of black freedom, these episodes illustrate enslaved people's direct engagement with local
and national politics. Moreover, they remind us that enslaved people's path-
ways of knowledge and communication did not stop at the border between
Indian Territory and the United States. When enslaved people considered the
possibilities that either a principal chief of the Choctaw Nation or a president
of the United States might set the stage for black people's liberation, they did
more than simply imagine the possibility that newly appointed political leaders
would change their lives. They communicated, moved, and acted in ways that
might accelerate the pace of that change and widen its consequences.[81]

Enslaved people in and around Indian Territory may have hoped for the
arrival of a powerful intercessor while they amassed weapons and plotted their
self-liberation, but they already had an extensive network of friends and allies
in place. Free black activists in the states protested slavery in Indian Territory as
vociferously as they denounced slavery in the United States. Through the pages
of publications such as *Frederick Douglass' Paper* and the *Douglass' Monthly*,
free black people reached out to their "brethren and sisters" enslaved in Indian
Territory, urging resistance and pledging unity. An 1851 open letter "To the
Christian men and women held in Slavery among the Choctaw Indians" encouraged self-liberation: "You are probably in circumstances in which it will be
very difficult for you to escape. But if you have the opportunity of emigrating
from that land of oppression, by all means improve it."[82] In 1859, keenly aware of
the crisis in Kansas and attuned to the possibility that proslavery white settlers
had Indian Territory in their sights, *Douglass' Monthly* exhorted the "Tous-
saints and Christophs among the negroes themselves" to rise up and extinguish
slavery.[83]

If Lincoln's election to the presidency and the early rumblings of secession
and war stoked the fires of black resistance, so, too, did they push Indians to reaf-
firm their commitment to preserving their territorial and political autonomy, including the institution of chattel slavery.[84] In January 1861 Jacob Folsom planned
on buying an enslaved boy to work on his farm, noting somewhat caustically
that he did so with the hope that Lincoln and the Republicans would not overrun Indian Territory and abolish slavery. Within a few months, almost as soon

as the war began, Indians found themselves facing off not against Free-Soilers and abolitionists but instead against Confederate intruders and squatters. In May 1861 Sampson Folsom fumed that "our lovely country [is] in the hands of Texanian filibusters—they are making inroads upon our soil. . . . [W]hat they will do next is to make *white settlement* in our midst. . . . [We must] keep out land *pirates* and abolitionists to maintain the supremacy of the laws of the land." Though Folsom once more invoked an abolitionist threat, it is hard to conceive of a wave of antislavery Texans flooding Indian Territory in 1861.

Enslaved people, too, feared the onslaught of the white raiders they sometimes called "Bushwackers." Ex-slave Kiziah Love, for example, recalled that right before the war, thieves stole slaves from Indian Territory to sell in the states. Elsie Pryor was one such person. She later explained that she had been "stolen by Bushwackers" while she was collecting water from a stream. Pryor was taken to Fort Smith, where she was sold to a white buyer.[85]

In the spring of 1861, Confederate forces attacked the U.S. forts that had been established to protect the borders and peoples of Indian Territory from white intruders and Southern Plains Indians. The Confederate army captured Fort Smith in Arkansas in May 1861, effectively closing off the lower Mississippi River and isolating Indian Territory from the Union. During this time, the Union withdrew its troops from Indian Territory, deploying them in theaters to the south and east. Choctaw and Chickasaw diplomats in Washington, D.C., urged their lawmakers back home to remain neutral regarding the impending crisis. Nonetheless, legislators quickly adopted resolutions averring their support of the Confederacy because "natural affections" and "social and domestic institutions" united Choctaws and Chickasaws with their "Southern friends" and "brethren."

On June 12, 1861, the nations entered a treaty with the Confederacy that dispensed with genteel euphemisms and directly addressed the subject of slavery. It confirmed the legality of chattel slavery and extended the Fugitive Slave Law to the nations, requiring the return of runaway slaves from the Confederacy and pledging to return any runaways from the Indian nations.[86] When the Choctaw and Chickasaw governments allied with the Confederacy in the summer of 1861, they severed their nations' existing treaty relations with the Union.

Unlike the Creek and Cherokee Nations, which split over these issues of slavery and nationalism, the Choctaw and Chickasaw Nations remained largely intact. No significant loyalist contingent of Choctaw or Chickasaw men and women coalesced in these nations as it did among the Creeks and Cherokees. The absence of a sizable loyalist faction, however, should not be taken as the sole or best indicator of popular sentiment regarding the issues of slavery and sovereignty. The few hundred loyalist Chickasaws later recounted the ways they suffered at the hands of Confederate Indians. They told of being driven out of their homes and exiled to Arkansas, and they claimed that Chickasaw governor Winchester Colbert ordered the confiscation of their property. They also told of rebel Indians capturing, imprisoning, and sometimes killing Unionist Chickasaws.[87]

Choctaw and Chickasaw men served with Confederate troops, fighting against loyalist Creeks as well as Union soldiers from the states. In the spring of 1863, Union forces gained control of Fort Gibson in the Cherokee Nation and in the following months defeated Confederate troops, including a Choctaw and Chickasaw regiment, in the Battle of Honey Springs some twenty-five miles south of the fort. The defeat withered Indians' confidence in their alliance with the Confederacy. Confederate troops torched commissaries, destroying much-needed supplies to prevent Union soldiers from seizing them. The loss at Honey Springs also set the stage for the Union to take Fort Smith in September 1863.

In the wake of Union victories at Gettysburg and Vicksburg, the defeat at Honey Springs eroded hopes in Indian Territory that the Confederacy would triumph in the war. Before news of General Robert E. Lee's surrender at Appomattox on April 9, 1865, reached Indian Territory, Indian leaders had already convened a Grand Council that included representatives from the Choctaw, Chickasaw, Cherokee, Creek, and Seminole Nations along with delegates from Native peoples in Kansas and the region west of Indian Territory. At this and a subsequent council meeting, Indian leaders began planning for their postwar future by addressing their diplomatic relationships with each other, as well as by setting an agenda for restoring treaty relations with the United States.[88]

Nearly a century of scholarship has assessed the causes and reasoning that compelled the Indian nations to enter treaty relations with the Confederacy. At issue in much of the discussion is the extent to which allying with the South either signaled the Indian nations' commitment to the racial ideology of chattel slavery or marked a nationalist strategy to preserve Indian sovereignty. Yet the two cannot be disentangled. Protecting sovereignty was also protecting slavery. The resolution adopted by the Chickasaw legislature in May 1861 suggests as much. After criticizing Lincoln and the federal government for withdrawing Union troops from Indian Territory and withholding the payment of annuity moneys, the resolution affirmed the "feelings and sympathies" that joined the Chickasaw Nation to the Confederacy. The Union's war of "conquest and confiscation," furthermore, threatened to unleash a tidal wave of slave insurrections that would rival "San Domingo in atrocious horrors."[89]

Though no large-scale slave insurrection erupted to set rivers of blood flowing in the Choctaw and Chickasaw Nations or anywhere else in Indian Territory, slave unrest in Choctaw country continued in 1861. Enslaved men continued to plan for the moment when they might rise up against their owners and also defeat slavery. On one occasion, the slaves owned by Robert Jones had acquired weapons and had to be "disarmed." Believing that the "feds" had reached Choctaw territory, they had decided the time was right to "rise and strike for freedom."[90] In his study of the border skirmishes between slavery's defenders and opponents in the Upper South and Lower North, historian Stanley Harrold insists upon recognizing the central roles played by runaway slaves. Harrold argues that enslaved people's resistance, specifically their escapes across the borders between slave and free states, catalyzed much of the fighting between proslavery and antislavery activists. In a similar vein, enslaved people's resistance and flight across the Indian Territory borders heightened Choctaw and Chickasaw slaveholders' fears about not simply slave insurrections but also uprisings that might attract both enslaved rebels from the states and white activists on either side of the slavery issue. Of course, enslaved people's resistance generally played out on the local level, but in Indian Territory, local events were frequently bound up in larger questions and debates over how Choctaws and Chickasaws could hold white intruders and a colonial government at bay. Understanding the full range and consequences of the struggles that developed between slaves and slaveholders requires understanding the ways both groups saw themselves in the context of local, regional, and national (whether U.S. or Indian) conditions.

4

The Treaty of 1866
Emancipation and the Conflicts over Black People's Citizenship Rights and Indian Nations' Sovereignty

For the enslaved men and women in the Choctaw and Chickasaw Nations, the end of the Civil War offered little reason for jubilation. Unlike their Cherokee, Creek, and Seminole counterparts, Choctaw and Chickasaw lawmakers did not abolish slavery either during or at the close of the war. The Union victory in the states did not automatically precipitate the abolition of slavery in the politically autonomous Indian nations, nor did it immediately restore treaty relations between the United States and Indian allies of the Confederacy. Months after the war's end and slavery's demise in the United States, Choctaw and Chickasaw lawmakers remained hesitant about declaring the end of chattel slavery and refused to contemplate the possibility of legally and socially redefining people of African descent as something other than slaves.

Finally, in the spring of 1866, the Choctaw and Chickasaw Nations, despite having separate governments, entered a joint treaty with the United States. The treaty abolished slavery in the two nations and presented a convoluted set of provisions regarding black people's legal freedom and civic status in the nations. In the Choctaw/Chickasaw 1866 treaty, much more so than in the Cherokee, Creek, and Seminole treaties of the same year, the issues of black people's status and rights were tightly interwoven with matters of U.S. Indian policy—namely, the unrelenting drive to curb tribal sovereignty and claim the better part of Indian Territory for the United States. The twinning of these issues generated considerable discord within all of the Indian nations as black people and Indians grappled with the social, economic, and political implications of both the abolition of slavery and an erosion of sovereignty.

The Choctaw/Chickasaw treaty of 1866 is noteworthy precisely because of the twisted path it laid out for establishing black people's freedom. Though the Choctaw and Chickasaw Nations were by 1866 once more separate entities, the treaty required them to act in concert regarding black people's freedom and citizenship rights. The treaty, furthermore, fused issues of black people's

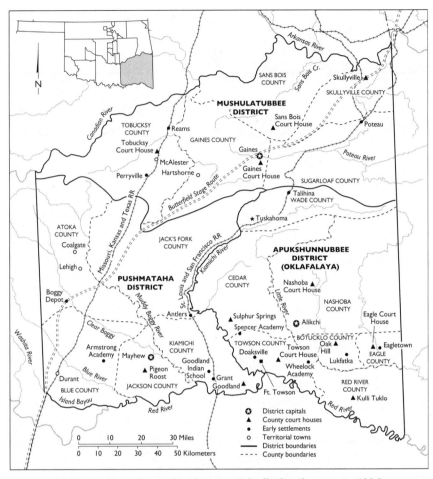

Map of Choctaw Nation, 1866. (In Clara Sue Kidwell, The Choctaws in Oklahoma: From Tribe to Nation, 1855–1970 *[Norman: University of Oklahoma Press, 2007])*

citizenship with matters related to Choctaw and Chickasaw land claims and annuity payments, making one contingent on the other.

In this respect, the Choctaw/Chickasaw treaty of 1866 is striking because it differs markedly from the Cherokee, Creek, and Seminole treaties, which laid out less-circuitous routes for former slaves' freedom and citizenship. The differences among the treaties offer a clear reminder that the population of Indian Territory was never homogenous, and, despite many broad similarities, the histories of black people's transition from slavery to freedom varied from one Indian nation to the next.

The 1866 treaties between the United States and the Choctaw and Chickasaw Nations were the last of their kind. In the years immediately after the Civil

War, U.S. lawmakers sought to move federal relations with Indian peoples in a new direction. The Ulysses S. Grant and Rutherford B. Hayes administrations pursued a peace policy that aimed to prevent violent conflicts between Indians, the U.S. military, and white settlers by confining Indian populations to reservations. Advocates of the peace policy hoped that staffing federal agencies with missionaries rather than bureaucrats would foster "civilization" among Indian populations and thus preclude their disintegration. By the 1870s, however, the peace policy was largely a failure, and the United States ceased making treaties with Indian peoples.[1] Still, the issues of slavery, racial classification, and land distribution that were central to the Choctaw, Chickasaw, Cherokee, Creek, and Seminole 1866 treaties would remain key points in U.S. policies toward these nations through the close of the nineteenth century. Indeed, the legacies of the 1866 treaties remain salient today for the descendants of those who were enslaved in the Indian nations.

BLACK PEOPLE IN THE Choctaw and Chickasaw Nations waited longer than most before gaining their freedom and a clear picture of their future. This did not mean that they did not have plans and ideas about what their lives as free people in the nations should look like. While Choctaw and Chickasaw leaders debated among themselves and negotiated with U.S. policy makers over the abolition of slavery and place of freed slaves in Indian Territory, black people pursued their own visions of freedom, which centered on social and economic independence from their former owners. In their efforts to make their freedom meaningful, former slaves helped shape the debates over race, citizenship, property, and sovereignty that engulfed the Indian nations and informed U.S.-Indian relations through the latter half of the nineteenth century.

From the months leading up to the war through the winter of 1865, enslaved people of all ages envisioned and pursued their liberation in ways that demonstrated their acute understanding of the local and national politics shaping the meanings of race, slavery, property, and freedom in both Indian Territory and the United States. As in so many places across the slaveholding South, enslaved people in the Choctaw and Chickasaw Nations neither needed nor waited for official declarations of slavery's demise to begin organizing their lives in accordance with their own visions of freedom. During the war, some number of slaves freed themselves from bondage by running away and establishing refugee camps near Union posts, while others joined the Union army as soldiers and laborers. Many black refugees from the Choctaw and Chickasaw Nations settled near Fort Smith, Arkansas, just east of Indian Territory. Whether they had fled the nations on their own or with the small contingent of Chickasaw and Choctaw loyalists, these refugees had left their loved ones behind in bondage.

Just before the end of November 1865, Robert Looman and other refugees near Fort Smith drafted a written petition that reached the assistant commissioner of the Freedmen's Bureau for Arkansas. The petitioners complained that slavery remained in tact in the Choctaw and Chickasaw Nations, where their families remained enslaved. Congress created the Bureau of Refugees, Freedmen and Abandoned Lands (known as the Freedmen's Bureau) in the spring of 1865 to supervise the transition from slavery to freedom. Freedpeople quickly called on the commissioned and retired army officers who staffed the bureau for assistance in locating lost relatives and settling disputes with former owners.

Though Indian Territory did not initially fall under the jurisdiction of the Freedmen's Bureau, black refugees from the Indian nations successfully gained the attention and assistance of the Arkansas bureau officers and other military personnel at Fort Smith. After receiving Robert Looman's complaint, the head of the bureau's Arkansas division initially entertained the notion of sending soldiers into the nations "to liberate" the slaves. A month later, hoping to stave off an exodus of self-liberated slaves from Indian Territory, army officers at Fort Smith decided they would "furnish an escort to a number of colored men" and accompany them into the Choctaw and Chickasaw Nations to visit their families.[2] If this Christmastime reunion cheered the refugees and their enslaved families, surely it also confirmed the efficacy of their enlisting a powerful and sympathetic ally. Not only does this episode remind us of former slaves' determination to remain connected with their families; it also highlights the gulf between slavery and freedom in the post–Civil War Indian Territory.

Slavery's delayed and protracted demise in Indian Territory, especially in the Choctaw and Chickasaw Nations, requires that we rethink the familiar timeline and geographic scope of abolition and Reconstruction. The Emancipation Proclamation (January 1, 1863) did not extend to Indian Territory, although in 1863 the loyalist faction of the Creek Nation acknowledged the proclamation's authority.[3] Though the Choctaw, Chickasaw, Cherokee, Creek, and Seminole Nations had allied with the Confederacy, they were not recognized as states in the Confederacy, leaving their governments and laws effectively untouched by General Lee's surrender.

Enslaved people in the Indian nations did not fall under the provisions of the Thirteenth Amendment, which Congress approved in January 1865 and the states ratified by December 1865. Though emancipation did not occur instantaneously in the southern states, the Thirteenth Amendment brought the debates and conflicts over slavery to an unequivocal end. At the same time, however, a new set of questions quickly emerged about how black people's freedom would be defined by law and in daily life. Congress and leading politicians, abolitionists, and reformers debated these issues and weighed the possibilities and consequences of greater federal involvement in defining and protecting black people's freedom.[4]

In the Choctaw and Chickasaw Nations, by contrast, the central point of contention in the months after the war ended was not resolving how black people's freedom would be defined. Rather, the question was whether the nations would abolish slavery and establish black people's freedom at all. These issues emerged as key points in the negotiations that culminated in the 1866 treaty that restored formal relations between the United States and the Choctaw and Chickasaw Nations.

When they allied with the Confederacy in 1861, the Choctaw, Chickasaw, Cherokee, Creek, and Seminole Nations severed their respective treaty relationships with the United States. In 1865, consequently, each of the Indian nations had to negotiate new treaties with the United States; the Choctaws and Chickasaws entered a joint treaty. Preliminary agreements in September 1865 and the final treaties in 1866 called for the abolition of slavery and the extension of citizenship to freed slaves in the Indian nations, effectively expanding Reconstruction to Indian Territory.

In the summer of 1865, President Andrew Johnson appointed Dennis N. Cooley, the commissioner of Indian Affairs, to head up the U.S. treaty commission and negotiate new treaties with the Choctaw, Chickasaw, Cherokee, Creek, and Seminole Nations. The other members of the U.S. treaty commission were Elijah Sells, the superintendent of Southern Indian Superintendency; Thomas Wistar, a prominent leader among the Quakers; Brigadier General William S. Harney; and Colonel Ely S. Parker, a member of the Seneca Nation and part of General Ulysses S. Grant's staff. Choctaw and Chickasaw delegates to the Fort Smith council reportedly responded favorably to Parker's presence on the council, though during his career in the Office of Indian Affairs, Parker would support federal policies designed to erode tribal sovereignty, including putting an end to U.S. treaty making with Indian peoples.[5]

Shortly before Cooley set out for Fort Smith, Arkansas, where the treaty council was to convene, he received his instructions from Secretary of the Interior James Harlan. Not long before his appointment as head of the Interior Department, Harlan, a Republican from Iowa, had served in the Senate. During his term, he had introduced a bill proposing the extension of the federal government over Indian Territory, which would set the stage for eventual statehood. The bill authorized the organization of Indian Territory as a formal territory of the United States and gave the president the power to name the secretary of Indian affairs as the governor of this new U.S. territory. Harlan's bill made it through the Senate by an almost 2-to-1 margin, but the House adjourned before voting on it. Once Harlan was named as secretary of the Interior Department, he pushed ahead with his plans for territorialization.

As Harlan's bill and subsequent instructions to Cooley indicate, western territorial expansion was very much on the minds of Reconstruction-era policy makers.[6] In his letter to Cooley, Harlan outlined a set of treaty provisions designed to hack away at the Indian nations' land claims and sovereign governments. The treaty commission was to "insist upon a cession by [the Indian nations] of all lands not needed," a determination that would be made by federal officials, not Indians. To underscore the seriousness of this demand, Harlan directed the commission to "impress upon them, in the most forcible terms, that the advancing tide of immigration is rapidly spreading over the country, and that the government has not the power or inclination to check it." Harlan also required that the treaties ensured the abolition of slavery and the enactment of "adequate measures" for granting former slaves full equality as tribal members.[7]

The Fort Smith treaty council opened on September 8, 1865, in a cloud of confusion. Commissioner Cooley began the proceedings with a short statement, informing the Indian representatives that the president of the United States required each nation to enter a new treaty with the United States. Chickasaw, Choctaw, Cherokee, Creek, Seminole, Wyandot, Osage, Seneca, and Shawnee delegates all responded that they had not been informed of the council's purpose—the renegotiation of treaties with the United States. Moreover, the Choctaw and Chickasaw delegates, who had been selected by the U.S. Indian agent, indicated that they only represented the few hundred Choctaw and Chickasaw loyalists and had no authority on behalf of their nations. Speaking through their black interpreter, Maharda Colbert, the Chickasaw delegates stated that they thought the council had been convened to reconcile the Choctaw and Chickasaw loyalists with their nations.

The leading men of the Choctaw and Chickasaw Confederate governments did not arrive at Fort Smith until almost a week later. They first met on their own at Armstrong Academy, the capital of the Choctaw Nation, to plan their strategy for dealing with the treaty commissioners from the United States.[8]

Nonetheless, Commissioner Cooley proceeded with the Fort Smith council, and on the second day, he read through the United States' requirements for new treaties. Prominent among the United States' demands were the creation

of a single territorial government, the abolition of slavery, and the "incorpo-
ration [of freedpeople] into the tribes on an equal footing with the original
members, or suitably provided for."[9] The U.S. Senate Judiciary Committee
had debated this explicit language of equality while drafting the Thirteenth
Amendment and ultimately struck it from the final text. Its inclusion in the
proposed treaty likely reflects Harlan's views on the subject of black people's
rights as free people; Harlan was among the Iowa Republicans who endorsed
black men's suffrage as early as 1866. Still, the treaty offered no further guidelines on the subject of freedpeople's status or rights in the Indian nations. The
vague language regarding ex-slaves' freedom in the Indian nations mirrored
the extent to which the definition of black people's freedom remained unclear
and contested in the United States.[10]

Choctaw and Chickasaw representatives responded to the U.S. treaty provisions regarding abolition and black people's standing in the nations in equally
ambiguous terms. The Chickasaw loyalists indicated that they were willing
"to make suitable provisions for [ex-slaves'] future homes." Chickasaw loyalist
Lewis Johnson added: "I have heard much said about the black folks. They suffered as much as we did. I have always understood that the President esteemed
the colored people, and we are willing to do just as our Father may wish, and
take them in and assist them, and let them help us." It is not clear, however, how
Johnson or other loyalists envisioned black people's future in the Chickasaw
and Choctaw Nations. Perhaps they imagined a return to the practices of kin-
based adoption and reciprocity that characterized earlier generations' interactions with outsiders and captives, or perhaps they had something else in mind.

Robert M. Jones, a wealthy Choctaw planter who owned over 200 slaves,
headed the Choctaw and Chickasaw Confederate delegation. He delivered
an opening statement to Cooley that historian Clara Sue Kidwell describes as
breathtakingly defiant. Jones maintained that the Choctaws believed the southern cause was "just" and that the two Indian nations had sided with the Confederacy to safeguard "our independence and national identity." The Choctaw
and Chickasaw delegation acknowledged U.S. authority over slavery in the
nations but took the position that the subject was "open to further negotiation."[11] In the end, the Fort Smith council simply restored diplomatic relations
between the Choctaw and Chickasaw Nations and the United States but did
not produce a formal treaty, leaving open myriad questions about the status of
some 5,000 enslaved people in the two Indian nations.[12]

After the Fort Smith council adjourned, Choctaw and Chickasaw lawmakers considered measures that would abolish slavery but preserve its social
and economic subordination of black people. Though Choctaw slaveholders

had "abandon[ed]" their property rights in slaves, Peter Pitchlynn, then the nation's principal chief, explained they expected that black people's freedom would nonetheless "be consistent with the rights of their late owners."[13] What emerged was a set of regulations that functioned like the Black Codes adopted in the southern states. On October 14, 1865, the Choctaw General Council decreed that "such persons as have to the present time, been considered as slaves" could either remain with their former masters or select a new employer and then enter into a written labor contract. Wages were set by a standardized schedule divided by ability into eight ranks, including children, but undistinguished by gender. The law not only coerced freedpeople into farmwork but also positioned them as sharecroppers by specifying that their wages would be the first lien on the crop. Vagrants, those former slaves without such contracts, were liable to arrest by the Choctaw lighthorsemen who would auction them to the highest bidder.[14]

Chickasaw governor Winchester Colbert addressed his nation's legislature in the first week of October. "Emancipation is inevitable," he told them, and he urged them to "bring about the manumission of slaves at the earliest practicable period." Colbert also informed the legislature that the good of the nation required them to "lay down a uniform rule of action for all in reference to slaves, so that there may be no confusion growing out of this subject among the people or among the slaves themselves."[15] Chickasaw lawmakers, however, only went so far as to approve a future constitutional amendment abolishing slavery. Citing a constitutional provision prohibiting the legislature from emancipating slaves without first compensating the slaveholder, lawmakers refused to abolish slavery outright.[16]

The legislature did authorize Colbert to instruct slaveholders to enter into labor contracts with their slaves. The following week, on October 11, 1865, Colbert issued a proclamation on the subject of slavery and labor. In it, he suggested that slaveholders implement a system of compulsory apprenticeship for minors and wage labor for adults while providing subsistence for the elderly and infirmed. Colbert informed the officers at Fort Smith of his proposal, noting that it should meet with their approval since it not only fulfilled the Fort Smith council requirements but also was much like the gradual emancipation laws implemented decades earlier by the northern states. Any declaration of universal emancipation, Colbert added, would have to come from the president or another U.S. authority.[17]

While Indian lawmakers implemented their plans for dismantling slavery, Robert Looman and other black refugees from the Choctaw and Chickasaw Nations approached U.S. military personnel for assistance. Slavery continued unabated, they complained. Not only did thousands of black people remain in bondage, but those who had freed themselves during the war risked capture and reenslavement. In September 1865, for example, Choctaw Michael Leflore kidnapped four men who had run away from his plantation to Arkansas during the war. Leflore brought the men back to his plantation, where they were tied up, beaten, and informed that they, as well as Leflore's other slaves, were not free. One of the kidnapped men escaped from Leflore's custody and brought the matter to the Freedmen's Bureau. Black people protested to bureau officers that those who "claim their freedom" were threatened and abused.[18] They informed the authorities that the Choctaws and Chickasaws equivocated as to the freedpeople's status in the nations and that black people were subjected to violent and often fatal assaults.

Writing from Fort Smith, Major General Hunt alerted the commissioner of Indian Affairs to the unsettled state of affairs: "I have had representations made to me by negroes from the territory that their lives are threatened, that some murders have been committed upon them, that they are informed by some that they are free, by others that they are still slaves and [they desire] to know which is their actual condition and what they should do." Hunt then elaborated on the subject of these alleged murders, stating that the accounts were unsubstantiated and that there were no witnesses or evidence of any murders. Not wanting to discredit or dismiss the freedpeople's concerns, however, Hunt concluded that "it is evident that an uneasy feeling prevails that may lead to mischief." He assured the commissioner that when he saw the Choctaw and Chickasaw delegates, who were soon expected to pass through Fort Smith on their journey to Washington, D.C., for the final treaty negotiations, he would apprise them of the government's unwillingness to tolerate any violence against former slaves.[19]

Hunt was not the only official to question the veracity of the freedpeople's accounts of violence, especially murder, perpetrated against them by the Choctaws and Chickasaws. This skepticism, combined with an appreciation of the tense atmosphere, suggests, however, that men such as Hunt were aware of local conditions but were unable or unwilling to see the freedpeople as entirely credible witnesses. They therefore intimated that the freedpeople might be fabricating some of their complaints. If the freedpeople brought unfounded accounts to the authorities or embellished when relating their own experiences, their deception might have reflected their appraisal of the most effective way to interact with the authorities. If the military or Indian agents intervened in only the most extreme cases of abuse, presenting grievous incidents of assault may have seemed a certain means of obtaining protection from less-violent or nonfatal attacks. If the authorities were willing to respond only to complaints of violence and not accusations of withheld wages or other types of exploitation, bringing assault cases forward may have provided freedpeople with a good starting point for airing other grievances. In any event, the regularity with which Indian agents and other military personnel indicated their knowledge of episodes of violence, repression, and threats reveals an awareness of a volatile, if not openly hostile, climate. In this regard, the immediate postemancipation experience was not unlike that in other parts of the former Confederacy. Freedpeople had to communicate their experiences of violence to the authorities in ways that were credible and likely to secure intervention without worsening an already adverse situation.[20]

Not long after the Fort Smith council, military personnel in the region deemed black people's condition "one of great hardship." In October 1865 Choctaws and Chickasaws had reportedly "commenced a most deadly persecution upon" their former slaves, beating them and shooting them.[21] In an effort to facilitate a smoother transition from slavery to freedom, the commissioner of Indian Affairs appointed Major General John Sanborn as a special commissioner of the Freedmen's Bureau to Indian Territory. Sanborn made his first report in November 1865, before he had traveled to the Choctaw and Chickasaw Nations. He based his evaluation of those nations on his communication with loyal Chickasaws who claimed to have information on the subject. According to Sanborn, despite the fact that both the Choctaw and Chickasaw National Councils had acknowledged "a change in the relations of the former masters and slaves," the majority of Choctaws continued to treat the freedpeople as slaves. "The public sentiment" in the Choctaw Nation, Sanborn concluded, was "radically wrong."

The Chickasaws' conduct was reportedly even more egregious. In that nation, Sanborn explained, the black people were still held as slaves, and the Chickasaws "entertain[ed] a bitter prejudice against them all." Sanborn's Chickasaw contact, the loyalist chief Lewis Johnson, claimed that Governor Colbert had stated publicly that Chickasaws "should hold the slaves until [the delegates] could determine at Washington whether or not they could get pay for them, and if they could not then they would strip them naked and drive them either south to Texas, or north to Fort Gibson."[22]

In Sanborn's second report, filed at the end of January 1866, his assessment had changed only slightly. He found that "there is still much that is wrong and cruel" in the way the Chickasaws and Choctaws treated their former slaves.[23] Even as slaveholders conceded that slavery was over and grudgingly hired black men and women as paid laborers and sharecroppers, the reports of antiblack violence did not subside. In one especially gruesome account, Sanborn reported, "the fresh skull of a negro is now hanging on a tree . . . with a bullet hole through it."[24] Rumors circulated that up to 600 freedpeople had been murdered in the Red River valley.[25] Military personnel in the region blamed Indians for isolated incidents and concerted campaigns of antiblack violence, but they also noted the regional circumstances that exacerbated Choctaw and Chickasaw hostility toward their former slaves.

In the southeastern corner of Indian Territory, wedged between Texas and Arkansas, the cattle and horses owned by Chickasaw and Choctaw farmers and planters made appealing targets for thieves. Early in 1865, before the war ended, an officer at Fort Gibson in the Cherokee Nation wrote to the secretary of the interior to complain about the government's standard method of supplying beef rations to Indian Territory. The "black men and reckless characters" employed to drive the herds into the territory could be counted on to turn around and leave the territory with stolen herds.[26] Not all rustlers, of course, were black men. In August 1865 Elijah Sells, superintendent of Indian Affairs, wrote that he had been informed of "a regular system" of cattle theft perpetrated through "the agency of irresponsible Indians, negroes and white men."[27] Choctaw and Chickasaw agitation about this loss of property found an easy outlet in their antipathy toward former slaves. Black people made convenient scapegoats, even more so when Chickasaws and Choctaws believed that freedpeople's communities included black migrants from the states. The presence of these unauthorized residents heightened the prevailing fear among many Indians that their land would be claimed not only by their former slaves but also by illegal intruders.

Claiming that the influx of freedpeople from the states to the communities of freedpeople in the Red River area contributed to cattle and horse rustling in that region, Choctaws and Chickasaws formed vigilante groups. Like vigilantes in the states, mounted Indian patrols monitored the labor and movement of freedmen, arresting unemployed freedpeople along with those black people who had moved into the territory from the states. Any black person found with a slaughtered cow or hog or a stolen horse was presumed to be a thief and risked summary execution by hanging.[28] Freedwoman Polly Colbert remembered both slave patrols and vigilantes, whom she called "Ku Kluxers."[29] Loring Folsom, in a letter to Peter Pitchlynn, who was serving as a Choctaw delegate to Washington, D.C., at the time, wrote of the ongoing tension between Choctaws and the freedpeople. Folsom recounted an incident in which a freedman and Choctaw woman were found in bed together. Folsom surmised that news of this scandal would mean that "the Klu Klax will be thick in this nation at a short notice [and] lots of such men in

Texas would come in a hurry for that business."[30] Although Choctaw and Chickasaw residents routinely supported measures to shore up their borders against illegal white settlers, the incursions of white vigilantes did not prove as troublesome.

Many of the military personnel and Freedmen's Bureau agents took the reports of brutality against freed slaves seriously, but their dramatic accounts of the violence and lawlessness in Indian Territory can also be read as a sign of their growing impatience with Indian governmental autonomy. After receiving Robert Looman's complaints about his family's continued enslavement, one Freedmen's Bureau officer looked forward to impressing upon "the Indians that the US is committed to protecting negroes' rights." He also hoped to find an Indian who had committed an "outrage" against a black person so he could punish and make an example of the offender. Sanborn, likewise, maintained that the federal government could not successfully protect former slaves in the Choctaw and Chickasaw Nations "until there is a proper military force stationed" at various posts in their territory. President Grant, who was inclined to think that Sanborn had overstated the extent of antiblack violence in the region, nonetheless endorsed the idea of placing Indian Territory under military control "for the purpose of protecting the Freedmen."[31]

Sanborn elaborated on the connections between black people's freedom and U.S. authority in Indian Territory, urging Interior Secretary Harlan to appropriate land in Indian Territory for former slaves. With a vision that vastly exceeded General William Sherman's now-infamous forty-acre land allowance to freedpeople on the Georgia coastal islands, Sanborn proposed extending the 1862 Homestead Act to freedpeople in Indian Territory. If black people were to receive 320-acre allotments, he reasoned, Indians would quickly submit to U.S. authority without "any open resistance, perhaps without a murmur, and the Freedmen will rejoice."[32]

The desire to see Indian Territory opened to U.S. settlers and under the control of U.S. rather than Indian law was not confined to military personnel, however. In the early weeks of 1866, dramatic reports of "murders of whites and blacks" appeared in the *New Era*, a Fort Smith newspaper supportive of Republican interests. The paper claimed that "the slave code is yet in full blast in the Choctaw and Chickasaw country, and the supreme law of the land, proclaiming the freedom of every human being, is ignored and derided." Not surprisingly, such accounts also included a call for a heightened military presence in the region. Some military officers, however, suspected the paper's editor of exaggerating wildly with the aim of undermining the Indian delegates' bargaining position in their final treaty negotiations with the United States.[33]

In the spring and summer of 1866, the Choctaw, Chickasaw, Cherokee, Creek, and Seminole Nations agreed to the final terms of their respective treaties with the United States. The treaties confirmed the abolition of slavery and laid out the terms of black people's citizenship in each nation. Yet the treaties did not present a unified course of action for the nations' leaders or former slaves. Rather, each treaty mapped a different route to black citizenship. The Seminoles' treaty granted "persons of African descent and blood" and their descendants "all the rights of native citizens." The Cherokee treaty conferred "all the rights of native Cherokees" upon ex-slaves and their descendants but also required that refugee freedpeople return to the nation within six months to secure their citizenship. Creek leaders signed a treaty that allowed former slaves up to one year to return to that nation, and it extended "all the rights and privileges of native citizens, including an equal interest in the soil and national funds" to former slaves and their descendants.

The years after 1866 proved to be a tumultuous time for former slaves throughout Indian Territory. On numerous occasions and for various reasons, Cherokee and Creek leaders contested freedpeople's right of return, challenged the legitimacy of citizenship claims made by black people who had never left, and excluded black people from annuity payments. Only former slaves in the Seminole Nation seemed unimpeded in the enjoyment of their rights as citizens in the years after the Civil War.[34]

The Choctaw/Chickasaw treaty also addressed the matter of freedpeople's citizenship and right of return but set forth a stunningly convoluted set of provisions that, in retrospect, could only result in confusion and turmoil. On April 28, 1866, commissioners representing the Choctaw and Chickasaw Nations approved a joint treaty of "permanent peace and friendship" with the United States. The Choctaw/Chickasaw 1866 treaty, like the Cherokee, Creek, and Seminole 1866 treaties, expanded on the laws and ideals governing Reconstruction in the southern states. But the Choctaw/Chickasaw treaty most firmly linked the issue of black people's citizenship in these Indian nations to federal policies designed to undercut Indian landholdings and tribal sovereignty.

The treaty language thus extended Congress's reach past the geopolitical boundaries of the states and added spectacularly new elements to Reconstruction's promotion of a strong national government, free-labor ideology, and protection of black people's civil rights. In language that echoed the recently approved Thirteenth Amendment, the second article of the Choctaw/Chickasaw treaty required the nations to abolish slavery and involuntary servitude. Choctaw delegates did not obtain the financial compensation for abolition they had desired.[35] The third article then laid out a lengthy and circuitous plan for establishing freed slaves' equal citizenship in the Indian nations. The sixth article granted right of way for two railroads through the nations, one running north-south and the other running east-west. Other sections proposed the creation of a unified government of Indian Territory composed of delegates from each nation or tribe, and also called upon the Choctaws and Chickasaws to "agree to such legislation as Congress and the President of the United States may deem necessary for the better administration of justice and the protection of the rights of person and property within the Indian Territory."[36]

The treaty sections that dealt with black people's freedom and the Choctaw and Chickasaw Nations' land did not address these issues as discrete matters but wove them together, effectively linking freedom and land as fungibles. Under the terms of their 1866 treaty, the Choctaw and Chickasaw Nations ceded around 4.6 million acres of land, known as the "Leased District," to the United States in exchange for $300,000. The treaty allowed the federal government to retain control of the money until Choctaw and Chickasaw lawmakers enacted the "laws, rules and regulations" needed to grant "all persons of African descent" and their descendants "all the rights, privileges, and immunities, including the right of suffrage, of citizens, except in the annuities, moneys, and public domain claimed by, or belonging to, said nations respectively ."

Eligibility for citizenship was limited to those black people who were "resident" in the nations in September 1865 when the Fort Smith council convened. Unlike the Cherokee and Creek treaties, the Choctaw/Chickasaw treaty did not allow a window of time for black war refugees to return to the nations.

The treaty's fourth article elaborated on the subject of freedpeople's rights and reiterated the call for Indian and black equality under the law. Black people were to be recognized as "competent witnesses in all civil and criminal suits and proceedings in the Choctaw and Chickasaw courts." In keeping with U.S. ideals of free labor, Indian employers were expected to enter "reasonable and equitable contracts" with freedpeople, providing "fair remuneration" for their labor. Lastly, black people, like Indians, were to have unrestricted access to the nations' land commons to build their own homes and farms.[37]

According to the treaty, the United States would pay out the $300,000 only if the Choctaw and Chickasaw Nations legally recognized black people's citizenship within two years (by 1868). Three-quarters of the money would be paid to the Choctaw Nation and one-quarter to the Chickasaw Nation, the proportions reflecting the relative size of their populations. The final amount disbursed, however, was to be reduced by $100 for every former slave who voluntarily emigrated from the Choctaw and Chickasaw Nations within ninety days of the citizenship legislation's enactment.

The treaty also included a contingency plan regarding black people's citizenship. If the nations failed to grant full citizenship to former slaves by June 1868, the federal government would no longer hold the $300,000 in trust for the Choctaw and Chickasaw Nations. Instead, the United States would retain the funds for "the use and benefit" of the former slaves in the Choctaw and Chickasaw Nations. If the Choctaw and Chickasaw Nations did not recognize black people as equal citizens by June 1868, the United States agreed that within ninety days, the federal government would remove "all such persons of African descent as may be willing to remove." Black people who opted to remain in the Choctaw and Chickasaw Nations forfeited their claims to a share of the $300,000 and would be subject to the same laws "as other citizens of the United States in the said nations."[38]

The treaty further compounded the issues of black people's citizenship and Indian nations' land claims in sections that proposed the survey and allotment of the Choctaw and Chickasaw lands. In these nations, as in the Cherokee, Creek, and Seminole Nations, custom and law had long recognized the people's collective ownership of the land. Even as the communal town fields of the late eighteenth century gave way to individual family farms, pastures, and plantations bounded by rough-hewn worm fences, individuals still owned only their improvements, livestock, and slaves but not the land.[39] The treaty of 1866 signaled Americans' growing impatience with Indian nations' collective land title and shoved them in the direction of private land ownership. Warming up for the mandatory allotment policies of the late 1880s, the treaty of 1866 placed the matter in the hands of Choctaw and Chickasaw legislators, leaving them to accept or reject the survey and allotment of their land in 160-acre parcels. If the Choctaw and Chickasaw governments agreed to this allotment scheme, land distribution would follow a racial grid that distinguished between "negroes" and "Indians" and limited black people to only forty-acre allotments.

After the 1866 treaty was ratified, Choctaw principal chief Peter Pitchlynn and Chickasaw governor Winchester Colbert credited their delegates with securing this unequal distribution of land.[40] Determined to protect their financial interests as established in earlier treaties, leading Choctaws had hired Baltimore attorney John H. B. Latrobe as their advocate in the 1866 treaty negotiations. Latrobe claimed the credit for authoring the treaty, though he also acknowledged the input of the Indian delegates. There is little in Latrobe's writing that explains the reasoning behind the complicated provisions regarding black people's citizenship. Historian Clara Sue Kidwell explains that the Choctaw and Chickasaw treaty delegates enlisted Latrobe's assistance because they wanted the federal government to resume payment of prewar annuities and other financial settlements and to prevent the United States from gaining control of the Leased District.[41]

The centrality of Indian nations and their land in the minds of federal policy makers during the post–Civil War period cannot be underestimated. The reasons for expanding federal authority and U.S. settlement westward into Indian Territory onto land taken from Indian peoples were as varied as the individuals who voiced them. Still, it is clear, as the 1866 treaties reveal, that the issues of slavery, emancipation, and black people's freedom went hand in hand with a significant assertion of federal power over the people and land in Indian Territory. Despite the apparent contradiction, the insistence upon defining freedpeople's citizenship in the Indian nations in terms of free labor and property rights and the simultaneous drive to extinguish Indians' political and territorial autonomy emerged from the same Reconstruction-era ideologies. These measures were not simply a sleight of hand to divert attention away from the assault on tribal governments and land claims. In the same manner that the "civilization programs" of the early nineteenth century had fused ideas about Indians' capacity for assimilation into the American mainstream with theories of racial hierarchy, many Reconstruction-era policy makers believed that ending tribal sovereignty and allotting Indian lands in severalty would uplift and not oppress Indians.[42]

The demands that the Choctaw, Chickasaw, Cherokee, Creek, and Seminole Nations emancipate their slaves, abolish slavery, and recognize former slaves and their descendants as citizens marked a dramatic intrusion into the nations' domestic affairs that did not go unnoticed or unchallenged by Indian leaders and their constituents. After the treaty was ratified, Principal Chief Pitchlynn and Governor Colbert delivered a joint statement to the Choctaw and Chickasaw Nations in which they explicated the treaty's provisions regarding black people's citizenship and the Indian nations' land. In their account of the treaty negotiations, Pitchlynn and Colbert indicated that the issue of land, namely control over the Leased District, became "complicated with . . . the negro question" because of U.S. insistence upon protecting and providing for "our late slaves." "Hence," they stated, "the connection of the two questions." As Pitchlynn and Colbert framed the situation, if the nations' legislatures recognized former slaves as citizens—"adopted" was the term generally used by Choctaws, Chickasaws, and black people—then the nations would gain favor with the United States. This was no small matter.

The Choctaw and Chickasaw Nations had been embroiled in financial disputes (known as the Net Proceeds claims) with the United States that dated back to the removal-era survey and sale of their Mississippi lands. Fulfilling their treaty obligations by adopting black people as citizens, Pitchlynn and Colbert explained, might "materially aid" the nations, "as it will undoubtedly produce a strong influence in favor of our yet unsettled claims and demands upon the United States." On the other hand, Pitchlynn and Colbert warned, excluding former slaves from citizenship could prompt the United States to create a colony of former slaves "in our immediate vicinity." They predicted the dire consequences of such a colonization plan, arguing that as the first all-black colony of former slaves in the United States, it would "be sustained and fostered by the government, and the friends of the negro, now so numerous and powerful." The colony would then attract "thousands of other negroes," and this rapidly growing black community would be "anything but desirable neighbors." By contrast, adopting their former slaves as citizens would allow Choctaws and Chickasaws to outnumber and dominate black people within the nations.[43]

Pitchlynn and Colbert's attentiveness to the subject of black colonization was hardly unwarranted. During the war, President Lincoln, members of his cabinet, and some senators had entertained various schemes for encouraging black emigration and colonization in Florida and the western United States, as well as in Haiti, Liberia, and Central America. Indian leaders' concerns about U.S. plans for colonizing freed slaves in the West had already surfaced in the Fort Smith negotiations. In fact, when the loyal Chickasaws were preparing to attend the council, they drafted a statement in which they opposed slavery, but noted: "We will not allow any other coloured persons to live amongst us." During the Fort Smith council, a Seminole delegate, similarly, stated that his people were willing "to provide for the colored people of our own nation, but do not desire our lands to become colonization grounds for the negroes of other States and Territories." Even the spokesman for the Osages, who had not been slaveholders, decried the possibility that the United States would settle black people from the United States in Indian Territory.[44]

The Choctaw/Chickasaw 1866 treaty conjoined the federal defense of black freedom and assault on Indian land and governments, and Indian leaders responded in kind. Historians, however, need not follow this trajectory. Focusing primarily on the federal policy agendas embedded in the treaty and Indian responses to the implicit and explicit assaults on their political autonomy and landholdings tells us almost nothing about the enslaved and emancipated black people in the Indian nations. The treaty conflated the issues of freedom and sovereignty, but scholars are not required to go down this path and frame both black people and the issue of their freedom primarily as a weapon for advancing the United States' colonial mission. Instead, we can consider the 1866 treaty and the issues it raised as illustrative of Reconstruction's complex, contradictory, and continental scope. Certainly, one goal was to erase the boundaries between Indian nations and the United States by extinguishing tribal governments and territories. To be sure, demanding the abolition of slavery and the recognition of black people as citizens represented a major intrusion into the Indian nations' sovereign affairs. But to cast this moment only as a strategic assault minimizes emancipation's profound meanings and consequences in black people's lives. It also obscures our view of the ways black people were already working to liberate themselves and assert their own expectations of freedom.

Especially in the years after the 1866 treaty went into effect, freedpeople, both men and women, organized and asserted themselves as political actors. Keenly aware of the ways the treaty fused black freedom and citizenship with Indian land loss and subjugation, freedpeople participated in and helped shape the intensifying debates engulfing the Indian nations over the meanings of race, property, citizenship, and sovereignty. In many respects, the story of emancipation and the early years of black people's freedom in Indian Territory falls in line with the broader, more-familiar narrative of the transition from slavery to freedom in the southern states. Black people in Indian Territory shared with black people in the states an understanding of emancipation as deliverance from a litany of physical and psychic abuses. Across the slaveholding South, freedpeople's expectations of and responses to freedom varied widely, reflecting the broad array of regional and local social, political, and economic conditions in the southern states.

In Indian Territory, too, the timing and circumstances of emancipation and the subsequent conditions of freedpeople's lives were hardly uniform. In the Choctaw and Chickasaw Nations, freedpeople recognized a collective history of enslavement that united black people across the Indian nations and the United States. In the decades after emancipation, black people in the Choctaw and Chickasaw Nations embarked on a freedom struggle that aimed in large measure to somehow reconcile the Diasporic experience of enslavement with the particular social and political conditions in the nations and Indian Territory.

5

Freedmen's Political Organizing and the Ongoing Struggles over Citizenship, Sovereignty, and Squatters

Though emancipation came late in the Choctaw and Chickasaw Nations, black people received the news of their liberation with joyous relief. The elderly Kiziah Love, a Choctaw freedwoman, recalled that when she learned of her freedom, she clapped her hands and thanked God that she was "free at last!" But the thrill of liberation was tainted with a heavy dose of uncertainty and apprehension.

From 1866 to 1868, black people waited to learn whether they would be granted citizenship in the Choctaw and Chickasaw Nations or the United States under the terms of the 1866 treaty. Neither party adhered to the treaty's provisions and June 1868 deadline, leaving an estimated 5,000 former slaves and their descendants with no certain standing in either the Indian nations or the United States.[1] From 1868 through the end of the nineteenth century, the Choctaw, Chickasaw, and U.S. governments continually disputed and sidelined the issue of freedpeople's citizenship.

Governmental inaction, however, did not dissuade freedpeople from organizing their lives in accordance with their own understandings and expectations of freedom. In the months and years following the 1866 treaty's ratification, black men and women in the Choctaw and Chickasaw Nations strove to make their freedom meaningful on a number of counts. Black men and women defined their freedom largely in terms of family, labor, land, and political participation. Matters of family, labor, and land were often intertwined, as people made decisions about where and with whom they would live and work. In some instances, families allied with each other, working collectively as sharecroppers, while other families fractured and set out in different directions. For many former slaves, freedom entailed claiming one of the fundamental rights traditionally associated with Choctaw or Chickasaw citizenship: using and improving unclaimed land to build their own homes and farms.

Black people's understandings of their freedom revolved around the ongoing and unresolved questions of their citizenship. Black people, especially men, insisted upon presenting their views and voicing their opinions in the public conversations about the 1866 treaty provisions regarding freedpeople's citizenship. When black men faced Indian leaders and U.S. authorities, they presented their own interpretations of the treaty's provisions, often taking both parties to task for failing to abide by the letter and spirit of the treaty. Black men's political participation in this context is especially noteworthy because of the ways they addressed the issues of race, land, and sovereignty that lay at the core of not only the 1866 treaty but also U.S. Indian policy and Choctaw and Chickasaw responses to American domination.

In the early months of freedom, black people found little to give them hope in the new order. The period between the Fort Smith council in September 1865 and the ratification of the Choctaw/Chickasaw treaty in April 1866 was an exhilarating but tumultuous time for the thousands of black people freed from slavery. Recalcitrant slaveholders, Indian and white vigilantes, and intractable lawmakers sought almost any opportunity that arose to keep black people as close to enslavement as possible. Judging from the records of their complaints and pleas for assistance during the winter of 1865–66, black people seemed to face violence, terror, and coercion at every turn. Indian leaders had made clear their reluctance to abolish slavery and their unwillingness to recognize black people's status and rights as citizens. This position was affirmed unequivocally in November 1866, when the Chickasaw and Choctaw legislatures each voted to refuse black people's citizenship and requested that the federal government remove former slaves from the nations in accordance with article III of the treaty.

Freedpeople were well aware of the repressive political and social climate in the Indian nations, and many could see no reason to remain in Indian Territory. Freedwoman Matilda Poe remembered that her mother replied, "Well, I'm heading for Texas," when she learned of her freedom. Matilda's father, however, exhibited greater reluctance to leave the Chickasaw Nation, although he and Matilda set out for Texas soon after her mother's departure.[2] One small group of former slaves left the Choctaw Nation and settled in Arkansas in September 1866. Jack Campbell's mother, similarly, left the territory for two years when she "got a chance to get to Fort Smith [Arkansas] and obtain some work."[3] The majority of black people, however, remained in Indian Territory.[4]

Beginning in the winter of 1866, large numbers of freedmen across the Choctaw and Chickasaw Nations organized mass meetings to discuss their options and agree upon a course of action. This initial round of collective protest likely drew on the earlier group formations and networks of communication. Black people emerged from slavery with many of the intellectual and social tools needed to identify and engage the political debates and policies that had the greatest bearing on their lives. No longer forced to hold clandestine gatherings or come together under the aegis of mission churches, freedmen openly announced meetings that attracted hundreds of participants and supporters. A small cohort of men planned the initial meetings and were quickly acknowledged as respected and trusted leaders who had the authority to speak and act on behalf of the wider community.

For Chickasaw freedmen, their first order of business entailed responding to the Chickasaw legislature's November 1866 unanimous vote of refusal to adopt former slaves as citizens and their concomitant directive to Governor Cyrus Harris to notify the U.S. government of their decision.[5] In December 1866 a group of 292 freedmen convened in Pickens County in the Chickasaw Nation to discuss the situation. The group selected five men—Charley Cohee, Squire Harren, Henry Cob, Isaac Alexander, and Richard Mobel—as the heads of their council. They drafted a petition to the U.S. Indian agent Martin Chollar, explaining that "the unfriendly and bitter feeling existing toward our people by the Chickasaws and their desire to get us off their lands" made removal the only viable option.[6] Relocating to land of their own, the petitioners insisted, would allow black men to support themselves and their families; they estimated that some 1,500 freedpeople were willing to leave the Chickasaw Nation. Even though Chickasaw lawmakers supported black removal, the freedmen's request gained little traction in Congress. Native American studies scholar Daniel F. Littlefield Jr. attributes this to the fact that Chickasaw delegates in Washington discredited the petition as the work of "contractors and speculators."[7]

According to the terms of the 1866 treaty, the Choctaw, Chickasaw, and U.S. governments had until the summer of 1868 to make a final decision regarding freedpeople's citizenship and, by extension, their residence. As the June 1868 deadline approached, Choctaw and Chickasaw freedmen convened a mass meeting in Boggy Depot, a large town on the western edge of Choctaw territory and not far from Chickasaw territory. Noting that the most recent session of the Choctaw legislature had also indicated its refusal to extend citizenship to former slaves, attendees at this meeting agreed that removal was the only means of ensuring black people's safety and prosperity. The participants in this meeting selected four delegates—James Squire Wolf, Squire Butler, Isaac Alexander, and Anderson Brown—to represent their cause in Washington. The secretary of the interior received the petition but explained that his department had never received the funds from Congress to underwrite the cost of removal and there was no land available for the freedpeople's relocation.[8]

The treaty deadline passed with inaction on both sides, and the question remained: were freedpeople now citizens of the Choctaw and Chickasaw Nations with the rights enumerated in the treaty, or had they become citizens of the United States by default?

Freedmen responded to the situation in two ways during the early months of 1869: they solicited the assistance of Valentine Dell, the editor of Fort Smith's *New Era*, a staunchly Republican newspaper; and they organized yet another convention. Dell, a member of the Arkansas state senate, was one of many politicians and reformers in the states who defended freedpeople's claims to land in Indian Territory and also advocated opening Indian Territory to U.S. settlement and governance. In February 1869 freedmen held a convention near Skullyville, a large town in the northeastern part of the Choctaw Nation. This meeting selected James Squire Wolf, Mahardy Colbert, and Anderson Brown as the delegates to present Congress with yet another request for removal. In their petition, they noted that they were asking that the United States "simply carr[y] out in good faith the promise made to our suffering people by the Government and [fulfill] treaty stipulations." Again, there was no federal action on the matter.[9]

By the summer of 1869, the commissioner of Indian Affairs instructed George Olmstead, the newly appointed U.S. Indian agent to the Choctaws and Chickasaws, to investigate and report on the conditions of freedpeople's lives. Olmstead was directed to determine whether freedpeople wanted to stay in or leave the nations. Recognizing freedpeople's ability to secure the attention of state and federal lawmakers, Choctaw and Chickasaw leaders monitored their gatherings and sought to regulate their contact with U.S. officials. Choctaw leaders, for example, requested that Olmstead and other investigators meet with freedpeople only in the regions heavily populated by black people. They also required investigators to provide advance notification of their meetings with freedpeople to the Choctaw and Chickasaw governors and other headmen, allowing them to attend the gatherings.[10]

In August 1869 Olmstead called a meeting with freedmen in the two nations along with Chickasaw governor Cyrus Harris, Choctaw principal chief Allen Wright, and other citizens of the two nations. Over 300 black men took part in this meeting. When Wright addressed the crowd, he warned: "Everybody is against you." He proposed that freedpeople follow in the footsteps of Simon Harrison, the manumitted preacher who had emigrated to Liberia in 1853. Wright urged the men to "leave the country and go to Liberia, where there is a home provided for freed people."[11] Given the opportunity to express their position on the question of whether or not to remain in the nations, the freedmen "decided in a body that they would remain." They arrived at this position, Olmstead explained, because "they preferred being with the people among whom they were raised than among others whom they did not know."[12] Still, the freedmen also indicated that they wanted U.S. and not Choctaw or Chickasaw citizenship.

One month after their meeting with Agent Olmstead, a group of Choctaw and Chickasaw freedmen assembled on their own. They met again at Skullyville. At this September 1869 convention, the participants concluded that because the Indian nations and the United States had failed to act under the 1866 treaty, it could no longer be considered valid or applicable in their lives. The group issued a number of resolutions, all of which attested to a sense of rootedness in the Choctaw and Chickasaw Nations. "We can claim no other country as ours except this Territory," declared one of the resolutions. "We desire to continue to live in it in peace and harmony with all others living therein." The Skullyville platform then addressed the question of citizenship. Only one month after expressing to the Indian agent and the Choctaw and Chickasaw leadership their desire for U.S. citizenship, the Choctaw and Chickasaw freedmen reversed course and declared: "We consider ourselves full citizens of those nations, and fully entitled to all the rights, privileges, and benefits as such, the same as any citizen of Indian extraction." Not only did the freedmen's petition call for recognition as Choctaw and Chickasaw citizens, but they also endorsed allotting land "to each inhabitant as his own" and also "opening this territory to white immigration."[13]

What had changed in the span of one month to bring about this shift? Did the group debate the relative merits and consequences of citizenship in the Indian nations and the United States? Did the change signal divisions among the participating freedmen? What role, if any, did men like Valentine Dell play in the discussion leading to the resolutions adopted at this convention? In the absence of detailed documentation, it is hard to arrive at firm conclusions. It is evident, however, that the September 1869 Skullyville meeting was not attended by either the U.S. Indian agent or Choctaw and Chickasaw leaders. The absence of these men perhaps afforded freedmen greater latitude to voice their thoughts and demands and even to assess the positions of their white allies.

Toward the end of the year, freedmen tried to organize a follow-up meeting to be held at Armstrong Academy in the southwestern corner of the Choctaw Nation. Choctaws and Chickasaws harassed politically active freedmen and ultimately prevented them from assembling. Black men known to be participants in these gatherings received death threats. Broadsides announcing the meeting's date and location were torn down and destroyed. Agent Olmstead apparently lent his support to the opposition by informing U.S. law enforce-ment at Fort Smith that two freedmen, James Ladd and Richard Brashears, sought to "disturb the peace and tranquility of the United States" by riling up the black people in the Indian nations.[14] Finally, on January 15, 1870, freed-men managed to convene again in Skullyville, and they added more points to the resolutions put forth at the first meeting. They decried the harassment of the leading and outspoken freedmen, especially the recent arrest of Richard Brashears, and they reasserted their demands for citizenship in the two na-tions. They were "less than ever inclined to leave our native country."[15]

What did black people mean by these references to their "native country" or the "people among whom they were raised"? In many respects, such phrases evoke a sense of cultural connection or identification with the indigenous peo-ples among whom black people had lived and labored for so long as slaves. In her study of slavery and emancipation in the Cherokee Nation, Celia Naylor highlights the "sociocultural ties and sense of belonging" that informed the ways people of African descent identified with Cherokee cultural beliefs, prac-tices, and structures.[16] Black people in the Choctaw and Chickasaw Nations, too, recognized and often highly valued the aspects of indigenous culture they had adopted. Choctaw freedman Lemon Butler, for example, acknowledged that some black people identified closely with Choctaw culture, speaking only the Choctaw language.[17] Other freedpeople pointed to the preparation and consumption of particular foods or their understanding of indigenous medical knowledge as signs of their cultural likeness with Choctaws and Chickasaws.[18] For many black people, the exchange and adaptation of language, foodways, and healing practices contributed to but did not fully shape their sense of in-dividual and collective identity within the Choctaw and Chickasaw Nations. Indeed, many black people knew too well that they had learned indigenous languages and cultural practices under the duress of enslavement.

Historian Michael Vorenberg's discussion of what he terms "affective citi-zenship" offers another useful way to understand freedpeople's expressions of cultural affinity with Native peoples. Referencing Benedict Anderson's notion of an "imagined community," Vorenberg frames his concept of "affective citi-zenship" to encompass the ways that an individual or group feels connected to a particular polity through shared language, beliefs, or residency. This sense of belonging, furthermore, does not require the polity to acknowledge such affective ties or reciprocate by granting legal recognition or citizenship. As Vorenberg explains, many free African Americans in the antebellum United States described themselves as U.S. citizens regardless of how they were defined by law. The concept of "affective citizenship" thus helps us understand that freedpeople might reference their cultural, social, and personal affinity with the Choctaws and Chickasaws and cast themselves as citizens of the nations even though Indian lawmakers insisted they had not and could not become legal citizens.[19]

While freedpeople, such as Lemon Butler, spoke of points of cultural connection with Choctaws and Chickasaws, they also knew that black people, as former slaves, constituted a distinct and marginalized group in the nations. Butler was one of the men involved in planning the failed meeting at Armstrong Academy in the winter of 1869. Ladd and Brashears sent a letter to Butler informing him of the upcoming convention and its agenda: "to obtain [our] rights as men and citizens of the nations." They asked Butler to "immediately send word to all the colored people of your section to meet there on the day named. Explain as much as possible the reason of the meeting, and see that there be a full attendance."[20] In their closing line, Ladd and Brashears captured the sentiment that animated former slaves' political action across Indian Territory and the southern states: "If we do not work for ourselves, who will?"[21]

The first wave of meetings and conventions between 1866 and 1869 secured widespread support among the black men in the Choctaw and Chickasaw Nations and also gained the attention of Indian leaders and federal policy makers. A cohort of leading black men emerged from these initial conventions, and for at least the next two decades, many of the same names regularly appeared on letters and memorials presented to Indian and federal authorities.

In many respects, freedmen's political activism in Indian Territory falls in line with the ways black men in the southern states came together, exchanged information, and voiced their demands. Like freedpeople in the southern states, black people in Indian Territory knew too well that the change in their legal status was not coeval with a shift in social, economic, and political relations. Black men in the Choctaw and Chickasaw Nations underscored their loyalty to the Union, reminded their Republican audiences of Indians' support for the Confederacy, and used a language of manhood that emphasized their eagerness to embrace the American ideals of free labor, private property, and marriage. In the petitions calling for removal and also in the petitions asserting the right to remain in the nations, freedmen cast themselves as loyal Unionists whose principal goals were to own land and homes, achieve self-sufficiency through their labor, and care for their wives and families.[22] Freedmen and freedwomen strove to make their freedom meaningful on multiple levels. In their daily lives, black people's understandings of what it meant to be free informed how they interacted with each other, their former masters, and other free people. At the same time, former slaves viewed their freedom in terms of the future and possibilities not yet realized. By agitating for citizenship and challenging Indian and U.S. policy makers to take action, freedpeople strove to effect change and bring the world more closely in line with their expectations.

During the first years after emancipation, freedpeople contemplated their future in the Choctaw and Chickasaw Nations but also faced the demands and pressures of living and working in the present. Despite freedmen's political organizing and collective protest, Choctaw and Chickasaw leaders did not view the abolition of slavery as the beginning of a discussion about categories of racial identification and the connections between race and citizenship in their nations. From the beginning, Choctaw and Chickasaw leaders had approached the issue of emancipation in terms of their property rights, namely their ownership of black people's bodies and labor. Like many southern slaveholders, Choctaw and Chickasaw leaders framed emancipation foremost as a labor crisis and endorsed measures to coerce black men, women, and children into labor contracts with their former masters.[23]

Most black people found themselves working on farms and plantations in the months after their emancipation, performing much of the same work they had done in slavery. In January 1866 Peter Pitchlynn's son Lycurgus wrote to his father that he had hired many of their former slaves to continue working on their plantations as sharecroppers. He made a contract with "Abe's family." Freedpeople organized their labor mainly in family units, with the husband entering a contract on behalf of his wife, children, and possibly other relatives as well. Freedpeople also aligned their families, combining to form larger blocs of workers and selecting leaders from within their ranks. In the first year of freedom on the Pitchlynn estate, for example, all of the farmhands "elected Solomon as their Capt[ain]."[24]

Eventually, many of Pitchlynn's former slaves set out to claim and work their own farms, but some continued to work, at least part-time, on his family's estate for years to come. In 1879 "Black Solomons crowd" entered a contract to farm Malvina Pitchlynn's land.[25] The Pitchlynns seemed relieved to have Solomon, one of the Pitchlynns' most trusted and favored slaves, on board. But Solomon may have had a different view of his prominent role. In addition to heading the work gangs, he participated regularly in the freedmen's mass meetings, and his name appears on their various petitions.

One of the hallmarks of freedom for former slaves across the South was the prospect of controlling one's labor by quitting undesirable employers. Mary Lindsay, a Chickasaw freedwoman, offered the following recollection of her relationship with her mistress after emancipation. According to Lindsay, her former mistress told her: "[T]hey say I got to pay you if you work for me, but

Ann Mickle and B. F. Kemp's former slave in a buggy. (Chickasaw Council House Collection; courtesy of the Oklahoma Historical Society)

I ain't got no money to pay you. If you stay on with me and help me I will feed and home you and I can weave you some good dresses if you card and spin the cotton and wool." Lindsay soon made two realizations: first, her mistress indeed had money, although she never paid her workers; and second, she had given Lindsay "just one dress."[26] Through a chance encounter with a young boy, Lindsay serendipitously learned that her own family lived nearby. She quit her mistress's place and set out on a ten-mile walk to the nearest town in search of them.

Freedmen and freedwomen placed a premium on taking charge of one's body and labor. Indeed, the value of such autonomy could outweigh potential financial gain. The black people formerly owned by the Pitchlynns' neighbor Cal Howell, for example, refused to work for him. Instead, they worked for the Pitchlynns, despite receiving a lesser share of the crop than Howell had offered.[27] Even though the Pitchlynns wrote sentimentally of their former slaves' continued loyalty and productivity after emancipation, things were not always as they seemed. One day, Lycurgus Pitchlynn found that "Ned and Ann, old Dans children," had departed without any word to their former master.[28]

Within a few years of emancipation, growing numbers of freedpeople began to claim and farm their own tracts of land. Both the Choctaw and Chickasaw Nations held their land in common, allowing their citizens the right to claim and improve small or large tracts of land depending on their resources. Despite the tenuous nature of their rights to claim and improve the land, many freed-people staked claims to land and balanced sharecropping with subsistence farming to support themselves. By the late summer of 1870, Agent Olmstead reported that black people's unresolved citizenship status had not deterred them from "labor[ing] for themselves and families."[29] In the early 1870s, Lemon Butler indicated that many freedpeople in the Choctaw Nation chose their own homes and improved "such quantities [of land] as we think we can cultivate." Butler sharecropped for his former master but also had his own "residence on another place."[30] Freedman Daniel Burton's parents took their seven children, left their deceased former master's property, and "established a home of our own where my parents spent their remaining days."[31] After emancipation, Charley Brown's parents "just picked out a place in this Choctaw Nation that was suitable to do some farming on . . . [and] just tried to raise what we called a living."[32]

By the 1870s, the turbulence and violence that had ushered in black people's freedom had died down, but Choctaw and Chickasaw leaders remained vigilant in their efforts to check black people's autonomy and prosperity. In 1871 Chickasaw officials insisted that freedpeople pay a dollar per person for a residency permit to remain in the nation. Increasingly, lawmakers pursued measures designed to restrict black people's access to land. Such efforts were not simply a manifestation of antiblack racism. Rather, they reflected a more-complex interplay of social, economic, and political issues related to the expansion of white settlement into and around Indian Territory.

Within five or six years of emancipation, wealthy Choctaws and Chicka-saws increasingly met their labor needs by renting their land to white farmers and laborers. The post–Civil War boom in western railroad construction drew white workers as well as prospective farmers, merchants, entrepreneurs, and speculators to the region. For Choctaws and Chickasaw who had expansive land claims, hiring white farmworkers or leasing their land to white tenants could be a profitable step. Historian Alexandra Harmon notes that some Choctaws and Chickasaws, as well as some Cherokees and Creeks, amassed considerable wealth in the 1870s through farming and stock-raising enterprises. Cherokee Cornelius Boudinot once observed that the wealthiest man in Indian Territory was Choctaw planter "Old Bob Jones," whose Red River plantations were reportedly worth $1.5 million.[33] Large planters, such as Robert Jones and Peter Pitchlynn, relied on both white and black tenants and laborers to work their land. Between 1877 and 1879, Malvina Pitchlynn, one of Peter Pitchlynn's daughters, wrote to her father with the details of their labor agreements with "white families" and "freedmen renters."[34]

Though many wealthy Choctaws and Chickasaws embraced the opportunity to enhance their family fortunes, lawmakers sought to exert strict governance and control over the white people who entered the nations. An 1877 Choctaw law prohibited leasing the public domain to noncitizens, but wealthy landlords circumvented the law by calling their white renters "laborers."[35]

For wealthy planters, securing white tenants or workers simultaneously generated income and excluded black people from access to land. During this time, Chickasaw lawmakers barred freedpeople from taking on hired hands by refusing to issue entry permits to noncitizens hired by black people.[36] The matter of black people's rights to use and profit from the public domain was clarified in an 1877 law that stated: "Negroes have no rights in the public domain and its natural appurtainces [sic] of the Choctaw and Chickasaw Nations except to as much land as they may cultivate for the support of themselves and families, and it shall not be lawful for negroes to sell or otherwise dispose of any timber for any purpose."[37] An 1872 law barred Choctaw citizens from selling timber, rock, and stone coal to railroads, suggesting that the law directed toward black people was intended for a similar purpose. The enactment of racially specific laws highlights the entrenched nature of ideologies of racial difference and hierarchy in the postemancipation period.

In some instances, white settlers and Indians held similar views of black people's desire to claim their own tracts of land. White tenants on Indians' plantations objected to living near black families who operated their own farms. Rhoda Pitchlynn, another of Peter Pitchlynn's daughters, had married one of her white renters, a man named D. L. Kennedy. In May 1877 Kennedy complained to his father-in-law: "Labor is very hard to find in this country, and farming is a perfect drag there are no negroes on the place, and haven't been for two years. They all have places of their own and are farming on their own."[38] Yet a shared disdain for black people's economic and social autonomy did not cement a bond between Choctaws, Chickasaws, and the white people who moved into their nations during the second half of the nineteenth century.

While Indians profited, sometimes quite handsomely, from their commercial ties to white merchants, investors, and laborers, they nonetheless remained wary of the rapidly growing influx of white people, especially men, from the states. Whether white men entered Indian Territory as legally permitted residents in the nations or as illegal intruders, Choctaw and Chickasaw leaders perceived them as a threat to personal security and the long-term stability of their nations' sovereignty. In 1872 Allen Wright, the governor-elect of the Choctaw Nation, explained to a visiting delegation from the U.S. Congress that his people remained skeptical of the expansion of American railroads into

Indian Territory and the accompanying spread of white settlement. Wright argued that white settlers had a long history of stealing Choctaws' property and falsely accusing them of crimes. "That was the trouble in Mississippi," he stated.[39]

When Choctaw and Chickasaw leaders contemplated the potential consequences of the growing numbers of white people in their nations, they framed their concerns in terms of race, gender, and class. Historian Clara Sue Kidwell argues that a central fear was that white men would obtain Indian citizenship by marrying Indian women and would then gain control of the nation's resources and governance.[40] An 1875 Choctaw law was aimed at preventing the nation from being "filled up with white persons of worthless character by so called marriages" to Choctaw women. The law required any white man from the states who sought to marry a Choctaw woman to do the following: prove that he did not have a wife in the states; obtain the signatures of ten Choctaw citizens-by-blood who had known him for over a year and would attest to his moral character; swear to obey Choctaw laws; and pay a five-dollar fee for the marriage license.[41] Though white men were usually the targets of such legislation and scrutiny, white women were not exempted from similar assessments of their racial character. In the 1880s, Choctaws and Chickasaws testified to federal authorities that white women, not Indian women, were prone to licentiousness.[42] In March 1876 Malvina Pitchlynn complained to her father that she was having a difficult time getting "good white men" to work her land. Three years later, Peter Pitchlynn received a letter from a friend complaining about the white people who had fled past crimes and debts and entered the Choctaw Nation: "Among all the thousands of whites that is sojourning or renting farmes, I don't know but only three white men that is honest and good men. . . . The balance is what would be termed trash."[43]

Federal authorities, employing their own set of race, gender, and class stereotypes, also gave attention to the character of white settlers and intruders in and around Indian Territory. In 1874 the commissioner of Indian Affairs included in his annual report a sketch of life in the Choctaw and Chickasaw Nations. He predicted that the nations would soon face serious difficulties arising from a steadily increasing stream of white people onto their lands. Federal officials, however, were not so concerned with wealthy Indians' loss of income or property to white thieves. Instead, many surmised that, rather than working for themselves, Indians had turned to white farmworkers in lieu of black slaves. That is, the presence of white workers on Indians' farms signaled Native people's "indolence and unthrift" rather than their prosperity.[44] Such pronouncements went hand in hand with praise for black people's industry and thrift. In 1872 one observer wrote of freedpeople in the Choctaw and Chickasaw Nations: "They are opening farms, building huts, fencing lands, raising grain, cattle, hogs, ponies . . . [and are] more provident than many of the Indians."[45] Through the latter decades of the century, this type of glowing assessment of black people's success in Indian Territory usually accompanied a call for opening the region to U.S. settlement and bringing the Indian nations under U.S. governance.

THROUGH THE 1870S, the question of freedpeople's citizenship remained embroiled in the Choctaw and Chickasaw Nations' dealings with the federal government over the nations' future in Indian Territory. Even as freedmen gained the attention of the federal officials, their actions and demands were received and evaluated within the broader context of U.S. Indian policy. The financial panic that gripped the United States in the early 1870s, resulting from a volatile mix of speculation, capitalist exploitation of labor, and corruption, contributed to the widespread belief in Congress that the Office of Indian Affairs was rotten with corruption and fiscal malfeasance.[46] In particular, lawmakers in Washington, as well as in the Choctaw Nation, turned their attention to Choctaw delegates' renewed lobbying efforts to secure payment of annuities and the outstanding claims from the 1830s (the Net Proceeds claims) owed to the nation by the United States. Bureaucrats at the Office of Indian Affairs, congressmen, Choctaws Peter Pitchlynn and Sampson Folsom, and their lawyer John Latrobe accused each other of deception and fraud.[47] In the various proposals and schemes devised to obtain payment of the Choctaw claims, Choctaw leaders and a variety of other interested parties raised the issue of freedpeople's citizenship and the seemingly mythical $300,000 discussed in the 1866 treaty.

By the end of 1870, a few hundred free black men and women, under the direction of Daniel C. Finn, an Arkansas attorney, submitted yet another petition to Congress. Borrowing language from the recently ratified Fifteenth Amendment to the U.S. Constitution, the petition protested black people's continued persecution by Choctaws "on account of our race, color, and previous condition of servitude." The petitioners indicated their desire for U.S. citizenship and requested that the $300,000 provided for in the 1866 treaty be paid to "the freedmen of the Choctaw and Chickasaw Nation." A total of 219 freedpeople (153 men and 66 women) left their marks on the petition, which was notarized by an Arkansas justice of the peace.[48]

Daniel C. Finn, a white attorney and speculator from New York who had moved to Arkansas after the Civil War, had visited a number of Choctaw and Chickasaw plantations in the Red River region. On one of Robert Jones's plantations, he "told many of these freedmen that [he] thought it was wrong for them to remain there, 'treated on Jones's plantation like dogs.' "[49] Finn "went to Pichlyn's [sic] farm, and to Jones's and Wheelock's plantations, to get signatures" for his petition to Congress. Finn was not engaged in charity work. He intended to deduct 5 percent from every $100 per capita payment made by the federal government to a freedman or freedwoman.[50] Freedwomen, along with freedmen, listened to his pitch and supported his endeavor. Because Finn sought to take a percentage of the per capita payments, his interests were best served by soliciting both female and male heads of household. Freedwomen entered their names on the petition and indicated whether they were widowed or single mothers; some women were unmarried and had no children.

Although the nature of Finn's interactions with the freedpeople is unknown except through his own description, neither the petition nor the supporting documents vary in significant or even perceptible ways from earlier descriptions of freedmen's actions and demands. Even if Finn pressured freedpeople into signing his petition, he certainly did not push them into accepting a new posture in regard to the questions of their citizenship and residency. The freedpeople who encountered Finn, moreoever, did not follow him blindly. By his own admission, some freedpeople accused him of giving them one petition to sign and then submitting a different one to Congress, a charge he denied. Other freedpeople rejected his overtures entirely. Lemon Butler recalled that after Finn left the Red River region, he headed to the northern end of the Choctaw Nation looking for more supporters of his petition. Butler noted that in his neighborhood, "the people would not sign it, and [Finn] turned back."[51] Butler and his brother attempted to track Finn and also reported him to the U.S. Indian agent.

In Congress, suspicions about lobbying and fraud in the Net Proceeds case, coupled with concerns about men like Finn, led to the formation of an investigative committee. Headed by Representative John P. C. Shanks of the House Committee on Indian Affairs, the committee was created to investigate allegations of fraud committed against Indians. The members extended the committee's purview to include matters related to freedpeople's standing in the Choctaw, Chickasaw, Creek, and Cherokee Nations. The committee visited Indian Territory in the summer of 1872 and interviewed a number of freedmen, as well as many Indians. The committee charged that many of the Choctaw delegates and their attorneys involved in the Net Proceeds case intended to defraud the Choctaw Nation. On the subject of freedpeople's citizenship in the Choctaw and Chickasaw Nations, however, the committee did not issue as strong an evaluation but rather offered the broad recommendation that "the permanent interest and welfare of both Indians and colored people demand the action of the Government."[52] Many Choctaws and Chickasaws took heart that Shanks, a Republican veteran of the Union army, was not sympathetic to Daniel Finn and did not endorse the removal and per capita compensation of freedpeople from the nations. Still, Choctaw and Chickasaw leaders knew that the issues of allotment and the opening of Indian Territory to white settlement and U.S. governance necessarily entailed dealing with the question of freed-people's citizenship.[53]

From the 1870s onward, Choctaw and Chickasaw leaders increasingly em-ployed a rhetoric of domination when discussing the subject of freedpeople's citizenship and the potential role of the federal government in resolving the matter. When Congress debated various bills that would have provided finan-cial relief to freedpeople in the two Indian nations and effectively recognize them as citizens of the nations, Choctaw and Chickasaw spokesmen cast their nations as the victims of U.S. domination and force. An editorial in a Choc-taw newspaper, for example, argued that if the Choctaw lawmakers did not extend citizenship to freedpeople, the federal government would surely "force [them] upon us." The editorial conceded that Choctaws would have to accept the United States' insistence upon black people's citizenship as the price of the Confederacy's defeat, "as the Southern whites did seven years ago."[54] Mem-bers of the Cherokee Nation supported Choctaw and Chickasaw lawmakers' unwillingness to grant citizenship to former slaves. An item in the Cherokee government's official newspaper, the *Cherokee Advocate*, argued that Congress was trying to "force" black people upon the nations. Choctaw and Chickasaw spokesmen also had the support of some congressmen, including Represen-tative Shanks, who positioned themselves as benevolent defenders of Indian peoples. Shanks, for example, argued that Congress should not force upon the Choctaws and Chickasaws either "these negroes whom they do not want" or "a division of their property [land] without their consent."[55] Indians debated and disagreed over whether to submit to U.S. plans for the allotment of their territory, but despite their differences of opinion, Choctaws and Chickasaws almost uniformly embraced a nationalist defense of their governments and their right to remain a separate people from the United States. One 1872 news-paper commentary, for example, suggested that because Indian Territory was home to "a distinct race, aboriginal to the country," it should be admitted to the United States as a state governed by Indians rather than subjected to feder-ally appointed territorial authorities.[56] Granting citizenship to former slaves, Choctaw and Chickasaw leaders repeatedly argued, threatened to undermine the stability of the nations' governments as well as their land title. In an 1876 speech to the Chickasaw legislature, Governor B. F. Overton urged lawmakers not to extend citizenship to black people. "If you do," he cautioned, "you sign the death-warrant of your nationality with your own hands."[57]

While Choctaw and Chickasaw spokesmen worried about the loss of their land to white settlers and squatters, they voiced a subtly different set of concerns about black people. It was not simply that as citizens, freedpeople would have legal rights to claim land and even receive equal allotments, but that black citizens would vote and potentially take charge of the nations' social and political affairs. One Chickasaw delegation to Congress, for example, pointed to the growing black population in the nation, noting that two of the four counties in the nation had black majorities. These delegates complained that the vast number of black people in the nation would take "control of our schools and government" if they were granted citizenship.[58] Such arguments appear less as a defense of Indian sovereignty than as an attempt to preserve the southern postemancipation racial hierarchy.

AS THE YEARS WORE ON, freedpeople in the Choctaw and Chickasaw Nations continued their quest for a resolution of their citizenship status, but the nature of their concerns and demands shifted somewhat. They continued to reference the citizenship provisions in the 1866 treaty, and they also continued to speak of their cultural connections to and family histories in the nations; but they increasingly framed their interests in a broader context, identifying with black people in the states and invoking a more collective history of slavery and emancipation.

In the months and years after emancipation, black people from Kansas, Arkansas, and Texas moved into the Choctaw and Chickasaw Nations. An untold number of these early migrants were people who had been enslaved in the Indian nations and had either fled or been removed by their masters during the war. The 1866 treaty had not left open a window of time for the return of freedpeople who had been war refugees. Rather, it only covered those "persons of African descent resident in the said nations at the date of the treaty of Fort Smith."[59] In the years after the treaty's 1868 adoption-or-removal deadline had passed, the question of how to handle these late arrivals added to the conflicts over black people's status and rights in the nations.

Chickasaw lawmakers contended that the black people who arrived in the nation after 1866 had never been enslaved by Chickasaws or Choctaws but were instead from the southern states. They charged that black soldiers, veterans of the Union army, remained in the West and infiltrated Indian Territory. Their allegations fused opposition to U.S. domination—namely, the presence of the military in their midst—with racist antipathy. Chickasaw leaders remained steadfast that black veterans were not wartime refugees from Indian Territory but intruders, men from the states who had no right to reside within the Choctaw or Chickasaw Nations. In one instance, Chickasaw leaders protested the presence of "a large number of colored soldiers from the States." They charged that the soldiers, along with "a large number of colored people from the States who had been attracted to this African stronghold in the Chickasaw nation," threatened to outnumber and thus overtake the Chickasaw Nation's government.[60]

From the very beginning of the citizenship debates, black men and women in the Choctaw and Chickasaw Nations had a decidedly different view of black veterans and others who arrived in Indian Territory after the war. In their early petitions to Congress, these freedpeople made clear their concern regarding the 1866 treaty's exclusion of black men who had enlisted in the Union army from the provisions for citizenship or removal. Two of the five resolutions issued at the January 1869 Scullyville convention addressed this subject. First, the freedmen at that meeting scorned the 1866 treaty's determination of who was eligible for adoption as "a most insidious clause" because it failed to include "a large number of our brethren, who at the time were either still in the Union army or had not ventured to return to their country." By 1869, these veterans were ineligible for either citizenship or removal under the treaty because, technically, they were intruders in the nations, having returned after the treaty's ratification. The next resolution called upon the federal government to act specifically in response to this situation. The freedmen entreated Congress "not to permit so cruel an outrage to be inflicted on its own defenders, and not to allow rebels to punish loyal men for their loyalty."[61]

Freedpeople found some support among federal officials for this argument. S. N. Clark, a special agent of the Freedmen's Bureau responsible for assessing conditions in Indian Territory, also faulted the treaty's failure to acknowledge the return of former slaves to the nations. That the treaty only covered only black people residing in the nations at the time of its ratification was, in Clark's estimation, "a good-sized mouse" in the meal. He reminded Congress that the preliminary treaty had been concluded barely four months after the war ended, and he estimated that hundreds of black people had been refugees from Indian Territory at that time. Many black women and children had been taken to Texas by their masters, while others had fled on their own to Kansas. Black men from the nations, according to Clark, had "remained true to the government, and, daring every peril and hardship in their effort to escape, came within our lines and joined our army." Clark further elaborated on this point, stating that the treaty thus failed to extend its "meager benefits" to "the only loyal people in the Territory."[62]

The limited scholarship on enslaved men in Indian Territory who joined the Union army indicates that many black men fled to Kansas with black refugees and loyalist Indians from the Cherokee and Creek Nations. There, they likely enlisted with the First and Second Kansas Colored Regiments and were later mustered out of service and given their final payment at Fort Leavenworth, Kansas.[63] While some of these men likely enlisted again and gained notoriety as the infamous buffalo soldiers who fought the Plains Indians, many returned to their families and communities in Indian Territory.[64]

Freedpeople in the two nations welcomed the veterans who returned to their families and also incorporated newcomers into their communities. The extent to which the black veterans who moved into Indian Territory were in fact former slaves of the Choctaw and Chickasaw Nations rather than former slaves from the surrounding area (Arkansas and Missouri) is unclear. Regardless, as the freedmen's petitions suggest, these men were embraced as "brethren." The term evokes a particular sense of the extended kinship networks that had sustained enslaved people and also suggests the ways in which freedpeople considered themselves connected to each other through the shared experience of slavery and liberation.

Through the second half of the century, black communities in the Choctaw and Chickasaw Nations insisted upon their cultural, historical, and legal claims to inclusion in the nations as citizens, but they also identified themselves as a distinctive group within the nations. From the 1870s through the end of the century, for example, black people in the Choctaw and Chickasaw Nations, as in the Cherokee, Creek, and Seminole Nations, commemorated their liberation from slavery with July 4th and Emancipation Day celebrations, a mainstay of many black communities across the United States. Communities organized parades, concerts, picnics, and barbecues and invited prominent local and national black leaders to give speeches. Despite the seeming irony of celebrating July 4th, many black people embraced its symbolic promises of universal freedom as part of their antislavery campaigns and also as part of their freedom celebrations. In 1872, for example, freedpeople in the Choctaw Nation held a July 4th celebration and invited visiting congressman John Shanks to join their barbecue and festivities. In the antebellum period, free black Americans mostly held annual celebrations of the August 1834 abolition of slavery in the British West Indies. After the Civil War, black people in the states and also Indian Territory modified the tradition somewhat by choosing June 19th as the day of their celebrations; known as "Juneteenth," the day marked the date in

1865 when news of the war's end and slavery's demise finally reached Texas. In the Choctaw and Chickasaw Nations, black people embraced the Juneteenth tradition, holding events in Ardmore (Chickasaw Nation), Atoka (Choctaw Nation), and McAlester (Choctaw Nation).[65]

It was this unity and sense of common cause among black people that frustrated Chickasaw leadership.[66] Those who had been enslaved by Choctaw and Chickasaw masters did not differentiate themselves from those who had been enslaved by white masters in the states. Black veterans received the praise and protection of their communities, especially when they were married to freedwomen from the Choctaw and Chickasaw Nations. In this way, women's domestic roles made their way into freedmen's political agendas. This can be inferred from an undated fragment of a letter reporting on the proceedings of a mass meeting of "the colored residents of the Choctaw & Chickasaw nation."[67] The letter discusses issues of concern specifically to Choctaw and Chickasaw freedwomen. These women, the letter states, resided in the nations at the time of the 1866 treaty and had "intermarried" with black men from the states.[68] The black people in the nations wanted the federal government to protect the men's right to remain in the nations with secure property and personal rights. The recurrent use of terms such as "colored residents" and "colored people" may reflect, however, either that both men and women attended this mass meeting or that both recounted their experiences and grievances to the attorneys who penned the letter. In any event, domestic relations occupied a prominent place in the freedpeople's perception and articulation of their rights and demands in the Choctaw and Chickasaw Nations.

FROM THE TIME THE 1866 treaty was ratified through the end of the nineteenth century, black people, Choctaws, Chickasaws, and white Americans debated the central question: in what nation did freedpeople from the Indian nations belong? As freedpeople and Indian leaders considered the question and fashioned their answers, they took positions that always addressed a larger set of issues and concerns. Arguments that framed citizenship as compensation or reparation for slavery, or as an acknowledgement of cultural affinity, or as the realization of a liberal notion of race-blind equality were all situated in a broader set of questions about the future security of Indian sovereignty in the face of U.S. domination. Freedpeople, no less than Choctaw and Chickasaw leaders, had to frame their positions in the context of local conditions and also larger national agendas.

The 1866 treaty was a remarkable failure in addressing the issue of black people's citizenship in the Choctaw and Chickasaw Nations. Yet we cannot simply dismiss the treaty as an anomaly. Reconstruction-era federal policy often failed to ensure adequate protection of black Americans' standing and rights as citizens of the United States.

For almost thirty years, the freedmen and freedwomen of the Choctaw and Chickasaw Nations continued their efforts to resolve the question of their citizenship. They had to maneuver between the repressive aims of Indian lawmakers and the emancipatory promises of federal officials. And they did so in ways that placed their needs and demands at the fore rather than making the interests of either the United States or the Choctaw and Chickasaw Nations the determining factor.

6

A New Home in the West
Allotment, Race, and Citizenship

For nearly half a century after emancipation, black people in the Choctaw and Chickasaw Nations lived without a clearly defined status in either the nations or the United States. Questions and conflicts over black people's citizenship and their attendant rights in the Indian nations persisted through the second half of the nineteenth century. Choctaw and Chickasaw leaders periodically entertained the prospect of recognizing former slaves and their descendants as citizens of their respective nations. Federal lawmakers, likewise, routinely discussed measures that proposed to resolve black people's uncertain standing in the Choctaw and Chickasaw Nations. Yet it was only when the United States made its final push to dismantle Indian governments and land title in Indian Territory that the issues of black people's citizenship status and rights in the Choctaw and Chickasaw Nations were finally addressed by Choctaw, Chickasaw, and U.S. lawmakers.

In the early 1870s, Chickasaw lawmakers briefly considered a measure to adopt former slaves as citizens. Nothing concrete emerged from this initiative. For the rest of the century, Chickasaw legislators consistently opposed extending citizenship to black people. In 1876 Chickasaw governor B. F. Overton warned the legislature that recognizing black people as citizens was tantamount to "sign[ing] the death-warrant of your nationality with your own hands."[1] Yet, within a few years, Chickasaw lawmakers once more entertained the question of black people's citizenship rights in the nation.

In the autumn of 1878, the Choctaw General Council initiated plans to work with Chickasaw leaders to resolve the question of black people's citizenship. Choctaw legislators authorized Principal Chief I. L. Garvin to appoint five men to a commission charged with "settling the status of freedmen, formerly slaves of the Choctaw and Chickasaw Nations." In March 1879 the Chickasaw legislature authorized a similar commission. The following month, the two groups met in Caddo, where they were joined by representatives of the United States. While Choctaw delegates supported extending citizenship to—"adoption" was the common term—former slaves and their descendants, Chickasaw delegates remained uncertain.[2]

At the same time, Indian leaders turned their attention to federal efforts to territorialize Indian Territory. Through the 1870s, Choctaw and Chickasaw political leaders reaffirmed their opposition to land allotment and the extension of U.S. authority over the land and peoples of Indian Territory. In 1878 Choctaw principal chief I. L. Garvin maintained that allotment would "inevitably lead to [Choctaw] ruin." Reminding his supporters of the United States' failure to fully compensate those Choctaws who had received allotments in Mississippi under the nation's removal treaty, Garvin insisted that Choctaws could not count on the federal government to act in good faith. Though the issues of allotment and black people's citizenship were not always treated in tandem, Choctaws and Chickasaws perceived each issue as a prime example of U.S. efforts to dominate and ultimately dismantle their nations.[3]

By 1880, the Choctaw General Council notified the U.S. Congress that they were unable to fulfill the 1866 treaty requirement that they reach an accord with Chickasaw lawmakers regarding the question of black people's citizenship. Choctaw legislators, consequently, informed Congress of their intention to act alone and "accept said freedmen as citizens of said Choctaw Nation." On May 21, 1883, the Choctaw General Council approved an Act to Adopt the Freedmen of the Choctaw Nation. It granted Choctaw citizenship to "all persons of African descent resident in the Choctaw Nation" when the 1866 treaty was ratified and also conferred citizenship upon their descendants.[4]

Black people's rights as citizens of the Choctaw Nation, however, were limited. While black people enjoyed the right of suffrage and were eligible "to hold any office of trust or profit," they were barred from the elective offices of principal chief and district chief. Black citizens were excluded from the nation's annuities and public domain, and their land claims were restricted to forty acres. Race, gender, and sexuality remained salient and explicit categories in the legal code. Laws criminalized and punished rape, polygamy, adultery, incest, bestiality, and "inter-marriage between Choctaws and Negroes." A marriage between a Choctaw and a white person, by contrast, was not defined as a felony.[5] The Choctaw legal code confirmed yet restricted black people's rights as citizens, creating a racially defined and inferior category of citizenship.

Even after the Choctaw General Council's 1883 adoption legislation, Chickasaw leaders stood firmly against the idea of black people's citizenship and continued to warn of the dire consequences of adopting black people as citizens. On one occasion, lawmakers declared: "The number of freedmen being so great, if adopted, will soon control our schools and government that we have been building and fostering for the past forty years. We love our homes, institutions, and government, and will not surrender them."[6] In 1885 the Chickasaw legislature reaffirmed its refusal to adopt black people as citizens. The Chickasaw governor Jonas Wolf boldly charged: "The Chickasaw people cannot see any reason or just cause why they should be required to do more for their freed slaves than the white people have done in the slaveholding States for theirs." He continued that "it was by the example and teaching of the white man that we purchased, at enormous prices, their slaves, and used their labor, and were forced, by the result of their war, to liberate our slaves at a great loss and sacrifice on our part, and we do not hold or consider our nation responsible in nowise for their present situation."[7] In the 1888 elections in the Chickasaw Nation, the National Party made opposing black people's citizenship part of its platform.[8]

As in the Cherokee and Creek Nations, Choctaw and Chickasaw lawmakers articulated national identity in the 1870s and 1880s ever more forcefully in terms of race and racial exclusion. Choctaw and Chickasaw leaders' positions regarding black people's citizenship unfolded against the backdrop of the late nineteenth-century U.S. campaign to assimilate Indians by finally dismantling their governments and allotting the nations' land in severalty. During the latter half of the nineteenth century, Native leaders often deployed this antiblack racism to invigorate an anticolonial defense of Indian sovereignty against the federal mandates for land allotment.[9]

THE LATE NINETEENTH-CENTURY federal campaign to assimilate Indians through the forced privatization of their lands is a well-established chapter in the history of U.S. Indian policy. In the late nineteenth century, eastern reformers, including Massachusetts senator Henry L. Dawes, clamored for an end to Indians' communal ownership of tribal lands as the primary means of precipitating Indians' assimilation.[10] In 1887, largely in response to the efforts of the self-proclaimed "friends of the Indians," Congress passed the General Allotment Act, commonly referred to as the Dawes Act. It gave the president the authority to dissolve Indian nations by allotting their lands in severalty. After receiving allotments, Indians eventually would be granted U.S. citizenship. Writing for the *Atlantic Monthly* in 1899, Dawes outlined the idealized vision of Indian reform as follows: "Every adult male landholder stands at the polls and in the courts in the full rights of American citizenship."[11]

Rather than setting forth a blueprint for immediate action, the Dawes Act sketched broad goals and left the details unfinished. For almost six years after the passage of the Dawes Act, the Choctaw, Chickasaw, Cherokee, Creek, and

Seminole Nations retained control of their land in Indian Territory—nearly 20 million acres—and remained exempt from the law's provisions.[12] In 1893, however, Dawes was appointed the head of the Commission to the Five Tribes, a three-man commission authorized to negotiate agreements with Indian leaders for the termination of their governments and land title.

The Dawes Commission headed to Indian Territory in the winter of 1893–94 and began meeting with representatives of the Indian nations as well as delegates representing black communities. Negotiations proceeded slowly, with Indian representatives unwilling to submit to allotment. In 1896 Congress strengthened the Dawes Commission's power by authorizing it to compile final rolls of the members of each nation and create a government for Indian Territory. The commission met with Choctaw and Chickasaw delegates in the winter of 1896 to draft an allotment agreement. Choctaw and Chickasaw representatives delayed before approving the final draft but signed the final agreement on April 23, 1897, at Atoka in the Choctaw Nation.

Under the Atoka Agreement, citizens of the two nations would receive 160-acre allotments, though Choctaw freedpeople would receive only forty acres. The agreement did not include provisions for freedpeople in the Chickasaw Nation. Under the terms of the agreement, everyone in the Choctaw and Chickasaw Nations would become citizens of the United States when the Indian governments were dissolved. In June 1898 Congress ratified an amended version of the Atoka Agreement as part of the Act for the Protection of the People of the Indian Territory, known as the Curtis Act. Under the provisions of the Curtis Act, both Choctaw and Chickasaw freedpeople would receive forty-acre allotments. It is important to note, however, that the Curtis Act recognized the uncertainty of Chickasaw freedpeople's standing in the Chickasaw Nation, thus opening the way to later challenges and disputes over the legitimacy of their allotments. The act established a timetable for allotment, extinguished the Native governments in Indian Territory, and brought Indian Territory under U.S. control.[13]

Choctaw principal chief Green McCurtain had entered the Atoka negotiations confident that Indian delegates could influence the terms of land allotment. McCurtain anticipated that acquiescing to U.S. demands for allotment might enable the Choctaw Nation to preserve its government for at least a few more decades. The Atoka Agreement, however, set March 4, 1906, as the date for the termination of the Choctaw government. McCurtain, acknowledging the failure of his efforts, conceded that the federal government was "much more powerful than we are" and described the agreement as "repugnant to our feelings and against our wishes."[14]

White reformers and lawmakers cited the nations' communal ownership of land as their primary violation of the ideals and practices of American economic culture. Observers charged that holding the land in common fostered indolence, leaving the majority of Choctaws, Chickasaws, Cherokees, Creeks, and Seminoles with little or no motivation to work for gain rather than subsistence. The Dawes Commission contended that many Indians lived in wooded areas, where "full-bloods still remain, eking out an existence on a few acres of corn raised in the small valleys, and the hogs raised on the acorns." In 1893 a writer for *Harper's New Monthly Magazine* lauded federal Indian policy that brought an end to "millions of fertile acres [lying] in unproductive wildness."[15] In contrast to this state of "arrested progress," reformers noted that tribal land policies imposed no limits on some men who claimed vast tracts of land and grew wealthy from overseeing the cultivation of commodity crops.[16]

Like poverty, prosperity also signaled to reformers and lawmakers that Indians were misusing their land. Racial ideology, specifically a belief in white superiority, offered a partial explanation for these seemingly contradictory assessments of land use in Indian Territory. Echoing longstanding assumptions about the children born to white-Indian marriages, Dawes and his peers concluded that "mixed-blood" Indians were "more industrious" than "full-bloods" in pursuing and profiting from commercial ventures. Reformers nonetheless took a dim view of enterprising Choctaws, Chickasaws, Creeks, Cherokees, and Seminoles who derived material success from hiring workers from the states to work as tenant farmers in Indian Territory rather than from their own efforts.[17] Historian Alexandra Harmon characterizes these divergent interpretations of Indian land-use patterns as follows: "Tribe members were damned if they did not get rich in the tribal system and damned if they did."[18]

As framed by interested politicians and reformers, the issues of land use, labor patterns, and the distribution of wealth in the Indian nations were intertwined with ideas about racial characteristics, republican ideals, and American economic and territorial expansion. Their work, Dawes explained to his reform-minded colleagues, was "not for the regeneration of a locality, but for a race."[19] The various strands of thought about Indian assimilation and land appropriation have been well rehearsed in the scholarship, which has explained the complex and often contradictory visions advanced by policy makers and also has considered the ways in which Native Americans engaged and resisted these ideas and plans. Increased attention to Indian leaders' varying responses to the Dawes-era calls for land reform, however, has not yet accounted for black people's participation in the debates over allotment. Federal lawmakers, for example, paid careful attention to black people's legal status in the Indian nations, especially their right to claim land. On the other hand, Dawes and his colleagues were less interested in the substance of black people's lives than they were in using the political and material conditions of their lives as a gauge of Indians' level of "civilization."

Unlike their Indian counterparts, black farmers in the Choctaw and Chickasaw Nations generally earned high praise from the Dawes Commission and other federal personnel in Indian Territory. Officials responsible for taking censuses of the Indian nations in 1890, for example, concluded that "the negroes are among the earnest workers in the Five Tribes." In the same year, an article in *New England Magazine* made a similar observation, attributing much of the labor responsible for the "improvements, cultivated farms, valuable ranches, coal mines, and other industries" in Indian Territory to black people.[20] Although black farmers in the Creek, Choctaw, Chickasaw, Cherokee, and Seminole Nations exercised their rights to use the common land under the same laws governing other tribal citizens, reformers viewed them from a different vantage point. Black people were routinely described as honest, law-abiding, and hardworking, and their success as agriculturalists was not only considered indicative of their industriousness but also used as additional proof of Indians' backwardness.[21]

Turning a blind eye to the laws of segregation and the often-brutal, if not deadly, social conditions in the states that barred millions of black people from acquiring property, Dawes and his colleagues rarely hesitated to criticize the Creek, Choctaw, Chickasaw, Cherokee, and Seminole governments for their persistent discrimination toward black people in matters of land use.[22] For example, the Dawes Commission concluded its 1894 report to Congress with a harsh appraisal of the Indian leaders' success at restricting black people's access to land, segregating schools, and barring black men from political participation. From the commissioners' perspective, however, Indians' mistreatment of black people did not mirror conditions in the states as much as it illuminated Native leaders' refusal to comply with the provisions of their 1866 treaties with the United States that had mandated the extension of equal citizenship to former slaves and their descendents. By implication, it also highlighted Indians' stunted appreciation of the social and economic ideals of individual rights.

FOR THE PEOPLE of African descent who had been enslaved and emancipated in the Choctaw, Chickasaw, Creek, Seminole, and Cherokee Nations, the late nineteenth-century discord over their standing as tribal citizens and, concomitantly, their access to the tribal lands was nothing new. At the end of the century, black people mobilized once again to protect their standing in the Choctaw and Chickasaw Nations and ensure their equal treatment during allotment. Networks that had facilitated freedmen's organizing in the postemancipation period remained critical in the latter years of the nineteenth century.

In the 1880s, for example, Choctaw freedmen followed closely the Choctaw General Council's actions regarding black people's adoption and rights in the nation. In the years before the council approved adoption legislation, freedmen convened and selected representatives to petition federal officials, demanding attention and advice regarding their uncertain status in the nation. Only weeks before the council approved the adoption of former slaves and their descendants, freedmen in Atoka County organized a mass meeting to protest the measure pending before the council. They objected to the provisions that established unequal citizenship for black people, specifically their exclusion from elected office, limits on land claims, and restrictions on marriages with black people from the states. Even after the adoption bill was enacted, freedmen in various counties across the Choctaw Nation continued to gather and discuss these issues.[23]

Once the Choctaw government recognized black people's citizenship, black men in the Chickasaw Nation embarked on a new campaign to obtain federal intervention regarding their status. In February 1884, a group of sixty-four freedmen convened near the town of Stonewall in the Chickasaw Nation and elected King Blue and Isaac Alexander to represent their interests to Congress. Though the matter of black people's citizenship gained the attention of Senator Dawes and others in Congress, no definitive steps were taken in Washington.

After the ratification of the Atoka Agreement, Chickasaw freedmen established a new organization—the Chickasaw Freedmen's Association—and hired two white attorneys (Joseph P. Mulen and Robert V. Belt) to bring their case to the federal government. Charles Cohee, Isaac Kemp, George Hall, and Mack Stevenson were elected to lead the freedmen's association.[24] Chickasaw freedpeople promptly protested their exclusion from the Atoka Agreement and once more organized a mass meeting. The Chickasaw freedpeople continued to benefit from the energy and efforts of the newly adopted Choctaw freedpeople, many of whom lived in the Chickasaw Nation. Choctaw freedpeople challenged the Atoka Agreement, demanding that they not be distinguished by race from Indians and not be limited to forty-acre claims during the process of allotment. Charles Fields, a Choctaw freedman, informed the Dawes Commission that he was worried that he would not receive "equal rights" and that this frightened him. Fields wanted this equality, he explained, because "the Indians raise[d] me from a boy."[25] In this regard, the adoption of the Choctaw freedpeople did little to divide the common interests of the Choctaw and Chickasaw freedpeople.[26]

Through the 1880s, leading black men in the Choctaw and Chickasaw Nations met separately and jointly and consistently sounded two themes in their speeches and petitions demanding full citizenship. They articulated affective ties to the Indian nations based on sociocultural connections as well as personal and family history; they also cited material interests, namely the desire to secure their land claims and protect their property. An 1880 statement by a freedman in the Choctaw Nation read: "We do not belong to the States, we belong to the Nation and here is where we want to die." In 1881 a group of Choctaw freedmen wrote to the U.S. secretary of the interior to explain their desire to remain in the Choctaw Nation: "This is our home we were brought here (the old heads) when we were young, we have given to the Indians a long life of labor and toil for which we received no pay." King Blue and Isaac Alexander delivered to Congress a statement from the Chickasaw freedmen's February 1884 meeting in Stonewall. Referring to black people's determination to remain in the nation, it read: "For many and grave reasons we do not elect to remove. As natives, we are attached to the localities of our birth and childhood; as men we are attached to the people amongst whom we have been born and bred."[27]

Choctaw and Chickasaw freedmen's organizations were sometimes assisted by black leaders and activists from the states. James Milton Turner, for example, a prominent black attorney from St. Louis, helped organize Choctaw freedmen's meetings to protest their unequal citizenship under the 1883 adoption legislation. Turner also devoted his attention to freedpeople in the Cherokee Nation, supporting their efforts to secure equal rights and allotments. Black clergy and missionaries from the states also lent their support to freedpeople's efforts to receive equal standing as citizens and allottees in the Choctaw and Chickasaw Nations.[28]

With federally mandated allotment on the horizon, freedpeople became ever more determined to safeguard their land claims and property in the nations. Conflicts over land use dated back to the immediate postemancipation period, but in the era of allotment, freedpeople sought to ensure they would indeed become landowners under the Atoka Agreement. When the issue of citizenship was still up for debate, Choctaw freedmen, for example, wrote to federal officials that they were deeply troubled by the prospect of forfeiting their homes and property in the nations. Interestingly, Choctaw records indicate that the few freedpeople who opted not to accept citizenship and left the nation after 1883 were those who had not claimed and improved any land and did not own much, if any, livestock or other property.[29]

THE CURTIS ACT authorized the Dawes Commission to compile tribal rolls, enumerating the citizens in each of the Indian nations and thus confirming their eligibility for allotment. The commission nevertheless distinguished between citizens, classifying them as Indians by blood, intermarried whites, or freedmen. Particular attention was given to Indians, who were further classified according to their blood quanta. Informed by late nineteenth-century racist pseudoscience, tribal censuses classified Indians by blood quanta to determine their eligibility for receiving allotments. Blood quanta served as the gauge of allottees' competency to own and manage their land and determined their property ownership rights and obligations, such as paying taxes or selling the land. Administrators hired by the Dawes Commission recorded Indians' blood quanta, calculating individuals' levels of Indian blood to eighths and sixteenths. This formulation, however, was designed to extend only to persons who claimed both Indian and white ancestry.

Attuned to the history of slavery and emancipation in Indian Territory, lawmakers devised a racial classification scheme that isolated black people as a racially distinct class within each tribe.[30] Tribal members who identified themselves as having black and Indian parents and grandparents were placed on the "Freedmen" rolls. Enrollment thus effaced family histories and the conditions of slavery that had shaped so many enslaved people's family trees. The commission's official distinction between black and Indian citizens of the nations furthermore lent an air of legitimacy to tribal leaders' antiblack racism. The creation of separate tribal rolls for "Indians" and "Freedmen" cemented racial categories and hierarchy in the federal oversight of enrollment and allotment and, consequently, precipitated immediate and long-term material and political consequences for enrollees as they navigated the enrollment process and adjusted to individual ownership of allotted land.[31]

Federal lawmakers and bureaucrats were no strangers to the task of assigning racial and political identities to the African Americans in Indian Territory. In 1865 and 1866, when the United States renegotiated its treaties with the Choctaw and Chickasaw Nations, the notion that black people and Indians shared cultural commonalities held sway. By the end of the century, however, when the concept of Indian assimilation gripped lawmakers and reformers, the similarities between Indians and black people in Indian Territory no longer seemed so obvious or natural. In the spring and summer of 1885, delegates from

Chickasaw freedmen filing for allotments, Tishomingo, Oklahoma. (I. T. W. P. Campbell Collection; courtesy of the Oklahoma Historical Society)

the Senate Committee on Indian Affairs traveled west to gather information on conditions in Indian Territory and hear testimony on the subject from people in the Choctaw, Chickasaw, Cherokee, Creek, and Seminole Nations and also from the U.S. Indian agents stationed in Indian Territory.[32] Anticipating the complete dissolution of tribal governments, the visiting senators focused their attention on issues of land use and the nature of political life in the Five Tribes. They questioned a wide array of men, probing the correlation between racial identity and economic and civic fitness by asking about the extent to which mixed-blood and full-blood Indians, as well as black people, took up commercial or subsistence farming, attended school, held elected office, and voted.

The questions put forth by the Senate subcommittee often assumed a racial difference between blacks and Indians. White soldiers stationed at forts in Indian Territory, for example, were asked to evaluate and compare Indians' and blacks' capacity for "voting and sitting on juries."[33] And one Creek leader was asked: "Do the Indians stand on one side in a district and the negroes on another? Do they divide upon race lines?"[34] On the subject of legalized segregation, the senators were more concerned with the availability of separate facilities for black people than with the implication that their citizenship had been compromised.[35] When Caesar Colbert, a Choctaw freedman, worried that the Choctaw government would continue to restrict black people's access to land even during allotment, one senator dismissed these concerns, saying: "You don't know what the Choctaws will do, and if they have not done it yet, I would not be much frightened beforehand."[36] Testimony about the constraints on black people's rights as tribal citizens did not arouse the senators' sympathies. Instead, they regarded the tribal governments' antiblack measures as further evidence of Indians' backwardness and thus justification for U.S. intervention. In its 1894 report, the Dawes Commission put it succinctly, explaining that under tribal governments, law-abiding and industrious freedpeople suffered at the hands of Indian leaders who "perverted" justice and "inflicted irreparable wrongs and outrages upon" them.[37]

In other instances, classifying the inhabitants of Indian Territory proceeded with less fanfare but equal confusion. Federal personnel responsible for taking the 1890 census in Indian Territory described the difficulties of reconciling their perceptions of people with the answers they received to the question, "Are you an Indian?" They noted, for example, that some people who appeared "white in color and features" were Indians "by remote degree of blood," while others claimed Indian political identity through marriage. Census takers also encountered "Negroes . . . who speak nothing but Indian languages, and are Indians by tribal law and custom." Other black people, however, identified themselves as Indians but were not acknowledged as such by the nations. The task of locating people in one set of racial categories when both their appearance and their self-identification defied the census takers' classification scheme resulted in a census that often reflected arbitrary decisions that did not accord with enrollees' self-identification and family histories.[38]

The racial categorization of the tribal rolls also shaped federal policy governing the property rights, or trust status, attached to land allotments. Individuals classified as having one-half or more Indian blood were exempt from taxation and prevented from selling their land. However, allottees listed as having less than one-half Indian blood were responsible for property taxes and were free to sell their land. Freedpeople and intermarried whites were included in the latter category. The gradations of restrictions reflected policy makers' and reformers' ideas that allottees' competency at managing their property and finances correlated directly with blood quanta and race. Ultimately, most allottees lost their land to unscrupulous purchasers, tax burdens, and financial necessity.

In 1907, when the Dawes Commission finally closed its tribal rolls, almost 6,000 Choctaw freedpeople, including minors, had been enrolled, and just over 4,600 Chickasaw freedpeople had been enrolled. By 1930, members of the

Choctaw, Chickasaw, Cherokee, Creek, and Seminole Nations held less than 2 million acres of land, compared to the 1890 total of nearly 20 million acres.[39] Black people's acquisition of land allotments under federal law had a number of paradoxical implications. The first is that reformers' plans for including Indians in the American mainstream drew heavily on the ideals of civic equality that had informed Reconstruction-era legislation establishing black people's freedom and citizenship. Indeed, some activists and politicians drew clear parallels, proposing the extension of the Fourteenth Amendment over Native Americans. Yet in the name of elevating "Indians," the so-called Indian reform laws classified black people as a distinct group of citizens in the Indian nations whose rights were not equal to those of other tribal citizens. The racial classification scheme, furthermore, effaced family and consanguinal ties between black people and Indians. Federal law brought this class of landowning black people into legal existence as "Freedmen" of the Indian nations and assured them of property ownership at precisely the moment when black people across the United States lived under expanding regimes of legal and extralegal exploitation and violence that prevented and punished the accumulation of property.[40] Once allotment was completed, the Indian governments were dissolved, and freedpeople in the Choctaw and Chickasaw Nations were recognized as citizens of the United States. Almost immediately after Oklahoma statehood in November 1907, state lawmakers enacted a series of laws imposing racial segregation and disfranchising black voters.

Even at the various times when freedpeople had expressed their willingness to remove from the nations to another site in Indian Territory, or when they indicated that they wanted U.S. citizenship, they never attempted to diminish or elide their ties to the Choctaw and Chickasaw Nations. Many had survived the trek west earlier in the century when the nations were removed from the Southeast. They had lived and labored in the new country, where the hunger and diseases that punctuated the early years in the West knew no boundaries of race or status. Born and raised in the Chickasaw and Choctaw Nations, the freedpeople had no intention of organizing a mass migration away from the region and culture that had defined their lives and their family histories. Adam Burris, once owned by Peter Pitchlynn, wrote to his daughter Suckey in 1880 and begged her to return to her family in the Choctaw Nation. Burris was sorry to have received Suckey's most recent letter and learn that she did not "want to com[e] back to live with us in the nation." Burris reported that the family was doing well and had "plenty to suport [sic] you and your children." This optimistic assessment notwithstanding, Burris went on to issue his unequivocal position regarding his daughter's future: "I can

Martha Jackson at her home near Fort Towson, Oklahoma. (Thomas Foreman
Home Collection; courtesy of the Oklahoma Historical Society)

not send you any money to pay house rent but if you will come home I will send you all the money to pay your expences to Caddo and Ben will meat you at Caddo with his wagon and team to bring you home. Aunt Miley says if you will come home she can suport your children." Missing no opportunity to drive his point home, Burris accounted for all of their relatives and assured his daughter of everyone's willingness to assist her and her children. His question, "Suckey if you was to stay out theare what would become of your children?," hung against this backdrop of family and community mutual aid. It was not just money—passage to the territory and a debt-free existence— that Burris offered his daughter; he wanted her "to come home & live with us . . . they is a family of your conections in this country."[41] It was these ties of family and history in the Choctaw and Chickasaw Nations that sustained the freedpeople throughout the nearly half a century between emancipation and citizenship.

Conclusion

Writing in 1980, Ralph Ellison mused on the nature of historical memory. In a passage evocative of W. E. B. Du Bois's conception of black Americans' "double-consciousness," Ellison wrote: "We possess two basic versions of American history: one which is written and as neatly stylized as ancient myth, and the other unwritten and as chaotic and full of contradictions, changes of pace, and surprises as life itself."[1]

Ellison, a native son of Oklahoma, sought to impress upon his readers the necessity of retrieving the unwritten past, by which he meant the history of black people in America, and acknowledging its messy complexity, plurality, and legacies.

Until recently, the history of black people's enslavement, emancipation, and freedom in the southern Indian nations has existed mainly in the realm of the unwritten. In its place, two other narratives about the black experience in Indian Territory have held sway among a wide variety of people. The first depicts slavery in the Indian nations as benign and inherently different from bondage in the United States. This narrative, which has proved remarkably enduring, refuses to see slavery as an institution grounded in race and gender ideologies that justified the ongoing commodification and brutal exploitation of people of African descent. Arguments that identify slaveholding as a means of cultural preservation and continuity might be considered in this context to the extent that they overlook issues of race, gender, and the exploitation of labor and reproduction.

The second prevailing narrative about black life in Indian Territory begins with the late nineteenth-century migration of black people from the southern states to Indian Territory during the era of allotment and Oklahoma statehood. Here, Indian Territory is not figured as a site of slavery, emancipation, and struggles for meaningful freedom and citizenship but becomes a site that is often cast as "the West," or at least as someplace that is not "the South." That is, Indian Territory is narrated as the place where black people from the southern states went to escape poverty, violence, and the painfully limited social and economic opportunities of the post-Reconstruction South. Indian Territory is not seen as another place of black exploitation but as a site where freedom, opportunity, creativity, and productivity might flourish. The touchstone image in this narrative is that of Tulsa's "Black Wall Street," a vibrant and thriving black neighborhood ultimately cut down by white-supremacist violence.[2]

Both narratives effectively erase the history of black people's enslavement, emancipation, and struggles for meaningful freedom and citizenship in the Indian nations. So, too, do they erase Indian peoples and Native American history from understandings of "the South." Recently, however, historians and anthropologists, most notably Tiya Miles, Celia Naylor, Claudio Saunt, David Chang, and Circe Sturm, have delved into the history of slavery, emancipation, and freedom and called attention to the complex meanings of race, family, cultural identification, property, and nationalism in the Cherokee and Creek Nations. This book adds to this ongoing scholarly discussion with the presentation of new material and questions that expand our understanding of the Native South, Indian Territory, and the United States. Beyond contributing to understandings of slavery and its legacies in the Choctaw and Chickasaw Nations and widening the terrain of black-Indian studies, this book also situates this particular history within the broader context of American slavery and emancipation.

Indeed, the Choctaw constitution of 1983 effectively disenfranchised descendants of former slaves, those who had received Choctaw citizenship in 1883. The current constitutions of both the Choctaw and Chickasaw Nations restrict citizenship to people who can trace their ancestry back to the Dawes rolls of Indians by blood. As black people's struggles to preserve their citizenship in the Cherokee Nation over the past decade have shown, the assumed opposition between black people's rights and Indian sovereignty has endured, and the legacies of slavery and emancipation remain very much a part of people's lives. The material presented in this book attempts to realign the seemingly entrenched antagonism of black freedom and Indian sovereignty. Situating the history of black people's slavery and freedom, as well as the history of Native peoples' struggles to maintain sovereignty, in a larger context of domination and colonialism may allow us to see a history of intersecting and overlapping contests for power and justice.

Notes

Abbreviations

ABCFM   Papers of the American Board of Commissioners for Foreign Missions, microfilm (Woodbridge, Conn.: Research Publications Inc., 1982–85)

NAMP   National Archives Microfilm Publications, National Archives and Records Administration, Washington, D.C.

OKHS   Oklahoma Historical Society, Oklahoma City, Okla.

UOK   Western History Collection, University of Oklahoma Library, Norman, Okla.

Introduction

1. Doran, "Population Statistics of Nineteenth-Century Indian Territory," 501.

2. Baker and Baker, *The WPA Oklahoma Slave Narratives*, 6–9.

3. For critiques of dependency theory, see Albers, "Labor and Exchange in American Indian History," 279; and Van Hoak, "Untangling the Roots of Dependency."

4. Perdue, *"Mixed Blood" Indians*; Ingersoll, *To Intermix with Our White Brothers*, chap. 6.

5. Petition to the President and Congress, September 5, 1810, in Carter, *The Territory of Mississippi, 1809–1817*, 106–7.

6. Hitchcock, *A Traveler in Indian Territory*, 187.

7. Moore, *Nairne's Muskhogean Journals*, 57

8. Quoted in Kidwell, *Choctaws and Missionaries in Mississippi*, 6

9. Carson, *Searching for the Bright Path*; O'Brien, *Choctaws in a Revolutionary Age*; St. Jean, "Trading Paths"; Atkinson, *Splendid Land, Splendid People*.

10. Quoted in Carson, *Searching for the Bright Path*, 102.

11. Quoted in Atkinson, *Splendid Land, Splendid People*, 214; Paige, Bumpers, and Littlefield, *Chickasaw Removal*, chap. 1.

12. Quoted in St. Jean, *Remaining Chickasaw in Indian Territory, 1830s–1907*, 8.

13. Quoted in Paige, Bumpers, and Littlefield, *Chickasaw Removal*, 27.

14. Ibid., 27–28.

15. Kappler, *Treaties*.

16. Kaczorowski, "To Begin the Nation Anew"; Fields, "Ideology and Race in American History."

17. Hoxie, *A Final Promise*; Greenwald, *Reconfiguring the Reservation*; Bailey, *Reconstruction in Indian Territory*.

18. Morgan, *American Slavery, American Freedom*; Foner, "The Meaning of Freedom in the Age of Emancipation"; Foner, *Nothing but Freedom*; Stanley, *From Bondage to Contract*; Penningroth, *Claims of Kinship*.

19. Sturm, *Blood Politics*; Saunt, "The Paradox of Freedom."

Chapter 1

1. There is a long historiography examining African Americans' relationships with southern Indians. See Jeltz, "The Relations of Negroes and Choctaw and Chickasaw Indians"; Johnston,

"Documentary Evidence of the Relations of Negroes and Indians"; Porter, "Relations between Negroes and Indians"; Porter, "Notes Supplementary to 'Relations between Negroes and Indians'"; and Willis, "Divide and Rule." For a detailed review of this historiography, see Miles and Krauthamer, "Africans and Native Americans." For more recent studies that focus on slavery, see Miles, *Ties That Bind* and *House on Diamond Hill*; Naylor, *African Cherokees*; and Saunt, *A New Order of Things* and *Black, White, and Indian*.

2. Etheridge, "The Making of a Militaristic Slaving Society." For a history of Chickasaws' colonial-era alliances and warfare, see St. Jean, "Trading Paths."

3. Perdue, *Slavery and the Evolution of Cherokee Society*, 16; Perdue, *Cherokee Women*. For descriptions of Choctaws' treatment of Chickasaw captives, see O'Brien, *Choctaws in a Revolutionary Age, 1750–1830*, chap. 3.

4. O'Brien, *Choctaws in a Revolutionary Age*, 44.

5. For detailed histories of French and English trade relations with Indians in the Mississippi valley, see White, *The Roots of Dependency*; Braund, *Deerskins and Duffels*; Saunt, *A New Order of Things*.

6. O'Brien, *Choctaws in a Revolutionary Age*, chaps. 3–5; Carson, *Searching for the Bright Path*, chaps. 3–4; Perdue, "Race and Culture," 704–5; White, *Roots of Dependency*, chap. 3; Atkinson, *Splendid Land, Splendid People*, chap. 2.

7. Moore, *Nairne's Muskhogean Journals*, 37.

8. Rowland and Sanders, *Mississippi Provincial Archives: French Dominion*, 3:303. For detailed history of early Choctaw-French relations, see Usner, *Indians, Settlers, and Slaves*.

9. In the winter of 1702, Henri de Tonti toured Choctaw and Chickasaw villages and reported to his French superiors that he had seen one Choctaw village where the residents could no longer cultivate their fields because of their proximity to a hostile Chickasaw settlement. The Choctaws' enemies, de Tonti explained, "do not give them any rest." Historian Patricia Galloway notes that de Tonti's report is significant in part because he locates some Choctaw villages to the west of the Tombigbee River. Their migration westward, Galloway explains, indicates an attempt to distance themselves from and defend themselves against Creek and Chickasaw raiders. Chickasaw settlements faced similar pressures from Choctaw warriors. By the 1720s, Chickasaws consolidated their villages in a region that became known as the Chickasaw Old Fields (in today's Lee County, Mississippi) and abandoned their outlying fields and settlements. Henri de Tonti to M. d'Iberville, February 23, 1702, translated and transcribed in Galloway, "Henri de Tonti du village des Chacta, 1702," 166–73; ibid., 151; Atkinson, *Splendid Land, Splendid People*, 11.

10. Mortgage of John Wright to Samuel Wragg, June 15, 1714, Charleston, South Carolina, quoted in Morgan, *Slave Counterpoint*, 482.

11. Norris, "Profitable Advice for Rich and Poor," 128–32. Emphasis in original.

12. Gallay, *The Indian Slave Trade*, 299. Between 1676 and 1720, 42,800 African slaves were imported into North America. For a statistical history of the transatlantic slave trade, see Curtin, *The Atlantic Slave Trade*.

13. Hall, *Africans in Colonial Louisiana*, 10, 34, 35, 60; Wood, *Black Majority*; Gomez, *Exchanging Our Country Marks*, chap. 1. Rothman, *Slave Country*, 78, 186; Berlin, *Generations of Captivity*, 146.

14. Forbes, *Africans and Native Americans*.

15. Quoted in Usner, *Indians, Settlers, and Slaves*, 58.

16. Quoted in ibid., 139; St. Jean, "Trading Paths," 108.

17. For studies of Euro-American efforts to prevent identification and alliances between southeastern Indians and enslaved Africans, see Willis, "Divide and Rule"; and McLoughlin, "Red Indians, Black Slavery, and White Racism." James Merrell redirects this scholarship in his study of the Catawbas, arguing that their nineteenth-century ideas about racial difference and

antipathy for black people were not innate and cannot be understood by focusing primarily on Euro-American efforts to foment animosity between Indians and Africans. See Merrell, "The Racial Education of the Catawba Indians."

18. For a description of Cherokee leaders' acknowledgment of their limited ability to capture and return fugitives, see Miles, *Ties That Bind*, 32. For a discussion of Creeks' willingness to harbor fugitive slaves, see Saunt, *A New Order of Things*, chap. 5.

19. Diron d'Artaguette to Maurepas, March 20, 1730, in Rowland and Sanders, *Mississippi Provincial Archives: French Dominion*, 1:76. For a detailed discussion of the Natchez rebellion, see Usner, *Indians, Settlers, and Slaves*, 65–76.

20. Rowland and Sanders, *Mississippi Provincial Archives: French Dominion*, 1:65.

21. Ibid., 1:180.

22. Ibid., 1:178, 179.

23. Quoted in Usner, *Indians, Settlers, and Slaves*, 74.

24. Etheridge, "The Making of a Militaristic Slaving Society." For discussion of shifts in gender roles among Creeks and Cherokees, especially in relation to decision making and diplomacy, see Saunt, *A New Order of Things*, chap. 6; and Perdue, "Native Women in the Early Republic."

25. French sources document a case from 1739 in which a group of warriors under Alibamon Mingo's command intercepted a messenger from a Chickasaw camp who was carrying a "letter for an English trader." The band of Choctaws took their captive with the "intention of having this messenger burned." A Choctaw woman, a chief's wife, interceded and adopted the captive, sparing his life. Rowland and Sanders, *Mississippi Provincial Archives: French Dominion*, 3:726.

26. Windley, *South Carolina*, 71.

27. Saunt, *A New Order of Things*, 175–77.

28. Usner, *Indians, Settlers, and Slaves*, chap. 3; White, *The Roots of Dependency*, chap. 3; Saunt, *A New Order of Things*, chaps. 6–9; Rothman, *Slave Country*, chap. 2.

29. Horsman, "The Indian Policy of an 'Empire for Liberty,' " 39.

30. Governor of Mississippi Territory, quoted in Rothman, *Slave Country*, 39. The 1789 Treaty of San Lorenzo established the boundary between the United States and Spanish territory, providing for the United States' use of the Mississippi River and Spain's evacuation from west Florida.

31. Petition to the President and Congress, 1807, in Carter, *The Territory of Mississippi, 1809–1817*, 106–7; Secretary of War to William Cocke, March 19, 1816, in ibid., 669; Horsman, "The Indian Policy of an 'Empire for Liberty,' " 44–45.

32. There is a growing body of scholarship exploring the multifaceted meanings of Native American women's work, but, as Laura Klein and Lillian Ackerman have argued, the nuances of Native women's lives remain unexplored in most ethnographic studies, and women are presented "only where they are expected." Klein and Ackerman, *Women and Power in Native North America*, 3. Theda Perdue and Nancy Shoemaker have made similar arguments, and their respective works provide critical rereadings of historical sources that depict Native women's labor patterns. See, for example, Perdue, *Cherokee Women*; Perdue, *Sifters*; Perdue, "Native Women in the Early Republic"; and Shoemaker, *Negotiators of Change*. On women's roles in the deerskin trade, see Braund, "Guardians of Tradition and Handmaidens to Change."

33. Bieder, "Scientific Attitudes toward Indian Mixed-Bloods in Early Nineteenth-Century America." Kirsten Fischer takes a new and innovative approach to the formation of racial categories in colonial America, looking at the ways in which nonelite men and women—Native American, African and African American, and Euro-American—engaged dominant race, gender, and class ideologies. Fisher, *Suspect Relations*. See Jennifer Morgan, *Laboring Women*, on early ideas about black women and labor.

34. Phelps, "Excerpts from the Journal of the Reverend Joseph Bullen, 1799 and 1800," 262.

35. Berkhofer, *The White Man's Indian*, 85.

36. Perdue, "Race and Culture," 704–6.

37. Horsman, "The Indian Policy of an 'Empire for Liberty,'" 48; William Simpson to Secretary of War, October 19, 1810, in Carter, *The Territory of Mississippi, 1809–1817*, 123.

38. Quoted in O'Brien, *Choctaws in a Revolutionary Age*, 102–3.

39. Mushulatubbee and Puchshanubbee to Rev. Worcester, June 4, 1820, printed in *Missionary Herald*, vol. 16, 379; DeRossier, "Pioneers with Conflicting Ideals," 176.

40. Greg O'Brien, for example, covers the ways in which ideas about spiritual authority remained intact among Choctaws and their leaders even as spiritual authority became disassociated from chiefs' authority to redistribute material goods and no longer served as the basis for political authority. O'Brien, *Choctaws in a Revolutionary Age*, 106.

41. Silas Dinsmoor to Secretary of War, October 23, 1810, in Carter, *The Territory of Mississippi, 1809–1817*, 127.

42. *Niles Weekly Register*, July 3, 1830; Agent Benjamin Smith to John Calhoun, February 29, 1824, Letters Received by the Office of Indian Affairs, NAMP, M234, roll 135.

43. Young, *Autobiography of a Pioneer*, 213–14.

44. Lincecum, "Life of Apushimataha," 416; Mississippi newcomer quoted in Carson, *Searching for the Bright Path*, 73.

45. See Usner, *Indians, Settlers, and Slaves*, for discussion of frontier exchange economy.

46. Gomez, *Exchanging Our Country Marks*, 23; McClinton, *The Moravian Springplace Mission to the Cherokees*, vol. 1, *1805–1813*, 114, 390, 393; Mitchell, *An Exposition of the Case of the Africans Taken to the Creek Agency*.

47. Journal of the Mission at Elliot, January 7, 1821, vol. 1, folder 12, ABCFM 18.3.4; Thomas Stuart to Rev. Green, January 24, 1832, vol. 1, folder 6, ABCFM 18.4.4; Benson, *Life among the Choctaw Indians*, 98, 116–17.

48. Usner, *Indians, Settlers, and Slaves*, 111.

49. Loring Williams to Jeremiah Evarts, June 1823, vol. 2, folder 173, ABCFM 18.3.4.

50. Libby, *Slavery in Frontier Mississippi*, 48–56; Loring Williams to Jeremiah Evarts, June 1823, vol. 2, folder 173, ABCFM 18.3.4; Journal of the Mission at Elliot, 7 January 1821, vol. 1, folder 12, ABCFM 18.3.4.

51. John Allen to Secretary of War, February 7, 1830, Letters Received by the Office of Indian Affairs, NAMP, M234, roll 136; Miles, *Ties That Bind*, 36.

52. Young, *Autobiography of a Pioneer*, 211–12.

53. Oliver Stark to Rev. C. B. Treat, August 22, 1854, vol. 8, folder 267, ABCFM 18.3.4

54. Jefferson quoted in Horsman, "The Indian Policy of an 'Empire for Liberty,'" 50.

55. Miles, *Ties That Bind*, 20–21.

56. Circe Sturm discusses the racial attitudes of Euro-American reformers and policy makers toward Indians who had Euro-American relatives. Sturm, *Blood Politics*, 56–57

57. Quoted in Littlefield, *The Chickasaw Freedmen*, 16.

58. Perdue, *"Mixed Blood" Indians*, 69. Missionary Cyrus Byington compiled a dictionary of the Choctaw language in the 1820s. According to Byington's work, the Choctaw word *nahollushi* meant "a quadroon; the child or descendant of a white man by a red woman." Byington, *A Dictionary of the Choctaw Language*, 266.

59. Kidwell, *Choctaws and Missionaries in Mississippi*, 17–19; Perdue, "Race and Culture," 710.

60. Pushmataha did not descend from a politically prominent family and clan but rose to prominence by virtue of his success as a warrior in the late eighteenth and early nineteenth century. White, *Roots of Dependency*, 111.

61. Perdue, *"Mixed Blood" Indians*, 46. For an extensive genealogy of the Colbert family, see Martini, *Chickasaw Empire*.

62. Last will and testament of John Pitchlynn, September 11, 1824, box 1, folder 2, Pitchlynn Papers, UOK.

63. William Cocke to Secretary of War, September 22, 1816, Lowrie and Franklin, *American State Papers: Indian Affairs*, vol. 2, 106–7; Mary Lindsay in Baker and Baker, *The WPA Oklahoma Slave Narratives*, 246–48.

64. Pitchlynn Diary Transcript, November 28, 1828, box 5, folder 2, Pitchlynn Papers, UOK.

65. Shoemaker, *A Strange Likeness*, 3.

66. McLoughlin, "A Note on African Sources of American Indian Racial Myths"; McLoughlin, "'The First Man Was Red.'" On the formation of race as timeless and natural in the Euro-American context, see White, *Dark Continent*. For discussions of Native people's ideas about blood and racial identity, see Meyer, *Thicker than Water*; Sturm, *Blood Politics*; Strong and Van Winkle, "Tribe and Nation"; Strong and Van Winkle, "'Indian Blood'"; and Wilson, "Blood Quantum."

67. Loring Folsom to Thomas Pitchlynn, June 12, 1849, box 9, folder 12, Pitchlynn Papers, UOK.

68. For works that focus on the formation and development of categories of race and gender in the context of chattel slavery, see Morgan, *Laboring Women*; Fischer, *Suspect Relations*; McCurry, *Masters of Small Worlds*; White, *Ar'n't I a Woman?*; and Camp, *Closer to Freedom*.

69. Morgan, *Laboring Women*, 145.

70. Matilda Poe in Butler and Butler, *The WPA Oklahoma Slave Narratives*, 324–25; Polly Colbert in ibid., 86; Elsie Pryor in Rawick, *Oklahoma Narratives*, 261; Jefferson L. Cole in ibid., 120–27. Interviews with Jordan Folsom and Anna Colbert in Indian Pioneer Papers Collection, UOK. In her examination of slavery in the Cherokee Nation, Tiya Miles finds that among small slaveholders, Cherokee women increasingly gave up agricultural labor, now the work of slaves, and focused their energies on domestic work, including spinning and weaving. Miles, *Ties That Bind*, 39. It seems unlikely, however, that no Indians worked in the fields with their slaves like middling white slaveholders often did in the southern states. Before Removal, some Choctaw women worked seasonally as hired hands on cotton plantations in Alabama and Mississippi, picking cotton alongside enslaved workers but receiving goods and cash wages. In the absence of documentation, especially from Choctaw women workers and small slaveholders, we cannot know for certain how the relations between Indian owners and black slaves who labored together compared to the interactions between Indian hired hands and slaves who worked for white planters. For descriptions of Choctaw women and men working as hired laborers for white farmers and planters, see Carson, *Searching for the Bright Path*, 82; Carson, "From Corn Mothers to Cotton Spinners," 9, 10, 15, 19; and Olmsted, *A Journey in the Back Country*, 174.

71. John Pitchlynn to Peter Pitchlynn, September 29, 1824, box 1, folder 4, Pitchlynn Papers, UOK; Armstrong Census, NAMP, A39; Senate Doc. 512, part 3, 23rd Cong., 2nd sess., 59; ibid., part 2, 405–7. In his biography of Peter Pitchlynn, W. David Baird writes of Pitchlynn that "by October [1832] he owned or had an interest in forty-five Negroes, all of whom prepared to make the trip west." Baird, *Peter Pitchlynn*, 46.

72. Carson, *Searching for the Bright Path*, 79–80.

73. Letter from Choctaw Chiefs (Mushulatubbee and Puchshanubbee) to Rev. Worcester, *Missionary Herald*, June 4, 1820, 379.

74. Cyrus Kingsbury to Jeremiah Evarts, August 8, 1825, vol. 3, folder 12, no. 4, ABCFM 18.3.4.

75. Kidwell, *Choctaws and Missionaries in Mississippi*, 111.

76. *The Constitution and Laws of the Choctaw Nation* (1840), 11, 17, 20, 22.

77. Ibid., 11, 12, 14, 20, 22, 27, 28. For discussions of race, citizenship and slavery in the Cherokee Nation, see Sturm, *Blood Politics*; Miles, *The Ties That Bind*; Naylor, *African Cherokees in Indian Territory*; and Yarbrough, *Race and the Cherokee Nation*.

78. Littlefield, *The Chickasaw Freedmen*, 13.

79. *The Constitution and Laws of the Choctaw Nation* (1840), 27.

80. This line of analysis draws from works on the naturalization of race and racial difference in the Americas in the eighteenth and nineteenth centuries by Jennifer Morgan and Kirsten Fischer. Morgan, *Laboring Women*; Fischer, *Suspect Relations*.

81. *Missionary Herald*, February 1824, 47; Cyrus Kingsbury to Reverend Fay, April 5, 1822, vol. 2, folder 145, ABCFM 18.3.4; Cyrus Kingsbury to Jeremiah Evarts, December 27, 1821, vol. 2, folder 144, ABCFM 18.3.4; G. W. Long to Major Smith, November 5, 1824, Letters Received by the Office of Indian Affairs, Chickasaw Agency, NAMP, M234, roll 135; Peter Pitchlynn to Rhoda Pitchlynn, September 10, 1837, box 1, folder 54, Pitchlynn Papers, UOK.

82. Matilda Poe and Kiziah Love in Butler and Butler, *The WPA Oklahoma Slave Narratives*, 259, 325.

83. William Cocke to Secretary of War, September 22, 1816; Lowrie and Franklin, *American State Papers: Indian Affairs*, vol. 2, 106–7.

84. Last will and testament of Sophia Pitchlynn, box 3, folder 47, Pitchlynn Papers, UOK; Matilda Poe in Baker and Baker, *The WPA Oklahoma Slave Narratives*, 324–25; Anna Colbert, Indian Pioneer Papers, UOK.

85. David Chang has written an outstanding study of the changing social, political, and legal meanings of race, property, and land. Chang, *The Color of the Land*. Rowena McClinton makes this argument in an unpublished paper cited in Miles, *Ties That Bind*, 39 cf. 73.

86. Peter Pitchlynn to James Fletcher, December 1842, box 2, folder 85, Pitchlynn Papers, UOK.

87. Turner B. Turnbull to Samuel Garland, December 22, 1863, box 3, folder 106, Pitchlynn Papers, UOK.

88. John Allen to Secretary of War, February 7, 1830, Letters Received by the Office of Indian Affairs, Chickasaw Agency, NAMP, M234, roll 136; James McDonald to John Calhoun, November 9, 1824, Letters Received by the Office of Indian Affairs, NAMP, M234, roll 169; Agent Upshaw to the Commissioner of Indian Affairs, December 6, 1847, and Bill of Sale and Deed (Susan Guest), in Special File 278: Negroes Stolen from John R. Guest and Overton Love, Chickasaw Indians, 1848–60, Special Files of the Office of Indian Affairs, 1807–1904, NAMP, 574, roll 76; Senate Report 295, 33rd Cong., 1st sess.

89. Carson, *Searching for the Bright Path*, 116.

90. Banner, *How the Indians Lost Their Land*, chap. 6; Carson, *Searching for the Bright Path*, 112–23. Clara Sue Kidwell writes about the Choctaws who elected to remain in Mississippi in *Choctaws and Missionaries*, chaps. 8–10. Also see Wells and Tubby, *After Removal: The Choctaw in Mississippi*.

91. Paige, Bumpers, and Littlefield, *Chickasaw Removal*, 40–43; Atkinson, *Splendid Land, Splendid People*, 231–32; Gibson, *The Chickasaws*, 178.

92. Evidence of inaccuracies includes the fact that some slaveholders such as the Harkins family are not on the census. Ann Llewellen and her mother, Susan Graham, are listed on the 1831 census as having 110 acres under cultivation. A letter from 1832 concerning Graham's desire to keep her land and remain in Mississippi indicates that "her hands (negroes) have been, ever since the spring of 1830 actually on and cultivating the land under her directions and control." These slaves were not listed on the census. There are also discrepancies between the Armstrong Census in the National Archives and the census data published in Senate Doc. 512. For example, Captain Anthony Turnbull in Greenwood Leflore's district is listed as owning five slaves on the Armstrong Census but not in Senate Doc. 512. Finally, a note on the census says it was made in

haste. Armstrong Census, 1831, NAMP, roll A39; Senate Doc. 512, part 3, 23rd Cong., 2nd sess., 59, 215.

93. Muster Roll, October 1837, Chickasaw Census and Muster Rolls, 1837–39, RG 75; Littlefield, *The Chickasaw Freedmen*, 10.

94. Armstrong Census, 1831, NAMP, roll A39; Senate Doc. 512, part 3, 23rd Cong., 2nd sess., 57, 59, 73, 85. Of the sixty-six slaveholders enumerated in the 1831 census of Choctaw towns, only eleven were identified as "white," but at least half of these men were married to Choctaw women. When considering the distribution of slaves among Choctaw and Euro-American slaveholders, the issue of racial categories must be addressed. Though many scholars have distinguished between Euro-American and Choctaw slaveholders in terms of race, Theda Perdue's writings on southern Indian women's marriages to Euro-Americans suggest the need to reevaluate this distinction. Marriages between the daughters of powerful Indian leaders and colonial traders, Perdue argues, brought potentially powerful and disruptive male outsiders under the social and spiritual control of the women and their kin. Absorbed into matrilineal kinship networks, Englishmen such as John Pitchlynn and Nathaniel Folsom and the French Charles Juzan were not regarded as foreigners by their families and neighbors, and perhaps they thus might be counted among the "Choctaw" slaveholders.

95. Armstrong Census, 1831, NAMP, roll A39; Senate Doc. 512, part 3, 23rd Cong., 2nd sess. For example of hiring, see Lycurgus Pitchlynn to Peter Pitchlynn, December 11, 1857, box 3, folder 4, Pitchlynn Papers, UOK.

96. Clara Sue Kidwell discusses the "whites and mixed-bloods [who] owned slaves." Kidwell, *Choctaws and Missionaries*, 80. Also see White, *The Roots of Dependency*, 132–36; Atkinson, *Splendid Land, Splendid People*, 23–4; and Akers, *Living in the Land of Death*, 140–42.

97. Armstrong Census, 1831, NAMP, roll A39; Senate Doc. 512, part 3, 23rd Cong., 2nd sess., 54–124.

98. Senate Doc. 512, part 3, 23rd Cong., 2nd sess., 46. For a history of racial terminology in the context of Black-Indian relations, see Forbes, *Africans and Native Americans*.

99. Wood, "Slave Labor Camps in Early America"; Rothman, *Slave Country*, chap. 5.

100. A clear and detailed discussion of the treaty provision that allowed Choctaws to remain in Mississippi and the federal government's mismanagement of Choctaw claims for land in Mississippi can be found in Kidwell, *The Choctaws in Oklahoma*, chap. 1; also see Kidwell, *Choctaws and Missionaries in Mississippi*, chaps. 8–10.

101. Halliburton, "Chief Greenwood Leflore and His Malmaison Plantation," 56–63. On Mississippi Choctaws, see Kidwell, "The Choctaw Struggle for Land and Identity in Mississippi"; Kidwell, *Choctaws and Missionaries in Mississippi*, chaps. 8–10; and Kidwell, *The Choctaws in Oklahoma*, chap. 1. See article XIV of the 1830 Treaty at Dancing Rabbit Creek in Kappler, *Treaties*.

102. Samuel Garland to Peter Pitchlynn, November 28, 1833, box 1, folder 39, Pitchlynn Papers, UOK; Baird, *Peter Pitchlynn*, 51.

103. Lowrie, *American State Papers, Class VIII, Public Lands*, vol. 7, 14; Armstrong Census; Senate Doc. 512, 23rd Cong., 2nd sess., 79, 84.

104. Senate Exec. Doc. 166, 50th Cong., 1st sess., 9; Susan Colbert interview, Indian Pioneer Papers, UOK.

105. Baird, *Peter Pitchlynn*, 46.

106. Susan Colbert interview, Indian Pioneer Papers, UOK. Colbert recalled that "Bob Shields" used his land to purchase her mother and grandmother from a Mississippi slaveholder. The Choctaw Removal census does not identify a Bob Shields (or Robert Shields) but does list James Shields as a captain in Greenwood Leflore's district. Removal records indicate that James Shields owned seven slaves in 1831.

107. Lowrie, *American State Papers, Class VIII, Public Lands*, vol. 7, 14; Senate Doc. 512, part 4, 23rd Cong., 2nd sess., 565–66.

108. William Colquhoun to General George Gibson, April, 20, 1832, Senate Doc. 512, part 2, 23rd Cong. 1st sess., 605–6.

109. Letters from Molly Nail, February 20, 1832, and October 13, 1832, Senate Doc. 512, part 3, 23rd Cong., 2nd sess., 210, 484; Senate Doc. 512, part 4, 23rd Cong., 2nd sess., 504–5.

110. J. H. Hook to William Armstrong, September 11, 1832, in Senate Doc. 512, part 1, 23rd Cong., 1st sess., 161–62.

111. Circular issued by George Gibson, August 12, 1831; William Armstrong to General George Gibson, October 28, 1832; William Armstrong to George Gibson, February 25, 1833, Senate Doc. 512, part 1, 23rd Cong., 1st sess., 30; Senate Doc. 512, part 2, 23rd Cong., 1st sess., 390–91, 405–7; Senate Doc. 512, part 3, 23rd Cong., 1st sess., 378. Other issues of confusion arose about the racial composition of Creek households; see Barbara Krauthamer, "A Particular Kind of Freedom."

112. Senate Doc. 512, part 2, 23rd Cong., 1st sess., 390–91; Senate Doc. 512, part 2, 23rd Cong., 1st sess., part 2, 604–6; Foreman, *Indian Removal*, 217, 224–26; Gibson, *The Chickasaws*, 189.

113. Jack Campbell in Rawick, *Oklahoma Narratives*, 90; William Nail interview in Indian Pioneer Papers, UOK.

114. Parsons, "Letters on the Chickasaw Removal of 1837," 280–81; Senate Doc. 512, part 3, 23rd Cong., 1st sess., 952–53, 1024–25, 1056–57. For a map of Removal routes, see Foreman, *Indian Removal*, 396–97.

115. Baird, *Peter Pitchlynn*, 49–50; Spalding, "Cyrus Kingsbury: Missionary to the Choctaws," 162–63.

116. Foreman, *Indian Removal*, 97–99, 222. U.S. Department of the Interior, *Annual Report of the Commissioner of Indian Affairs, 1838*, 76; Baird, *Peter Pitchlynn*, 49.

117. Muster Roll, October 1837, Entry 253, Census & Muster Rolls, 1837–1839, RG 75.

118. John Pitchlynn to Peter Pitchlynn, January 30, 1834, box 1, folder 40, Pitchlynn Papers, UOK.

119. Rhoda Pitchlynn to Peter Pitchlynn, August 30, 1841, box 1, folder 65; Rhoda Pitchlynn to Peter Pitchlynn, September 23, 1841, box 1, folder 67; Rhoda Pitchlynn to Peter Pitchlynn, October 26, 1841, box 1, folder 70; Lavinia Pitchlynn to Peter Pitchlynn, December 14, 1841, box 1, folder 72; all in Pitchlynn Papers, UOK. For a discussion of Indian health issues during Removal, see Akers, "Removing the Heart of the Choctaw People."

120. Schwartz, *Birthing a Slave*.

121. Mary Lindsay in Butler and Butler, *The WPA Oklahoma Slave Narratives*, 246.

Chapter 2

1. Raboteau, *Slave Religion*, chap. 5.

2. Portnoy, *Their Right to Speak*, 23–25; Kingsbury quoted in Kidwell, *Choctaws and Missionaries*, 25.

3. Kidwell, *Choctaws and Missionaries*, 35; Atkinson, *Splendid Land*, 218.

4. Quoted in Portnoy, *Their Right to Speak*, 25.

5. Quoted in Kidwell, *Choctaws and Missionaries*, 27.

6. In 1831 Perry's widow owned fifteen slaves, making her the fourth-largest slaveholder in her district. Armstrong Roll, A39.

7. Kidwell, *Choctaws and Missionaries*, 29, 37–41.

8. Atkinson, *Splendid Land*, 219; Paige, Bumpers, and Littlefield, *Chickasaw Removal*, 1–14. One account described Colbert as having "a large well cultivated farm, about 30 or 40 likely

slaves and a white overseer to superintend them—a good stock of cattle and hogs." Peyton Short, "Tour to Mobile, Pensacola &c. by Peyton Short of Kentucky," 6.

9. Kingsbury to Evarts, August 8, 1825, vol. 3, folder 12, ABCFM 18.3.4; Kidwell, *Choctaws and Missionaries*, 37, 41; Deloria, *Custer Died for Your Sins*, chap. 8.

10. Kidwell, *Choctaws and Missionaries*, 41.

11. Ibid., 38, 68.

12. Treaty of Doak's Stand in Kappler, *Treaties*; Kidwell, *Choctaws and Missionaries*, 45–49.

13. Kingsbury to Rev. David Greene, December 25, 1844, vol. 8, folder 7; Kingsbury to Rev. David Green, May 31, 1845, vol. 8, folder 13, ABCFM 18.3.4.

14. Quoted in Miles, *Ties That Bind*, 93.

15. See Portnoy, *Their Right to Speak*, chap. 3; Guyatt, " 'The Outskirts of Our Happiness.' "

16. *Missionary Herald*, vol. 18, 290; Loring Williams to Jeremiah Evarts, June 18, 1822, vol. 2, folder 169, ABCFM 18.3.4. Williams initially called his mission Newell, but the American Board changed the name to Bethel. Kidwell, *Choctaws and Missionaries*, 57.

17. Paige, Bumpers, and Littlefield, *Chickasaw Removal*, 15.

18. Raboteau, *Slave Religion*, chap. 5.

19. Gomez, *Exchanging Our Country Marks*, 20, 23.

20. Ibid., 11.

21. Ibid., 8; Stuckey, *Slave Culture*, 24.

22. Sobel, *Trabelin' On*, 191.

23. Littlefield, *The Chickasaw Freedmen*, 9.

24. Loring Williams to Jeremiah Evarts, June 1823, vol. 2, folder 173, ABCFM 18.3.4; Loring Williams to Jeremiah Evarts, June 18, 1822, vol. 2, folder 169, ABCFM 18.3.4; Journal of the Mission at Elliot, January 7, 1821, vol. 1, folders 12–24, ABCFM 18.3.4; Journal of the Mission at Elliot, September 31, 1819, printed in *Missionary Herald*, vol. 16, no. 7, July 1820, 319.

25. Cyrus Kingbury journal, February 27, 1820, reprinted in *Missionary Herald*, vol. 16, no. 8, August 1820, 366; Journal of the Mission at Elliot, March 1820, reprinted in *Missionary Herald*, vol. 16, no. 8, August 1820, 364; Journal of the Mission at Elliot, February 18, 1821, vol. 1, folios 12–24, ABCFM 18.3.4.

26. Loring Williams to Jeremiah Evarts, June 1823, vol. 2, folder 173, ABCFM 18.3.4. Cyrus Kingsbury to Reverend C. B. Treat, February 1, 1854, vol. 8, folder 102, ABCFM 18.3.4. Cornelius, *When I Can Read My Title Clear*, 12, 20–22, 64, chap. 5, especially 107–9; Cornelius, *Slave Missions and the Black Church in the Antebellum South*, 127–30.

27. Choctaws and Chickasaws, for example, may have believed that the quakes arrived as the fulfillment of the Shawnee prophet Tecumseh's prophecy. In the late summer of 1811, Tecumseh had met with Chickasaw, Choctaw, and Creek leaders seeking to rally them to join his pan-Indian cultural and military resistance movement against the United States. Legend has it that Choctaw and Chickasaw headmen declined his overtures and shortly afterward some Creek leaders resisted his call, too. Tecumseh is said to have responded by prophesying that the ground would shake and destroy the Creek's Tuckhabatchee town (in present-day Alabama). On December 16, 1811, the first of the New Madrid quakes leveled the houses in Tuckhabatchee. According to Moravian missionaries in Georgia, the quakes left Cherokees and also the black people they enslaved in the grip of fear and anxiety. Some people attributed the quake to divine retribution for Cherokees' acculturation. Feldman, *When the Mississippi Ran Backwards*, 181; Miles, *House on Diamond Hill*, 148–49.

28. Phelps, "Excerpts from the Journal of the Reverend Joseph Bullen," 262; Littlefield, *The Chickasaw Freedmen*, 8; Cyrus Kingsbury to Thomas McKenny, May 5, 1826, vol. 4, folder 278, ABCFM 18.3.4. For descriptions of Chickasaw towns, see Atkinson, *Splendid Land*, 186.

29. For discussion of black people as playing roles in the missionaries' assimilation project, see Littlefield, *The Chickasaw Freedmen*, 5–10.

30. Gibson, *The Chickasaws*, 116; Bethel Journal, reprinted in *Missionary Herald*, vol. 19, no. 4, April 1823, 116; Loring Williams to Jeremiah Evarts, June 18, 1822, vol. 2, folder 169, ABCFM 18.3.4; Littlefield, *Chickasaw Freedmen*, 15–17.

31. Edmond Flint in Rawick, *Oklahoma Narratives*, 128–29.

32. My argument here is not that the sources are unreliable but that they reflect the thoughts of a much later generation of enslaved people, most of whom were children during their enslavement in Indian Territory, not Mississippi. And the interviews also reflect the conditions of both the interview process and the Depression. For studies that have used the WPA narratives to study the intersections of African American and Native American history, see Naylor, *African Cherokee*; Lovett, "'African and Cherokee by Choice'"; Bay, *The White Image in the Black Mind*. For discussions of the possibilities and limitations of the sources, see Blassingame, "Using the Testimony of Ex-Slaves"; and Shaw, "Using the WPA Ex-Slave Narratives to Study the Impact of the Great Depression."

33. Phelps, "Excerpts from the Journal of the Reverend Joseph Bullen," 271.

34. Loring Williams to Jeremiah Evarts, June 18, 1822, vol. 2, folder 169, ABCFM 18.3.4

35. For references to "brush arbors," see Kiziah Love and Polly Colbert in Butler and Butler, *The Oklahoma WPA Narratives*, 89, 260.

36. Israel Folsom to Peter Pitchlynn, August 22, 1842, box 1, folder 81, Pitchlynn Papers, UOK; Kidwell, *Choctaws and Missionaries*, 73–76.

37. Loring Williams to Jeremiah Evarts, June 18, 1822, vol. 2, folder 169, ABCFM 18.3.4; Loring Williams to Jeremiah Evarts, June, 1823, vol. 2, folder 173, ABCFM 18.3.4; Gibson, *The Chickasaws*, 177.

38. Creel, *"A Peculiar People,"* 149.

39. Ibid., 180–85.

40. Loring Williams to Jeremiah Evarts, June 18, 1822, vol. 2, folder 169, ABCFM 18.3.4; Raboteau, *Slave Religion*, chap. 5.

41. Camp, *Closer to Freedom*, 7.

42. Quoted in Gibson, *The Chickasaws*, 177.

43. Bethel Journal, reprinted in *Missionary Herald*, April 1823, 116.

44. Loring Williams to Jeremiah Evarts, June 1823, vol. 2, folder 173, ABCFM 18.3.4

45. Ibid.

46. Journal of Elliot Mission, 1822, folders 31–37, vol. 1, ABCFM 18.3.4; Loring Williams to Jeremiah Evarts, June 1823, vol. 2, folder 173, ABCFM 18.3.4.

47. Minges, *Slavery in the Cherokee Nation*, especially chap. 3; McLoughlin, *The Cherokees and Christianity*, 223. Interestingly, a number of leading Keetowahs were also slaveholders.

48. *Choctaw Telegraph*, September 6, 1849, and October 18, 1849; Morrison, "Notes from the *Northern Standard*," 83–84.

49. George Harkins to Peter Pitchlynn, October 19, 1853, box 2, folder 65; Robert Jones to Peter Pitchlynn, July 12, 1854; both in Pitchlynn Papers, UOK.

50. Israel Folsom to Cyrus Kingsbury, December 20, 1847, vol. 8, folder 49, ABCFM 18.3.4; Kidwell, *Choctaws and Missionaries*, 161.

51. Loring Williams to Jeremiah Evarts, February 14, 1824, vol. 2, folder 174, ABCFM 18.3.4; Kidwell, *Choctaws and Missionaries*, 96. Missionaries were rarely surprised when Choctaws and Chickasaws took exception to their methods of education and correction and looked elsewhere for teachers and schools. Cyrus Kingsbury wrote to the Office of Indian Affairs in the spring of 1826: "The system of labour adopted and [pursued?] in our schools has been the principal ground of objection on the part of the natives, and was I believe the primary reason for them

wishing to have a school in Kentucky." Cyrus Kingsbury to the War Department, Office of Indian Affairs, May 5, 1826, vol. 4, folder 278, ABCFM 18.3.4.

52. Loring Williams quoted in Kidwell, *Choctaws and Missionaries*, 96.

53. Camp, *Closer to Freedom*, xvii, chap. 1.

54. *The Constitution and Laws of the Choctaw Nation* (1847), 21–22; Cyrus Kingsbury to Rev. David Greene, May 31, 1845, vol. 8, folder 13, ABCFM 18.3.4; Littlefield, *The Chickasaw Freedmen*, 13.

55. Saunt, *Black, White, and Indian*, 70–74; Miles, *Ties That Bind*, 112.

56. Missionaries made this argument in an 1848 letter to Reverend Selah Treat, the Secretary of the American Board, Annual Report of the ABCFM, 1848, 98; Kidwell, *Choctaws and Missionaries*, 81–83.

57. Cyrus Kingsbury to Jeremiah Evarts, December 27, 1821, vol. 2, folder 144, ABCFM 18.3.4. Despite making the argument about costs, they spent $4,164 in 1822 to hire slaves and paid $1,884 in wages to free workers. Kingsbury to Reverend Fay, April 5, 1822, vol. 2, folder 145, ABCFM 18.3.4.

58. Cyrus Byington to Jeremiah Evarts, May 12, 1824, vol. 2, folder 154, ABCFM 18.3.4; Loring Williams to Jeremiah Evarts, April 1824, vol. 2, folder 177, ABCFM 18.3.4; Cyrus Kingsbury to Reverend Fay, April 5, 1822, vol. 2, folder 145, ABCFM 18.3.4.

59. *Annual Report of the American Board of Commissioners to Foreign Missions* (1848), 83, 91; Cyrus Kingsbury to Reverend Greene, May 25, 1847, vol. 8, folder 38, ABCFM 18.3.4.

60. American Board was criticized at "public conventions" in Ohio and Illinois. *Annual Report of the American Board of Commissioners to Foreign Missions* (1848), 99.

61. "The American Board and Its Slaveholding Mission Churches," *National Era*, February 7, 1850.

62. "To the Christian men, and women held in Slavery among the Choctaw," *Frederick Douglass' Paper*, December 11, 1851. " 'The Board' and Slavery," *North Star*, October 13, 1848.

63. "The American Board of Foreign Missions," *Provincial Freeman*, April 14, 1855.

64. Cyrus Kingsbury to Reverend Fay, April 5, 1822, vol. 2, folder 145, ABCFM 18.3.4; Cyrus Kingsbury to Reverend Greene, December 27, 1844, vol. 8, folder 8, ABCFM 18.3.4.

65. Cyrus Kingsbury to Reverend Fay, April 5, 1822, vol. 2, folder 145, ABCFM 18.3.4. Cyrus Kingsbury to Reverend Greene, December 27, 1844, vol. 8, folder 8, ABCFM 18.3.4. On course of instruction, see Sheehan, *Seeds of Extinction*, 132.

66. Whipple, *Relation of the American Board of Commissioners to Foreign Missions to Slavery*, 47, 89.

67. Cyrus Kingsbury to Reverend Fay, April 5, 1822, vol. 2, folder 145, ABCFM 18.3.4; Kingsbury to Jeremiah Evarts, December 27, 1821, vol. 2, folder 144, ABCFM 18.3.4; Reverend Greene to Prudential Committee, January 24, 1857, vol. 6, folder 59 or 60, ABCFM 18.3.4. Missionaries continued to hire slaves through 1860–61; see U.S. Department of the Interior, *Annual Report of the Commissioner of Indian Affairs, 1860*, 141, 147.

68. Cyrus Kingsbury to Jeremiah Evarts, September 11, 1821, vol. 2, folder 86; Cyrus Kingsbury to Jeremiah Evarts, December 27, 1821, vol. 2, folder 144; Cyrus Kingsbury to Reverend Fay, April 5, 1822, vol. 2, folder 145; Loring Williams to Jeremiah Evarts, February 14, 1824, vol. 2, folder 174; all in ABCFM 18.3.4.

69. Cyrus Kingsbury to Reverend Fay, April 5, 1822, vol. 2, folder 145, ABCFM 18.3.4; Cyrus Byington to Jeremiah Evarts, April 15, 1822, vol. 2, folder 146, ABCFM 18.3.4; Cyrus Kingsbury to Reverend Greene, December 27, 1844, vol. 8, folder 8, ABCFM 18.3.4; Kidwell, *Choctaws and Missionaries*, 83.

70. Henry Copeland to Rev. Treat, February 8, 1856, vol. 7, folder 226, ABCFM 18.3.4.

71. Reverend Green to Prudential Committee, January 24, 1857, vol. 6, folder 59, ABCFM 18.3.4.

72. Cyrus Kingsbury to Reverend David Greene, December 25, 1844, vol. 8, folder 7, ABCFM 18.3.4.

73. Jacobs, *Incidents in the Life of a Slave Girl*, 301.

74. Littlefield, *The Chickasaw Freedmen*, 8; Cyrus Kingsbury to Reverend David Greene, December 25, 1844, vol. 8, folder 7, ABCFM 18.3.4; Cyrus Kingsbury to Reverend David Greene, February 27, 1847, vol. 8, folder 34, ABCFM 18.3.4; Reverend David Greene to the Committee, January 24, 1857, vol. 6, folder 59 or 60, ABCFM 18.3.4. As early as 1836, the American Board's Prudential Committee had admonished missionaries against buying slaves and holding them liable for their purchase price. In the Choctaw Nation, missionaries continued to buy and manumit slaves, using their own money rather than American Board funds to finance the purchases.

75. Cyrus Kingsbury to Reverend Greene, December 25, 1844, vol. 8, folder 7; Cyrus Kingsbury to Reverend Greene, February 27, 1847, vol. 8, folder 34; Cyrus Kingsbury to Reverend Greene, May 25, 1847, vol. 8, folder 38; all in ABCFM 18.3.4

76. I estimate $500 to $600 because Copeland writes that he paid Mrs. Wright $475, which was the balance due on Phillis in the summer of 1855. Correspondence indicates that Phillis had worked for four years (from 1850 to 1854), without wages or compensation. In addition to the $475 he paid, Copeland raised another $60 to go toward Phillis's price. Henry Copeland to Reverend Treat, May 26, 1852, vol. 7, folder 8; Henry Copeland to Reverend Treat, February 9, 1854, vol. 7, folder 206; Henry Copeland to Rev. Treat, July 9, 1855, vol. 7, folder 220; Henry Copeland to Rev. Treat, February 8, 1856, vol. 7, folder 226; John Edwards to Rev. Treat, June 5, 1856, vol. 7, folder 259; all in ABCFM 18.3.4.

77. *The Constitution and Laws of the Choctaw Nation* (1847), 32–35.

78. Washington, *Sojourner Truth's America*, 196–97, 283; Jones, *All Bound Up Together*, 93–95.

79. 1860 free census; Armstrong Roll, A39 and Senate Doc. 512; Senate Report 5013 part 2, 59th Cong., 2nd sess., 1541.

80. Choctaw Chiefs to Prudential Committee, April 24, 1850, vol. 6, folder 76, ABCFM 18.3.4; Cyrus Kingsbury to Reverend Greene, July 2, 1847, vol. 8, folder 40, ABCFM 18.3.4. Cyrus Kingsbury and Sampson Folsom to George Manypenny, November 13, 1854, box 2, folder 51, Pitchlynn Papers, UOK; Littlefield and Littlefield, "The Beams Family: Free Blacks in Indian Territory."

81. Peter Pitchlynn to John C. Spencer, Secretary of War, March 25, 1842, box 1, folder 79, Pitchlynn Papers, UOK;

82. *The African Repository*, January 15, 1841, 19–20.

83. Spalding, "Cyrus Kingsbury: Missionary to the Choctaws," 206.

84. Cyrus Kingsbury to Jeremiah Evarts, October 6, 1825, vol. 3, folder 14, ABCFM 18.3.4.

85. Portnoy, *Their Right to Speak*; Guyatt, "'The Outskirts of Our Happiness.'"

86. Laurie, *Beyond Garrison*, chap. 1; Washington, *Sojourner Truth's America*, 115–16; Cyrus Kingsbury to Reverend Greene, July 2, 1847, vol. 8, folder 40, ABCFM 18.3.4.

87. *Choctaw Intelligencer*, June 20, 1850.

88. James, "The Wings of Ethiopia," 130–31; Sidbury, *Becoming African in America*, 197–201; Burrowes, *Power and Press Freedom in Liberia*, 23–54.

89. For an example of slaves in the Cherokee Nation forming Liberia society, see Sidbury, *Becoming African in America*, 193; and Perdue, *Slavery and the Evolution of Cherokee Society*, 93–95.

90. Spalding, "Cyrus Kingsbury," 207.

91. *The African Repository*, vol. 19, January 1843, 36; Henry Copeland to Reverend Treat, February 9, 1854, vol. 7, folder 206, ABCFM 18.3.4.

92. *Annual Report of the American Colonization Society*, January 18, 1853, 4; *Annual Report of the American Colonization Society*, January 17, 1854; *Annual Report of the American Colonization Society*, January 20, 1857, 16.

93. Morrison, "Diary of Rev. Cyrus Kingsbury," 63; *The African Repository*, vol. 29, no. 3, March 1853, 71.

94. Miller, *Dear Master: Letters of a Slave Family*, 58–63, 70–71.

95. *Frederick Douglass' Paper*, November 19, 1852; Morrison, "Diary of Rev. Cyrus Kingsbury"; *The African Repository*, vol. 28, January 1853, 5; ibid., June 1853, 181; ibid., April 1873, 127. Contributors from the Choctaw Nation continued to send donations to the ACS for Harrison's support. *The Home and Foreign Record of the Presbyterian Church in the United States*, vol. 7, April 1856, 120.

96. Simon Harrison to Reverend McLain, September 10, 1853, printed in *The African Repository*, vol. 30, April 1854, 115–17; Simon Harrison to Cyrus Kingsbury, printed in *The African Repository*, vol. 33, June 1857, 171–72.

Chapter 3

1. Foreman, *Indian Removal*, 76; Baird, *Peter Pitchlynn*, 46; Armstrong Census, A39; John Pitchlynn to Peter Pitchlynn, March 10, 1833, box 1, folder 36, Pitchlynn Papers, UOK.

2. U.S. Department of the Interior, *Annual Report of the Commissioner of Indian Affairs, 1836*, 14; *Annual Report of the Commissioner of Indian Affairs, 1837*, 20–22; *Annual Report of the Commissioner of Indian Affairs, 1838*, 76.

3. Baird, *Peter Pitchlynn*, 50. See the letter from Solomon, a man owned by Pitchlynn, describing the work he and other enslaved men performed on one of Pitchlynn's plantations. Though the letter is written in Solomon's voice, it is unlikely that he actually wrote it. In the years after emancipation, an ex-slave named Solomon Pitchlynn left his mark, rather than signature, on a number of political petitions drafted by leading freedmen. See chapter 4. Solomon to Peter Pitchlynn, March 8, 1860, box 3, folder 62, Pitchlynn Papers, UOK.

4. U.S. Department of the Interior, *Annual Report of the Commissioner of Indian Affairs, 1836*, 14; *Annual Report of the Commissioner of Indian Affairs, 1837*, 20, 22; *Annual Report of the Commissioner of Indian Affairs, 1838*, 76; *Annual Report of the Commissioner of Indian Affairs, 1841*, 69; *Annual Report of the Commissioner of Indian Affairs, 1842*, 72; Fite, "Development of Cotton Industry."

5. There were 568 slaves in Kiamichi County; 398 slaves in Towson County; 440 slaves in Red River County; 280 slaves in Eagle County; 365 slaves in Blue County; and 302 slaves in Skullyville County. 8th U.S. Census, Arkansas, Slave Schedule, 1860, NAMP, M653, roll 54. Polly Colbert in Baker and Baker, *The WPA Oklahoma Slave Narratives*, 86.

6. Powers, "Notes on Doaksville," 543; In 1850 there were nine slaveholders in the United States who owned 500 or more slaves, and in 1860 that number increased to thirteen. Soltow, "Economic Inequality in the United States in the Period from 1790 to 1860," 825.

7. 1860 census data for Skullyville County in 8th U.S. Census, Arkansas, Slave Schedule, 1860, NAMP, M653, roll 54; U.S. Department of the Interior, *Annual Report of the Commissioner of Indian Affairs, 1850*, 122, 137; *Annual Report of the Commissioner of Indian Affairs, 1846*, 55, 64.

8. U.S. Department of the Interior, *Annual Report of the Commissioner of Indian Affairs, 1846*, 55, 64; *Annual Report of the Commissioner of Indian Affairs, 1841*, 85; *Annual Report of the Commissioner of Indian Affairs, 1854*, 147.

9. Wright, "John Hobart Heald," 318. Robert Jones owned steamboats and was a partner in a mercantile business in Doaksville. Choctaw Samuel Garland owned a mercantile outfit in Columbus, Mississippi. Wright, "Early Navigation and Commerce along the Arkansas and Red Rivers in Oklahoma," 82, 86. Kidwell, *The Choctaws in Oklahoma*, 28. Morrison, "Colbert Ferry on Red River, Chickasaw Nation, Indian Territory"; Kiziah Love in Baker and Baker, *The WPA Oklahoma Slave Narratives*, 258.

10. Byington, *A Dictionary of the Choctaw Language*, 319, 419; Wright, "Organization of Counties in the Choctaw and Chickasaw Nations," 325.

11. Doran says that unlike the Indian population, the enslaved population was not decimated by the unforgiving conditions of Removal and instead "thrived both before and after emigration. . . . [T]he overall growth in slave population was dominantly caused by natural increase." Doran, "Negro Slaves of the Five Civilized Tribes," 346. His use of the verb "thrived" should not be interpreted to mean anything other than "expanded."

12. Burnham, "An Impossible Marriage," 203. For more on the legal, ideological, and physical meanings of enslaved women's reproductive capacity, see Morgan, *Laboring Women*; and Schwartz, *Birthing a Slave*.

13. Kiziah Love in Baker and Baker, *The WPA Oklahoma Slave Narratives*, 259.

14. Camp, *Closer to Freedom*.

15. Ed Butler in Rawick, *Oklahoma Narratives*, 87.

16. Solomon to Peter Pitchlynn, March 8, 186[?], box 3, folder 62, Pitchlynn Papers, UOK.

17. Kiziah Love in Baker and Baker, *The WPA Oklahoma Slave Narratives*, 257; Jefferson L. Cole in Rawick, *Oklahoma Narratives*, 120–27; Matilda Poe in Baker and Baker, *The WPA Oklahoma Slave Narratives*, 324–25. For discussion of children's lives in slavery, see King, *Stolen Childhood*; and Schwartz, *Born in Bondage*.

18. Peter Pitchlynn to Rhoda Pitchlynn, September 10, 1837, box 1, folder 54, Pitchlynn Papers, UOK.

19. Israel Folsom to Peter Pitchlynn, August 22, 1842, box 1, folder 81, Pitchlynn Papers, UOK.

20. *Choctaw Telegraph*, September 6, 1849, OKHS.

21. Thomas Pitchlynn to Peter Pitchlynn, March 30, 1851, box 2, folder 19, Pitchlynn Papers, UOK.

22. Kidwell delves into the changing nature of political power and "the relation of the individual to the national government" in her study of the Choctaw Nation in Oklahoma. Kidwell, *The Choctaws in Oklahoma*, 41.

23. For history of slave patrols in the states, see Hadden, *Slave Patrols: Law and Violence in Virginia and the Carolinas*.

24. *The Constitution and Laws of the Choctaw Nation* (1852), 61.

25. *Constitution, Laws, and Treaties of the Chickasaws* (1860), 57–58, 91, 146–47, 166–67.

26. Kiziah Love in Baker and Baker, *The WPA Oklahoma Slave Narratives*, 259; Polly Colbert in Baker and Baker, *The WPA Oklahoma Slave Narratives*, 89.

27. Matilda Poe in Baker and Baker, *The WPA Oklahoma Slave Narratives*, 325.

28. Wiethoff, *The Insolent Slave*, chap. 1.

29. Henry Copeland to Reverend Treat, June 21, 1852, vol. 7, folder 195, ABCFM vol. 7, roll 761.

30. See chapter 2 for discussion of mistresses beating slaves and limiting their movement.

31. John Pitchlynn to Peter Pitchlynn, January 30, 1834, box 1, folder 40, Pitchlynn Papers, UOK.

32. Edmond Folsom to Peter Pitchlynn, August 12, 1832, box 1, folder 30, Pitchlynn Papers, UOK. *The Constitution and Laws of the Choctaw Nation* (1840), 11, 17, 20, 22.

33. *The Constitution and Laws of the Choctaw Nation* (1840), 13. *Constitution, Laws, and Treaties of the Chickasaws* (1860), 79. On alcohol trade with Euro-Americans, see Carson, *Searching for the Bright Path*, 75–76; White, *Roots of Dependency*, 84–91; and Atkinson, *Splendid Land, Splendid People*, 146, 220.

34. Camp, *Closer to Freedom*; Penningroth, *The Claims of Kinfolk*.

35. For a genealogy of the Harkins family, see Cushman, *History of the Choctaw, Chickasaw, and Natchez Indians*, 352–53. It seems that the slaves involved in this case were owned by Peter Pitchlynn and in the possession of his daughter Lavinia Harkins. An 1848 Choctaw law

confirmed married women's and men's right to retain ownership of the property each party brought to the union. Husbands and wives had the right to dispose of their own property but could not dispose of each other's property without consent. Property acquired during the marriage was considered communal, but the right of disposal lay with the husband. "An Act Married Persons Each to Retain the Right of Their Property," *The Constitution and Laws of the Choctaw Nation* (1852), 58.

36. Lycurgus Pitchlynn to Peter Pitchlynn, December 31, 1858, box 3, folder 37; Loring Folsom to Peter Pitchlynn, January 1859, box 3, folder 38; Lycurgus Pitchlynn to Peter Pitchlynn, January 3, 1859; all in Pitchlynn Papers, UOK.

37. The search party included Lycurgus Pitchlynn (Lavinia's younger brother), Loring Folsom (married to Malvina Pitchlynn, Lavinia's younger sister), James Harkins, and George Harkins. Loring Folsom to Peter Pitchlynn, January 1859, box 3, folder 38, Pitchlynn Papers, UOK.

38. Lycurgus Pitchlynn to Peter Pitchlynn, January 3, 1859, Pitchlynn Papers, UOK. For discussions of Christmas celebrations, see Raboteau, *Slave Religion*, 224.

39. Loring Folsom to Peter Pitchlynn, January 1859, box 3, folder 38; Lycurgus Pitchlynn to Peter Pitchlynn, January 3, 1859, box 3, folder 39, Pitchlynn Papers, UOK.

40. Loring Folsom to Peter Pitchlynn, January 1859, box 3, folder 38, Pitchlynn Papers, UOK.

41. "An Act Murder," *The Constitution and Laws of the Choctaw Nation* (1852), 60–61.

42. Loring Folsom to Peter Pitchlynn, January 1859, box 3, folder 38; Lycurgus Pitchlynn to Peter Pitchlynn, January 3, 1859, box 3, folder 39, Pitchlynn Papers, UOK. Donna Akers writes of Lavinia Pitchlynn's actions: "She evidently decided that Lucy would be burned, continuing a traditional prerogative afforded women in the southern nations that went back into antiquity." Akers, *Living in the Land of Death*, 142.

43. Cyrus Byington to Walter Lowrie, January 12, 1861, reprinted in McLoughlin, "The Choctaw Slave Burning," 117.

44. Lycurgus Pitchlynn to Peter Pitchlynn, January 3, 1859, box 3, folder 39, Pitchlynn Papers, UOK.

45. It seems that Prince, Lucy, and Adam were owned by Peter Pitchlynn but in the possession of Lavinia Pitchlynn and Richard Harkins. Though there are no clear records documenting ownership, Peter Pitchlynn's correspondence is filled with references to his slaves "Adam" and "Solomon."

46. Loring Folsom to Peter Pitchlynn, January 1859, box 3, folder 38; Lycurgus Pitchlynn to Peter Pitchlynn, January 3, 1859, box 3, folder 39; both in Pitchlynn Papers, UOK.

47. McLoughlin, "The Choctaw Slave Burning," 116.

48. Cyrus Byington to Walter Lowrie, reprinted in McLoughlin, "The Choctaw Slave Burning," 117.

49. McLoughlin, "The Choctaw Slave Burning"; Kidwell, *The Choctaws in Oklahoma*, chap. 3; Akers, *Living in the Land of Death*, 136–41. Though Akers is not interested in probing the lives of the enslaved people involved in this incident, she offers an insightful critique of American abolitionists' reactions to the story. She calls attention to the ways American outrage was informed by anti-Indian racism.

50. Peter Pitchlynn to Lycurgus Pitchlynn, April 21, 1849, box 2, folder 9; Peter Pitchlynn to Lycurgus Pitchlynn, July 8, 1849, box 2, folder 14; Charles Fishback to Peter Pitchlynn, July 10, 1849, box 2, folder 15; Lycurgus Pitchlynn to Peter Pitchlynn, December 11, 1857, box 3, folder 4; all in Pitchlynn Papers, UOK.

51. Naylor, *African Cherokees in Indian Territory*, 59; Edmond Folsom to Peter Pitchlynn, August 12, 1832, box 1, folder 30, Pitchlynn Papers, UOK; "Horrid Murder," *Choctaw Intelligencer*, January 29, 1851, OKHS; 8th census, 1860, Arkansas, Slave Schedule, NAMP, M653,

roll no. 54. For other accounts of slaves killing their owners, see Kaye, *Joining Places*, chap. 4; and McLaurin, *Celia, a Slave*.

52. In his 1849 narrative, Henry Bibb wrote of his brief enslavement in the Cherokee Nation. In Bibb's estimation, it was easier to run away from an Indian (Cherokee) master because of their generally lax attitude toward slaves. But Bibb's characterization of slavery in the Cherokee Nation does not accord with the recent scholarship by Tiya Miles, Celia Naylor, and Circe Sturm. Whether designed to highlight the cruelty of white masters or indicative of an anomalous experience, Bibb's narrative cannot be read on its own as a universal or even representative experience. See Bibb, *Narrative of the Life and Adventures of Henry Bibb*, 150. Also available online at the University of North Carolina, Documenting the American South, http://docsouth.unc.edu/neh/bibb/bibb.html. Also see Miles, *Ties That Bind*, 42–33; and Naylor, *African Cherokees*, chap. 1.

53. Notice for "Aleck" in *Choctaw Intelligencer*, February 19, 1851, OKHS. "A Chance for Slave-Catchers," *National Era*, April 10, 1851, is the reprint of Folsom's notice from the *Fort Smith Herald* and *Cherokee Advocate*. Folsom did regain possession of Aleck but not his horse, saddle, or shotgun. See *Choctaw Intelligencer*, March 12, 1851.

54. Loring Folsom to Peter Pitchlynn, June 19, 1856, box 2, folder 84, Pitchlynn Papers, UOK.

55. This case is described in more detail in Littlefield Jr. and Underhill, "Slave 'Revolt' in the Cherokee Nation, 1842," 121–31; and Naylor, *African Cherokees in Indian Territory*, 43–46.

56. *The Constitution and Laws of the Choctaw Nation* (1847), 32–35.

57. Krauthamer, "Blacks on the Border," chaps. 1 and 2.

58. *Choctaw Intelligencer*, August 1, 1850; July 12, 1850; March 12, 1851; and April 9, 1851, OKHS. Morrison, "Notes from the *Northern Standard*, 1842–49," 269–70.

59. See chapter 2.

60. *Choctaw Intelligencer*, June 27, 1850; and August 1, 1850, OKHS; Morrison, "Note on Abolitionism in the Choctaw Nation," 76–84.

61. Berry, *Black Resistance, White Law*, 55–57; Rhodes, *Mary Ann Shadd Cary*, 27–28.

62. Daniel F. Littlefield explains that the 1838 decision and the subsequent extension of the Fugitive Slave Act of 1850 to Indian Territory resulted from a protracted and convoluted case involving the sale of the free-black Beams family in the Choctaw Nation to two white men from the United States. With the support of some Choctaws who knew the Beams family, as well as the assistance of missionaries, the Beams family evaded capture for many years. The family eventually won its cases in the U.S. Circuit Court by 1858. See Littlefield Jr. and Littlefield, "The Beams Family: Free Blacks in Indian Territory," 16–35.

63. For a history of property laws and ownership in the wake of the Treaty of Guadalupe Hidalgo, see Montoya, *Translating Property*. For a discussion of U.S. national politics in the 1850s, see Wilentz, *The Rise of American Democracy*.

64. For a discussion of the sectional crisis and fighting in Kansas, see Freehling, *The Secessionists at Bay*, 61–79; and Harrold, *Border War*.

65. Allen Wright to Peter Pitchlynn, March 30, 1854, box 2, folder 34, Pitchlynn Papers, UOK.

66. U.S. Department of the Interior, *Annual Report of the Commissioner of Indian Affairs, 1854*, 132. Thompson McKenney to PP, February 14, 1854, box 2, folder 29, Pitchlynn Papers, UOK; Abel, *The American Indian as Slaveholder and Secessionist*, 29–62; Kidwell, *The Choctaws in Oklahoma*, 25; "A Southerner's Viewpoint of the Kansas Situation, 1856–1857," 43–56; Chapman, "Removal of the Osages from Kansas, part 1," 287–305; Miller, "Surveying the Southern Boundary Line of Kansas," 104–39; U.S. Department of the Interior, *Annual Report of the Commissioner of Indian Affairs, 1854*, 132.

67. George Harkins to Peter Pitchlynn, April 27, 1856, box 2, folder 78, Pitchlynn Papers, UOK; Sampson Folsom to Uni Oshi Ma (Peter Pitchlynn), December 9, 1857, box 3, folder 2,

Pitchlynn Papers, UOK; Meserve, "Chief Allen Wright," 314–21; Wilentz, *The Rise of American Democracy*; Foner, *Free Soil, Free Labor, Free Men*.

68. Thomas Pitchlynn to Peter Pitchlynn, March 30, 1851, box 2, folder 19; George Harkins to Peter Pitchlynn, August 12, 1856, box 2, folder 87; Robert Jones to Peter Pitchlynn, November 29, 1857; all in Pitchlynn Papers, UOK.

69. U.S. Department of the Interior, *Annual Report of the Commissioner of Indian Affairs, 1856*, 147–48; *National Era*, October 13, 1859; *Douglass Monthly*, November 1859. An 1862 article in the *New York Times* contended that the "slaveocracy" had hoped to expand into Indian Territory. "Western Missouri and Kansas," *New York Times*, January 12, 1862.

70. Littlefield, *The Chickasaw Freedmen*, 12; Kidwell, *Choctaws in Oklahoma*, chap. 2, especially 25–27; J. Wall to Peter Pitchlynn, November 11, 1850, box 2, folder 17, Pitchlynn Papers, UOK.

71. Slavery remained intact in both nations. In the years immediately after the division, the Chickasaw legislature enacted its own slave code. Laws, as described earlier in this chapter, laid out the punishments for harboring runaway slaves; barred slaves from possessing livestock, weapons, and liquor; and branded white abolitionists as "unfriendly and dangerous to the interests of the Chickasaw people" and mandated their expulsion from the nation. See *Constitution, Laws, and Treaties of the Chickasaws* (1860), 80.

72. Lycurgus Pitchlynn to Peter Pitchlynn, March 22, 1858, box 3, folder 18; George Harkins to Peter Pitchlynn, April 19, 1858, box 3, folder 21; Peter Pitchlynn and Sampson Folsom to Charles Nix, Secretary of Indian Affairs, September 3, 1858, box 3, folder 32; all in Pitchlynn Papers, UOK.

73. "Constitution of the Choctaw Nation," *Acts and Resolutions of the General Council of the Choctaw Nation* (1859), 22.

74. Tandy Walker quoted in Kidwell, *The Choctaws in Oklahoma*, 46. The entry for Tandy Walker on the slave schedule of the 1860 census indicates that he owned sixteen slaves in Skullyville County. 8th U.S. Census, Arkansas, Slave Schedule, 1860, NAMP, M653, roll no. 54. According to Annie Heloise Abel, the U.S. Indian Agent to the Choctaws, Douglas H. Cooper, wrote a memo in 1854 predicting that the nation would become "a sort of Canada" if measures were not taken to rein in abolitionist missionaries. See Abel, *The Indian as Slaveholder and Secessionist*, 41–42; and George Harkins to Tandy Walker, published broadside, Beinecke Library, Yale University.

75. George Harkins to Tandy Walker, published broadside, Beinecke Library, Yale University; Peter Pitchlynn and Sampson Folsom to Charles Mix, Secretary of Indian Affairs, September 3, 1858, box 3, folder 32, Pitchlynn Papers, UOK. The 1860 census lists George Harkins as the owner of nineteen slaves in Towson County. 8th U.S. Census, Arkansas, Slave Schedule, 1860, NAMP, M653, roll no. 54.

76. George Harkins to Peter Pitchlynn, April 19, 1858, box 3, folder 21; Lycurgus Pitchlynn to Peter Pitchlynn, June 2, 1858, box 3, folder 26; both in Pitchlynn Papers, UOK. Kidwell cites this letter from Lycurgus as evidence of his criticism of the Skullyville Constitution. I disagree and interpret his letter as criticizing the Doaksville Constitution instead. In this letter, however, Lycurgus Pitchlynn writes: "This abolition constitution is to be submitted on the 1st Wednesday of July to the people of the Choctaw nation for ratification or rejection." According to Kidwell's account of the constitutional crisis, the Doaksville Constitution was drafted in May 1858 and was presented, along with the Skullyville Constitution, for a popular vote on July 4, 1858. See Kidwell, *The Choctaws in Oklahoma*, 51; and "Acts and Resolutions Passed at the Called Session in June 1858," in *Acts and Resolutions of the General Council of the Choctaw Nation* (1859), 31–32.

77. On party politics, see Wilentz, *The Rise of American Democracy*; Lycurgus Pitchlynn to Peter Pitchlynn, March 22, 1858, box 3, folder 18, Pitchlynn Papers, UOK; and Sampson Folsom to Peter Pitchlynn, February 12, 1860, box 3, folder 61, Pitchlynn Papers, UOK.

78. Israel Folsom to Peter Pitchlynn, July 1860, box 3, folder 76, Pitchlynn Papers, UOK; Jubal B. Hancock to Peter Pitchlynn, September 16, 1860, box 3, folder 82, Pitchlynn Papers, UOK; White, "The Texas Slave Insurrection," 223–28.

79. Lycurgus Pitchlynn to Peter Pitchlynn, August 19, 1860, box 3, folder 80; Israel Folsom to Peter Pitchlynn, July 24, 1860, box 3, folder 76; both in Pitchlynn Papers, UOK.

80. Peter Howell to Peter Pitchlynn, October 1860, box 3, folder 83, Pitchlynn Papers, UOK. Thanks to Kristina Southwell in the Western History Collections at the Library of the University of Oklahoma for identifying Paraclifta.

81. Historian Steven Hahn characterizes this type of action as "naïve monarchism" and explains that it was a nearly ubiquitous element in slave insurrections across the Americas. Rebels in the West Indies, South America, and the United states believed at various times that a new ruler might set them free but for the obstructionist stance of the disloyal opposition. See Hahn, *A Nation under Our Feet*, 60. I find this characterization too dismissive of enslaved people's knowledge and actions.

82. Letter "To the Christian men and women held in Slavery among the Choctaw Indians," *Frederick Douglass' Paper*, December 11, 1851.

83. "Non-Extension versus Abolition of Slavery," *Douglass' Monthly*, October 1859.

84. David Chang makes a similar argument about the Creek Nation, noting that their decision to side with the Confederacy was both a "racist defense of slavery and its class privileges" and "a nationalist defense of Creek lands as sovereignty." See Chang, *The Color of the Land*, 36.

85. Jacob Folsom to Peter Pitchlynn, January 9, 1861, box 3, folder 92; Sampson Folsom to Peter Pitchlynn, May 14, 1861, box 3, folder 94; both in Pitchlynn Papers, UOK. Kiziah Love in Baker and Baker, *The WPA Oklahoma Slave Narratives*, 262; Elsie Pryor in Rawick, *Oklahoma Narratives*, 262.

86. Abel, *The American Indian as Slaveholder and Secessionist*, 73–75; 122 (n. 195); *The Statutes at Large of the Provisional Government of the Confederate States of America*, 321–22. *Documents of American Indian Diplomacy*, 611; Prucha, *American Indian Treaties*, 261–64. Article XLVII of their treaty with the Confederacy declared: "The institution of slavery in the said nations is legal and has existed from time immemorial; that slaves are taken and deemed to be personal property; that the title to slave and other property having its origin in the said nations shall be determined by the laws and customs thereof; and that the slaves and other personal property of every person domiciled in said nations shall pass and be distributed at his or her death in accordance with the laws, usages and customs of the said nations, which may be proved like foreign laws, usages and customs, and shall everywhere be held valid and binding within the scope of their operation."

87. House Report 98, 42nd Cong., 3rd sess., 737–39.

88. Kidwell presents a detailed yet concise account of Indian involvement in the war in *The Choctaws in Oklahoma*, chap. 5. For older though lengthier treatments, see Abel, *The American Indian in the Civil War* and *The American Indian and the End of the Confederacy*.

89. Chang, *The Color of the Land*, 36; Prucha, *American Indian Treaties*, 263; Abel, *The American Indian as Slaveholder and Secessionist*, 122.

90. Lycurgus Pitchlynn to Peter Pitchlynn, [n.d.] 1861, box 3, folder 91, Pitchlynn Papers, UOK. 8th U.S. Census, Arkansas, Slave Schedule, 1860, NAMP, M653, roll 54.

Chapter 4

1. Hoxie, *A Final Promise*, chap. 1.

2. General John W. Sprague to Major General Reynolds, November 20, 1865; General John W. Sprague to O. O. Howard, December 18, 1865; both in Records of the Arkansas Bureau of Refugees, Freedmen and Abandoned Lands, 979, Records of the Assistant Commissioner for

Arkansas, NAMP, roll 1. Francis Springer to General Sprague, December 4, 1865, Registers and Letters Received by the Commissioner of the Bureau of Refugees, Freedmen, and Abandoned Lands, 1865–1872, NAMP, 752, roll 22.

3. Naylor, *African Cherokees*, 151. In the Creek Nation, the loyalist faction entered a treaty with the United States that abolished slavery and established black people's equal standing under Creek law. See Saunt, *Black, White, and Indian*, 104. For an extended discussion of slavery and emancipation in the Seminole Nation, see Mulroy, *The Seminole Freedmen*, especially chaps. 3, 6, and 7.

4. Foner, *Reconstruction*. For a history of the Thirteenth Amendment, see Vorenberg, *Final Freedom*.

5. Armstrong, *Warrior in Two Camps*, 114–17. In 1871, in his capacity as commissioner of Indian Affairs, Parker advocated putting an end to U.S. treaty making with Indian peoples, calling upon the government to "cease the cruel farce of thus dealing with its helpless and ignorant wards." See Kidwell, *The Choctaws in Oklahoma*, 92.

6. Richardson, *West from Appomattox*, chaps. 2 and 3.

7. James Harlan to D. H. Cooley et al., August 16, 1865, reprinted in Abel, *The American Indian and the End of the Confederacy*, 219–26.

8. Report of the Secretary of the Interior, House Exec. Doc. 1, part 2, 39th Cong., 1st sess., 497–98, 500–502; Cyrus Bussey to Peter Pitchlynn, August 2, 1865, box 4, folder 33, Pitchlynn Papers, UOK; Peter Pitchlynn to Winchester Colbert, August 9, 1865, box 4, folder 36, Pitchlynn Papers, UOK; Winchester Colbert to Peter Pitchlynn, August 24, 1865, box 4, folder 38, Pitchlynn Papers, UOK. For longer descriptions of the Fort Smith council, see Abel, *The American Indian and the End of the Confederacy*, chap. 6; and Kidwell, *Choctaws in Oklahoma*, chap. 6.

9. Report of the Secretary of the Interior, House Exec. Doc. 1, part 2, 39th Cong., 1st sess., 502.

10. Foner, *Reconstruction*, 66–68; Vorenberg, *Final Freedom*, chap. 2; Dykstra and Hahn, "Northern Voters and Negro Suffrage," 208–9.

11. House Exec. Doc. 1, 504, 518, 529. For a discussion of Indians' thinking about the meaning of freedom in their respective nations, see Saunt, "The Paradox of Freedom," 63–94; and Kidwell, *The Choctaws in Oklahoma*, chap. 6.

12. "Agreement with the Cherokee and Other Tribes in the Indian Territory, 1865," in Kappler, *Treaties*, 1050–52. House Exec. Doc. 1, 440, has population estimates of 3,000 slaves in the Choctaw Nation and 2,000 in the Chickasaw Nation.

13. Peter Pitchlynn to Denis Cooley, September 21, 1865, reprinted in Abel, *The American Indian and the End of the Confederacy*, 285.

14. "An act temporarily providing for such persons as have been to the present time considered as slaves," Records of the Choctaw General Council, microfilm roll CTN-9, OKHS; Debo, *The Rise and Fall of the Choctaw Republic*, 99–101.

15. Colbert's address to the legislature is reprinted in Abel, *The American Indian and the End of the Confederacy*, 286–87.

16. Ibid., 289; Littlefield, *The Chickasaw Freedmen*, 23–25.

17. Colbert's Proclamation is reprinted in Abel, *The American Indian and the End of the Confederacy*, 288–89. Governor Winchester Colbert to Major General Henry J. Hunt, October 11, 1865, Doc. 110, *Annual Report of the Commissioner of Indian Affairs, 1869*, 357–58.

18. J. W. Ballard, November 30, 1865; Francis Springer to General Sprague, November 28, 1865; both in Registers and Letters Received by the Commissioner of the Bureau of Refugees, Freedmen and Abandoned Lands, 1865–1872, NAMP, M752, roll 22.

19. Brevet Major General Henry Hunt to the Honorable D. H. Cooley, Commissioner of Indian Affairs, November 28, 1865, Records of the Office of Indian Affairs, Letters Received, folder H1105-I1350, NAMP, 234, roll 836.

20. Dylan Penningroth makes a similar point in his analysis of former slaves' efforts to file claims with federal officials for property that was lost or destroyed during the war. See Penningroth, *Claims of Kinfolk*, chap. 4.

21. Assistant Commissioner Leard to O. O. Howard, October 24, 1865, Registers and Letters Received by the Commissioner of the Bureau of Refugees, Freedmen, and Abandoned Lands, 1865–1872, NAMP, M752, roll 21.

22. U.S. Department of the Interior, *Annual Report of the Commissioner of Indian Affairs, 1866,* 283–84; Bvt. Maj. Gen. John Sanborn to James Harlan, January 5, 1866, NAMP, M234, roll 837.

23. U.S. Department of the Interior, *Annual Report of the Commissioner of Indian Affairs, 1866,* 286; Littlefield, *The Chickasaw Freedmen,* 30–38; Debo, *The Rise and Fall of the Choctaw Republic,* 100; Abel, *The American Indian and the End of the Confederacy,* 296–98.

24. General Sanborn's report, January 8, 1866, Letters Received by the Office of Indian Affairs, 1824–1881, Southern Superintendency, 1851–1871, NAMP, M234, roll 837.

25. Capt. W. Wood to Lt. Col. J. Craig, January 29, 1866; John Sanborn to Maj. Gen. Hunt, January 9, 1866; John Levering to Maj. Gen. Reynolds, February 7, 1866; all in Letters Received by the Office of Indian Affairs, 1824–81, Southern Superintendency, 1851–1871, NAMP, M234, roll 837.

26. Col. William A. Phillips to Secretary of the Interior, January 17, 1865, Doc. 91-A, *Annual Report of the Commissioner of Indian Affairs, 1865.*

27. Elijah Sells to D. H. Cooley, August 5, 1865, in House Exec. Doc. 1, 39th Cong., 1st sess., 449.

28. In his multivolume history of Oklahoma, Joseph Thoburn wrote that he interviewed Choctaw and Chickasaw men who told him of their participation in the Vigilante Committee. Annie Abel quotes part of a letter from an officer at Fort Gibson who wrote about receiving freedmen's accounts of murder and assault and concluded that "the blacks are suffering a reign of terror" at the hands of Confederate Choctaws and Chickasaws. Thoburn and Wright, *Oklahoma,* 375–76. Debo, *The Rise and Fall of the Choctaw Republic,* 99–100. Abel, *The American Indian and the End of the Confederacy* 273 (n. 518).

29. Polly Colbert in Baker and Baker, *The WPA Oklahoma Slave Narratives,* 89. Colbert also said that she suspected that her master, Mr. Holmes, "was one of de leaders" of this Klan activity.

30. Loring Folsom to Peter Pitchlynn, August 29, 1870, box 4, folder 48, Pitchlynn Papers, UOK.

31. Francis Springer to General Sprague, December 4, 1864, Registers and Letters Received by the Commissioner of the Bureau of Refugees, Freedmen, and Abandoned Lands, 1865–1872, RG 105, NAMP, M752, roll 22; Grant, *1866,* 496.

32. Major General John Sanborn to James Harlan, January 5, 1866, NAMP, M234, roll 837.

33. "Letter from the Indian Nations and Texas," *New Era,* January 31, 1866; Captain W. Wood to Lt. Col. J. Craig, January 29, 1866; John Levering to Maj. Gen. Reynolds, February 7, 1866, Letters Received by the Office of Indian Affairs, 1824–81, Southern Superintendency, 1851–1871, NAMP, M234, roll 837.

34. Sturm, *Blood Politics,* 74–75, 171–74; Naylor, *African Cherokees,* chaps. 5 and 6; Saunt, *Black, White, and Indian,* chaps. 6 and 7; Mulroy, *The Seminole Freedmen,* chaps. 6 and 7. The Cherokee, Creek, and Seminole treaties can be found in Kappler, *Treaties.*

35. After the Fort Smith Council, on October 9, 1865, the delegates reported to the Choctaw General Council. They advised that the council instruct the men selected to go to Washington, D.C., for the final treaty negotiations "to insist upon the payment for the negroes to be emancipation in this nation. Though if the U.S. will not remunerate it shall not be an obsticle

[*sic*] to the completion of a Treaty." They also urged that the treaty delegates "request that no negro troops be stationed at any post in the Choctaw or Chickasaw nations." Statement to the General Council of the Choctaw Nation, October 9, 1865, Records of the Choctaw General Council, microfilm roll CTN-9, OKHS.

36. Kappler, *Treaties*.

37. Treaty with the Choctaw and Chickasaw, 1866, in Kappler, *Treaties*, 918–20. On federal efforts to promote free-labor ideology and labor contracts during Reconstruction, see Stanley, *From Bondage to Contract*. For a history of the commons and land use in Indian Territory, see Chang, *The Color of the Land*; and Alexandra Harmon, *Rich Indians*, chap. 4.

38. Treaty with the Choctaw and Chickasaw, 1866, in Kappler, *Treaties*, 918–31. The "leased district" had been the subject of negotiations between the Choctaws, the Chickasaws, and the United States since the 1850s. See Kidwell, *The Choctaws in Oklahoma*, chap. 2.

39. Israel Folsom to Peter Pitchlynn, February 24, 1870, box 4, folder 47, Pitchlynn Papers, UOK.

40. Address of Peter P. Pitchlynn and Winchester Colbert, July 12, 1865, box 5, folder 8, Pitchlynn Papers, UOK.

41. John H. B. Latrobe, "An Address to the Choctaw and Chickasaw Nations, in Regard to Matters Connected with the Treaty of 1866," Ayer Collection, Newberry Library; Semmes, *John H. B. Latrobe and His Times, 1803–1891*, 544–45; Kidwell, *Choctaws in Oklahoma*, 79–80.

42. Harmon, *Rich Indians*, 136, 157; Hoxie, *A Final Promise*, especially chap. 2.

43. Address of Peter P. Pitchlynn and Winchester Colbert, July 12, 1865, box 5, folder 8, Pitchlynn Papers, UOK.

44. Statement of Loyal Chickasaws, September 17, 1865, Letters Received by the Office of Indian Affairs, 1824–1881, Southern Superintendency, 1851–1871, NAMP, M234, roll 837; House Exec. Doc. 1, part 2, 39th Cong., 1st sess., 508–9; Foner, *Fiery Trial*, 199–259; Abel, *The American Indian and the End of the Confederacy*, 270, cf. 514.

Chapter 5

1. Arriving at an accurate count of the number of freedpeople in the nations is as challenging as determining the number of enslaved people. The 1860 census enumerates 2,297 enslaved people owned by Choctaws and 917 people owned by Chickasaws. By contrast, wartime estimates placed the enslaved population in the Choctaw Nation at 3,000 and that of the Chickasaw Nation at 2,000. Early twentieth-century censuses of the Choctaw and Chickasaw Nations counted 5,994 former slaves and their descendants in the Choctaw Nation and 4,670 former slaves and their descendants in the Chickasaw Nation. House Exec. Doc. 1, vol. 2, 39th Cong., 1st sess., 440; Saunt, "The Paradox of Freedom," 65, cf. 6.

2. Matilda Poe in Baker and Baker, *The WPA Oklahoma Slave Narratives*, 326.

3. Jack Campbell in Rawick, *Oklahoma Narratives*, 90–91.

4. Address of Peter Pitchlynn and Winchester Colbert, July 12, 1866, box 5, folder 8, Pitchlynn Papers, UOK; House Misc. Doc. 46, 42nd Cong., 2nd sess., 7.

5. The legislature also consented "to the sectionizing and allotment of the lands in severalty . . . as is provided for in the treaty of April 1866." House Misc. Doc. 29, 42nd Cong., 1st sess., 1; House Misc. Doc. 46, 8; Senate Exec. Doc. 166, 50th Cong., 1st sess., 2.

6. Senate Doc. 157, 55th Cong., 1st sess., 15–16.

7. Littlefield, *The Chickasaw Freedmen*, 52.

8. Senate Exec. Doc. 82, 40th Cong., 2nd sess.

9. Senate Doc. 157, 55th Cong., 1st sess., 20–21; Senate Exec. Doc. 166, 50th Cong., 1st sess., 3.

10. House Misc. Doc. 46, 42nd Cong., 2nd sess., 11.

11. Testimony of Allen Wright, House Report 98, 42nd Cong., 3rd sess., 564.

12. House Exec. Doc. 1, 41st Cong., 2nd sess.; *Annual Report of Commissioner of Indian Affairs, 1869,* 407–9.

13. Senate Misc. Doc. 106, 41st Cong., 2nd sess., 2.

14. Senate Report 744, 45th Cong., 3rd sess., 158.

15. Senate Misc. Doc. 106, 41st Cong., 2nd sess., 3.

16. Naylor, *African Cherokees in Indian Territory,* 5.

17. House Report 98, 42nd Cong., 3rd sess., 466.

18. Interview with Jane Battiest, Indian Pioneer Papers, microfiche 43, UOK; Polly Colbert and Kiziah Love in Baker and Baker, *The WPA Oklahoma Slave Narratives,* 87, 259; Jack Campbell and Jefferson L. Cole in Rawick, *Oklahoma Narratives,* 92, 122.

19. Vorenberg, "Abraham Lincoln's 'Fellow Citizens'—Before and after Emancipation," 152.

20. Senate Misc. Doc. 106, 41st Cong., 2nd sess., 5.

21. Ibid.

22. Stanley, *From Bondage to Contract;* Saville, *The Work of Reconstruction;* Cullen, "I's a Man Now," 489–501.

23. For a lively and innovative discussion of southern slaveholders' views of emancipation as a labor crisis, see Guterl, *American Mediterranean,* chap. 4.

24. Lycurgus Pitchlynn to Peter Pitchlynn, January 9, 1866, folder 44, Pitchlynn Papers, UOK.

25. Loring Folsom to Peter Pitchlynn, July 28, 1879, folder 91, Pitchlynn Papers, UOK.

26. Mary Lindsay in Baker and Baker, *The WPA Oklahoma Slave Narratives,* 251.

27. Lycurgus Pitchlynn to Peter Pitchlynn, January 9, 1866, folder 44, Pitchlynn Papers, UOK.

28. Lycurgus Pitchlynn to Peter Pitchlynn, January 9, 1866, folder 44, Pitchlynn Papers, UOK.

29. Report of Agent Olmstead, September 15, 1870, *Annual Report of the Commissioner of Indian Affairs, 1870,* 291.

30. Testimony of Lemon Butler, July 4, 1872, House Report 98, 42nd Cong., 3rd sess., 463.

31. Daniel Webster Burton in Rawick, *Oklahoma Narratives,* 85.

32. Ibid., 75.

33. Harmon, *Rich Indians,* 138–41.

34. Malvina Pitchlynn to Peter Pitchlynn, March 12, 1878, box 4, folder 83; Loring Folsom to Peter Pitchlynn, July 28, 1879, box 4, folder 91; both in Pitchlynn Papers, UOK.

35. Debo, *The Rise and Fall of the Choctaw Republic,* 111.

36. Littlefield, *The Chickasaw Freedmen,* 83.

37. Bill no. 26, October 27, 1877, Coleman Cole Collection, UOK.

38. K. L. Kennedy to Peter Pitchlynn, May 28, 1877, box 4, folder 73, Pitchlynn Papers, UOK.

39. House Report 98, 42nd Cong., 3rd sess., 565.

40. Kidwell, *The Choctaws in Oklahoma,* chap. 8.

41. *The Vindicator,* vol. 1, no. 35, November 17, 1875, in Coleman Cole Collection, UOK.

42. Testimony of Sampson Cole, Senate Report 1278, part 2, 49th Cong., 1st sess., 243–44.

43. Malvina Pitchlynn Folsom to Peter Pitchlynn, March 12, 1876, box 4, folder 83; Calvin Robinson to Peter Pitchlynn, April 29, 1879, box 4, folder 89, Pitchlynn Papers, UOK.

44. U.S. Department of the Interior, *Annual Report of the Commissioner of Indian Affairs, 1874,* 71. See Harmon, *Rich Indians,* for a more detailed discussion of racial stereotypes in the context of Indian land use and wealth.

45. House Misc. Doc. 46, 16.

46. On the U.S. financial crisis of the early 1870s as it related to the West, see Richardson, *West from Appomattox*. For a discussion of the financial crisis and the construction of railroads in and around Indian Territory, see Kidwell, *The Choctaws in Oklahoma*, chap. 7.

47. For a detailed discussion of the negotiations and allegations surrounding the Net Proceeds Case, see Kidwell, *The Choctaws in Oklahoma*, chap. 9.

48. House Misc. Doc. 46, 1–6.

49. "Brief of D. C. Finn's Testimony," in House Report 98, 42nd Cong., 3rd sess., 466–67.

50. Finn's involvement with the Choctaw and Chickasaw freedpeople was not his only foray into freedpeople's affairs in the Indian Territory. In 1876 Finn inserted himself into the conflict brewing over the impeachment of Creek principal chief Lochar Harjo. Finn wrote letters and petitions to the federal government purportedly from Harjo and the Creek Executive Office at Okmulgee. In addition, Finn put together petitions with the names of Creeks and freedpeople requesting that the Creek annuity and land be divided so the loyalists and former rebels could maintain separate governments. Again, Finn took a position that had the potential to advance his financial interests under the aegis of protecting the freedpeople's welfare in accordance with Republican sympathies. Vertical file on Daniel C. Finn, Kansas Historical Society. Debo, *The Road to Disappearance*, 223–25.

51. House Report 98, 42nd Cong., 3rd sess., 465.

52. Kidwell, *The Choctaws in Oklahoma*, 130–31; House Report 98, 461.

53. *The Vindicator*, July 11, 1872, 5; *The Vindicator*, September 14, 1872.

54. *The Vindicator*, October 12, 1872.

55. *Cherokee Advocate* and Shanks quoted in Littlefield, *The Chickasaw Freedmen*, 63.

56. *The Vindicator*, October 5, 1872; Harmon, *Rich Indians*, chap. 4.

57. Overton quoted in Littlefield, *The Chickasaw Freedmen*, 64.

58. Memorial to the Congress of the United States in Letter from the Commissioner of Indian Affairs Relative to the Freedmen in the Chickasaw Nation, Senate Exec. Doc. 166, 50th Cong., 1st sess., 10.

59. Kappler, *Treaties*.

60. Memorial of the Chickasaws Relating to the President's Message of February 17, 1892, Senate Misc. Doc. 82, 52nd Cong., 1st sess., 2.

61. Senate Misc. Doc. 106, 41st Cong., 2nd sess., 3.

62. Senate Exec. Doc. 71, 41st Cong., 2nd sess., 2.

63. The First Kansas was redesignated the new 79th U.S. Colored Infantry Regiment on December 13, 1864. See Wilson, *The Black Phalanx*, 220–46; Hargrove, *Black Union Soldiers in the Civil War*, 51–60. Abel does not discuss black men's military participation, but she does provide an exceptionally detailed account of the organization of loyal Indians by Union commanders. See Abel, *The American Indian in the Civil War, 1862–1865*, 37–123.

64. Billington, "Buffalo Soldiers in the American West, 1865–1900"; Carroll, *The Black Military Experience in the American West*; Fowler, *The Black Infantry in the West, 1869–1891*; Savage, *Blacks in the West*, chap. 3.

65. *The Vindicator*, July 11, 1872; House Report 98, 466; Littlefield, "Juneteenth and August Fourth Celebrations." For a discussion of Emancipation Day celebrations in the United States, see Kachun, *Festivals of Freedom*.

66. Memorial of the Chickasaw Nation to the President of the United States, in Senate Exec. Doc. 166, 50th Cong., 1st sess., 10.

67. Letter fragment in folder "Missing Parts." Entry no. 604, Letters Received Relating to Choctaw and Other Freedmen, RG 75, National Archives, Washington, D.C.

68. Although the letter is undated, the reference to women who resided in the nation in 1866 and were thus covered by the Treaty and the indication that the complaints were being lodged

against both the Choctaw and Chickasaw Nations suggests that the letter was written before 1885, when Choctaw legislators approved a measure to adopt, or grant citizenship to, freedpeople.

Chapter 6

1. B. F. Overton quoted in Littlefield, *The Chickasaw Freedmen*, 66. For discussion of Chickasaw plans to extend citizenship to black people in the 1870s, see ibid., chap. 3.

2. Bill no. 40, Resolution Authorizing the Principal Chief to Appoint Five Commissioners to Confer with Like Commission on the Part of the Chickasaw Nation, Choctaw Nation Papers, UOK; Senate Exec. Doc. 166, 50th Cong., 1st sess., 4.

3. "Message of I. L. Garvin," *Star Vindicator*, October 19, 1878, box G-25, folder 2, Choctaw Nation Papers, UOK; "Resolution Approved by I. L. Garvin," *Star Vindicator*, November 16, 1878, box G-25, folder 5, Choctaw Nation Papers, UOK.

4. Bill no. 16, Freedmen Bill, November 2, 1880, box 12, folder 15, Choctaw Nation Papers, UOK; An Act to Adopt the Freedmen of the Choctaw Nation, May 21, 1883, box 15, folder 1, Choctaw Nation Papers, UOK; Littlefield, *The Chickasaw Freedmen*, 67.

5. An Act to Adopt the Freedmen of the Choctaw Nation, May 21, 1883, box 15, folder 1, Choctaw Nation Papers, UOK; Littlefield, *The Chickasaw Freedmen*, 70–71. In October 1883 the General Council repealed the section of the adoption law that covered black people's eligibility to hold office. An Act to Repeal Section Eight of a Freedmen Bill Approved May 21, 1883, October 26, 1883, box 15, folder 48, Choctaw Nation Papers, UOK; Durant, *Constitution and Laws of the Choctaw Nation*, 206.

6. Senate Doc. 157, 55th Cong., 1st sess., 22–23.

7. "An Act Rejecting the Adoption of the Freedmen in the Chickasaw Nation," October 22, 1885, reprinted in Senate Doc. 157, 55th Cong., 1st sess., 28–29.

8. Littlefield, *The Chickasaw Freedmen*, 150.

9. See Sturm, *Blood Politics*, for a study of the ways antiblack racism informed and shaped Cherokee nationalism in this period.

10. U.S. Department of the Interior, *Annual Report of the Board of Indian Commissioners, 1886*.

11. Dawes, "Have We Failed with the Indian?," 283.

12. Debo, *And Still the Waters Run*, 6.

13. Burton, *Indian Territory and the United States*; Wicket, *Contested Territory*; Hoxie, *A Final Promise*, chap. 5; Littlefield, *The Chickasaw Freedmen*, chaps. 8 and 9.

14. "Editorial of Views of Chief," in *Minco Minstrel*, October 19, 1894, Jefferson Gardner Papers, Choctaw Nation Manuscript Collection, packet 1, folder 2, UOK; McCurtain quoted in Kidwell, *Choctaws in Oklahoma*, 149.

15. McAdam, "An Indian Commonwealth," 884

16. Senate Misc. Doc. 24, 53rd Cong., 3rd sess., 8.

17. Senate Misc. Doc. 24, 53rd Cong., 3rd sess., 10.

18. Harmon, "American Indians and Land Monopolies in the Gilded Age," 128. Also see Harmon, *Rich Indians*, chap. 4.

19. *Twenty-Ninth Annual Report of the Board of Indian Commissioners, 1897*, 30.

20. U.S. Bureau of the Census, 11th U.S. Census, 1890, *Extra Census Bulletin*, 7; Crawford, "Oklahoma and the Indian Territory," *New England Magazine* 8, June 1890, 454.

21. This sentiment echoed that of antebellum observers who alleged that Indians were kinder and gentler slaveholders than their white counterparts because they failed to appreciate the ideals of owning private property, specifically slaves, and profiting in the market economy through the exploitation of enslaved people's labor and reproduction.

22. Harmon addresses the ways in which both Indians and non-Indians "overlook the shortcomings of their own systems," but she does not extend this discussion to Indians' and non-Indians' ideas about black people's rights to claim land and their land use patterns in either the United States or the Five Tribes.

23. Resolution of the Freedmen of Atoka County, May 1883, box 1, folder 1883, Letters Received Relating to Choctaw and Other Freedmen, RG 75; Littlefield, *The Chickasaw Freedmen*, 71.

24. Senate Doc. 182, 102, 110, 113.

25. Senate Report 1278, part 2, 49th Cong., 1st sess., 298.

26. In 1897 a committee of Choctaw freedmen wrote to Indian Agent D. M. Wisdom. They protested their treatment by the Dawes Commission and both the Choctaw and Chickasaw leaders in the Atoka agreement. Senate Doc. 149, 55th Cong., 1st sess.

27. Nelson Coleman to James F. A. Sisson, July 19, 1880, box 1, folder 1880, RG 75; Letter from Choctaw Freedmen to Secretary of the Interior, August 15, 1881, box 1, folder 1881, RG 75; Printed Memorial of the Freedmen of the Chickasaw Nation to Congress, box 1, unmarked folder 2, RG 75.

28. George W. Dallas to Secretary of the Interior, January 3, 1881, box 1, folder 1881, RG 75; James Milton Turner to James McLean, June 2, 1883, box 1, folder 1883, RG 75; Senate Exec. Doc. 111; Naylor, *African Cherokees*, 168; Littlefield, *The Chickasaw Freedmen*, 71.

29. R. H. Butler and others to Secretary of the Interior, August 30, 1881, box 1, folder 1881, RG 75; Census Roll of Choctaw-Chickasaw Freedmen, 1885, National Archives Microfilm publication P2128, roll 1, RG 75, Records of the Bureau of Indian Affairs; Choctaw Freemen, 1885–1897, Choctaw National Records, CTN roll 7, OKHS.

30. For a study of tribal responses to the federal government's imposition of categories of blood quanta on the Five Tribes, see Sturm, *Blood Politics*; and Metcalf, "Lambs of Sacrifice." On race and pseudoscientific thought, see Frederickson, *The Black Image in the White Mind*; Horsman, *Race and Manifest Destiny*; Jacobson, *Whiteness of a Different Color*; and Stepan, "The Hour of Eugenics." For a history of Indians' thinking about the symbolic meanings of blood, see Meyer, *Thicker than Water*. For works discussing Native Americans' engagement with Euro-American concepts of race, see Perdue, *"Mixed Blood Indians"*; Saunt and others, "Rethinking Race and Culture in the Early South"; Shoemaker, "How Indians Got to Be Red"; and Merrell, "The Racial Education of the Catawba Indians."

31. On racial categories and the U.S. Census in the nineteenth century, see Nobles, *Shades of Citizenship*; Dominguez, "Exporting U.S. Concepts of Race"; Harris, "Whiteness as Property"; and Hodes, "The Mercurial Nature and Abiding Power of Race."

32. Senate Report 1278, part 1, 49th Cong., 1st sess., 1–2.

33. Senate Report 1278, part 2, 49th Cong., 1st sess., 204, 359.

34. Ibid., 158.

35. Ibid., 152, 170.

36. Ibid., 296.

37. Senate Misc. Doc. 24, 53rd Cong., 3rd sess., 12.

38. U.S. Bureau of the Census, 11th U.S. Census, 1890, *Extra Census Bulletin*, 3, 6. Other observers arrived at similar conclusions, expressing their findings in the language of blood and race. A writer for *Harper's Monthly Magazine*, for example, contended that "few Indians can boast of blood uncontaminated by that of the African," while another magazine noted that blacks and Creeks had "intermarried to a great extent." McAdam, "An Indian Commonwealth," 891; Crawford, "Oklahoma and the Indian Territory," 454. On tribal resistance to U.S. census takers, see Biolsi, "The Birth of the Reservation," 125–29.

39. Senate Report 969, 54th Cong., 1st sess.; Debo, *And Still the Waters Run*, 379; Biolsi, "The Birth of the Reservation," 119–25; Hoxie, *Final Promise*, chap. 5. Approximately 23,405 people

of African descent in the Choctaw, Chickasaw, Cherokee, Creek, and Seminole Nations stood to gain ownership of land through the allotment process. This is the number of black people who were included on the final tribal rolls for receiving land allotments, but the number does not include those who were rejected from the final rolls and thus were ineligible for allotments. Angie Debo, *And Still the Waters Run*, 47.

40. On the history of segregation in southern states, see Schechter, *Ida B. Wells-Barnett*; Feimster, *Southern Horrors*; Mack, "Law, Society, Identity"; Kantrowitz, *Ben Tillman*; and Ayers, *The Promise of the New South*. Daniel F. Littlefield Jr. has written a study of violence and lynching in Indian Territory, linking local episodes of anti-Indian violence to U.S. colonial policies toward the Indian nations. Littlefield, *Seminole Burning*.

41. Adam Burris to Suckey Burris, April 13, 1880, box 4, folder 101, Pitchlynn Papers, UOK.

Conclusion

1. Ellison, *Going to the Territory*, 124; Du Bois *The Souls of Black Folk*.

2. Brophy, *Reconstructing the Dreamland*; Hirsch, *Riot and Remembrance*; Ellison, *Going to the Territory*, 130–33; Chang, *The Color of the Land*, 195–96.

Bibliography

Primary Sources

MANUSCRIPT COLLECTIONS

Atlanta, Ga.
  Georgia State Archives, Rare Books Collection
    David B. Mitchell, *An Exposition of the Case of the Africans Taken to the Creek Agency by Capt. William Bowen, on or about the 1st of December, 1817* (1821)
Chicago, Ill.
  Newberry Library, Ayer Collection
    John Latrobe, *An Address to the Choctaw and Chickasaw Nations in Regard to Matters Connected with the Treaty of 1866*
New Haven, Conn.
  Beinecke Library, Yale University
    C. C. Carpenter, "Grand Rush for the Indian Territory" (broadside)
    George W. Harkins, "To the Choctaw People, Brethren, and Friends: Letter to Tandy Walker" (broadside, 1858)
    Peter Pitchlynn, *Remonstrance, Appeal, and Solemn Protest of the Choctaw Nation Addressed to the Congress of the United States* (1870)
Norman, Okla.
  University of Oklahoma Library, Western History Collection
    Choctaw Nation Papers
    Coleman Cole Collection
    Jefferson Gardner Collection
    Indian Pioneer Papers
      Microfiche, http://digital.libraries.ou.edu/cdm/landingpage/collection/indianpp
    Peter Perkins Pitchlynn Collection
Oklahoma City, Okla.
  Oklahoma Historical Society
    Chickasaw Roll of 1818
    Records of the Five Civilized Tribes, microfilm
      Choctaw Nation
        CTN7, Census and Citizenship-Freedmen, 1885–97
        CTN9, Records and Documents of the General Council, 1864–76
        CTN10, Records of the General Council, Senate, and House of Representatives, 1872–1883
Topeka, Kans.
  Kansas Historical Society
    Vertical file on Daniel C. Finn
Washington, D.C.
  National Archives and Records Administration
    Records of the Bureau of the Census, Record Group 29

8th U.S. Census, 1860, Arkansas, Slave Schedules, National Archives Microfilm
Publications, M653, roll 54
Records of the Bureau of Indian Affairs, Record Group 75
Office of Indian Affairs, Letters Received, National Archives Microfilm Publication
M234, rolls 134, 135, 136, 169, 836, 837
1831 Choctaw Armstrong Roll, National Archives Microfilm Publication A39
Special Files of the Office of Indian Affairs, 1807–1904, National Archives Microfilm
Publication M574, roll 76
Enrollment Cards for the Five Civilized Tribes, 1898–1914, National Archives Microfilm
Publication M1186, roll 49
Chickasaw and Choctaw Records, Letters Sent, Entry 252
Chickasaw Removal Records, Muster Roll, October 1837, Chickasaw Census and Muster
Rolls, 1837–39, Entry 253
Letters Received Relating to Choctaw and Other Freedmen, Entry 604
Rolls of Choctaw Freedmen, Entry 605
Records of the Bureau of Refugees, Freedmen, and Abandoned Lands, Record Group 105
Records of the Assistant Commissioner for the State of Arkansas Bureau of Refugees,
Freedmen, and Abandoned Lands
General Records, Letters and Telegrams Sent, National Archives Microfilm Publication
M979, roll 1
Registers and Letters Received by the Commissioner of the Bureau of Refugees, Freedmen,
and Abandoned Lands, 1865–1872, National Archives Microfilm Publication M752,
rolls 21, 22
Records of the Office of the Secretary of War, Record Group 107
General Records, 1791–1947, Correspondence, Letters Received by the Secretary of War,
National Archives Microfilm Publication M221, roll 47
Woodbridge, Conn.
American Board of Commissioners for Foreign Missions
Papers of the American Board of Commissioners for Foreign Missions, microfilm;
Research Publications Inc., 1982–85
Chickasaw Mission, vol. 1 (ABC 18.4.4) microfilm reel 779
Choctaw Mission, vol. 1 (ABC 18.3.4) microfilm reel 755
Choctaw Mission, vol. 2 (ABC 18.3.4) microfilm reel 755
Choctaw Mission, vol. 3 (ABC 18.3.4) microfilm reel 756
Choctaw Mission, vol. 4 (ABC 18.3.4) microfilm reel 757
Choctaw Mission, vol. 6 (ABC 18.3.4) microfilm reel 759
Choctaw Mission, vol. 7 (ABC 18.3.4) microfilm reel 761
Choctaw Mission, vol. 7 (ABC 18.3.4) microfilm reel 762

NEWSPAPERS AND MAGAZINES

African Repository (Washington, D.C.)
African Repository and Colonial Journal (Washington, D.C.)
Afro-American Advocate (Coffeyville, Kans.)
Atlantic Monthly
Choctaw Intelligencer (Doaksville, Choctaw Nation, Indian Territory)
Choctaw Telegraph (Doaksville, Choctaw Nation, Indian Territory)
Douglass' Monthly (Rochester, N.Y.)
Frederick Douglass' Paper (Rochester, N.Y.)

Harper's New Monthly Magazine
Missionary Herald (Boston, Mass.)
National Era (Washington, D.C.)
New England Magazine (Boston, Mass.)
New Era (Fort Smith, Ark.)
New York Times
Niles' Weekly Register
North Star (Rochester, N.Y.)
Provincial Freeman (Ontario)
The Vindicator (New Boggy, Choctaw Nation)

GOVERNMENT DOCUMENTS

Twenty-Ninth Annual Report of the Board of Indian Commissioners, 1897. Washington, D.C.: Government Printing Office, 1898.

U.S. Bureau of the Census. 11th Census, 1890. *Extra Census Bulletin: The Five Civilized Tribes in Indian Territory*. Washington, D.C.: Government Printing Office, 1890.

U.S. Department of the Interior. *Annual Report of the Commissioner of Indian Affairs, 1835*. Washington, D.C.: Government Printing Office, 1835.

———. *Annual Report of the Commissioner of Indian Affairs, 1836*. Washington, D.C.: Government Printing Office, 1836.

———. *Annual Report of the Commissioner of Indian Affairs, 1837*. Washington, D.C.: Government Printing Office, 1837.

———. *Annual Report of the Commissioner of Indian Affairs, 1838*. Washington, D.C.: Government Printing Office, 1838.

———. *Annual Report of the Commissioner of Indian Affairs, 1841*. Washington, D.C.: Government Printing Office, 1841.

———. *Annual Report of the Commissioner of Indian Affairs, 1842*. Washington, D.C.: Government Printing Office, 1842.

———. *Annual Report of the Commissioner of Indian Affairs, 1843*. Washington, D.C.: Government Printing Office, 1843.

———. *Annual Report of the Commissioner of Indian Affairs, 1846*. Washington, D.C.: Government Printing Office, 1846.

———. *Annual Report of the Commissioner of Indian Affairs, 1850*. Washington, D.C.: Government Printing Office, 1850.

———. *Annual Report of the Commissioner of Indian Affairs, 1854*. Washington, D.C.: Government Printing Office, 1854.

———. *Annual Report of the Commissioner of Indian Affairs, 1860*. Washington, D.C.: Government Printing Office, 1860.

———. *Annual Report of the Commissioner of Indian Affairs, 1865*. Washington, D.C.: Government Printing Office, 1865.

———. *Annual Report of the Commissioner of Indian Affairs, 1866*. Washington, D.C.: Government Printing Office, 1866.

———. *Annual Report of the Commissioner of Indian Affairs, 1869*. Washington, D.C.: Government Printing Office, 1869.

U.S. House of Representatives. *Annual Report of the Secretary of the Interior, 1865*. H. Exec. Doc. 1, Pt. 1, 39th Cong., 1st sess. Washington, D.C.: Government Printing Office, 1865.

———. *Annual Report of the Secretary of the Interior, 1865*. H. Exec. Doc. 1, Pt. 2, 39th Cong., 1st sess. Washington, D.C.: Government Printing Office, 1865.

———. *Annual Report of the Secretary of the Interior, 1869.* H. Exec. Doc. 1, Pt. 3, 41st Cong., 2nd sess. Washington, D.C.: Government Printing Office, 1869.

———. *Copy of Act Passed by Chickasaw Legislature on Freedmen of Chickasaw Nation.* H. Misc. Doc. 29, 42nd Cong., 1st sess. Washington, D.C.: Government Printing Office, 1868.

———. *Investigation of Indian Frauds.* H. Rpt. 98, 42nd Cong., 3rd sess. Washington, D.C.: Government Printing Office, 1873.

———. *Petition of Freedmen of Choctaw and Chickasaw Nations.* H. Misc. Doc. 46, 42nd Cong., 2nd sess. Washington, D.C.: Government Printing Office, 1872.

———. *Remonstrance of Col. Peter Pitchlynn, Choctaw Delegate, against the Passage of the Bill to Unite under one Government the Several Tribes West of the Mississippi River.* H. Misc. Doc. 35, 30th Cong., 2nd sess. Washington, D.C.: Government Printing Office, 1849.

———. *United States v. Choctaw and Chickasaw Nations, Etc.* H. Doc. 920, 61st Cong., 2nd sess. Washington, D.C.: Government Printing Office, 1910.

U.S. Senate. *Allotment of Land to Choctaw and Chickasaw Freedmen, Etc.* Sen. Doc. 183, 55th Cong., 1st sess. Washington, D.C.: Government Printing Office, 1897.

———. *Argument Made by Judge McKennon before the Committee on Indian Affairs of the House of Representatives Relative to the Condition of Affairs in the Indian Territory.* Sen. Doc. 182, 54th Cong., 1st sess. Washington, D.C.: Government Printing Office, 1896.

———. *Correspondence on the Emigration of Indians, 1831–1833.* Sen. Doc. 512, parts 1, 2 & 3, 23rd Congress, 2nd sess. Washington, D.C.: Duff Green, 1834; 1835.

———. *Letter from the Secretary of the Interior, Transmitting a Letter from the Commissioner of Indian Affairs Relative to the Freedmen in the Chickasaw Nation.* Sen. Exec. Doc. 166, 50th Cong., 1st sess. Washington, D.C.: Government Printing Office, 1888.

———. *Letter from the Secretary of the Interior, Transmitting, in Compliance with Senate Resolution of February 7, 1882, Copy of Report of the Acting Commissioner of the General Land Office of April 25, 1881, in Reference to the Right of Occupation by Settlers of Any Portion of the Indian Territory.* Sen. Exec. Doc. 111, 47th Cong., 1st sess. Washington, D.C.: Government Printing Office, 1882.

———. *Letter of the Acting Secretary of the Interior, Transmitting Copy of a Communication and Accompanying Copy of a Memorial from Certain Freedmen of the Choctaw Nation, Relative to Their Rights as Members of That Tribe.* Sen. Doc. 149, 55th Cong., 1st sess. Washington, D.C.: Government Printing Office, 1897.

———. *Letter of the Secretary of War Communicating, in Compliance with a Resolution of the Senate of the 16th Instant, a Copy of the Report of S. N. Clark, Special Agent of the Freedmen's Bureau, upon the Condition of the Freedmen in the Choctaw and Chickasaw Indian Nations.* Sen. Exec. Doc. 71, 41st Cong., 2nd sess. Washington, D.C.: Government Printing Office, 1870.

———. *Memorandum of the Case of the Chickasaw Freedmen, Brief and Argument, by R. V. Belt, Their Attorney.* Sen. Doc. 157, 55th Cong., 1st sess. Washington, D.C.: Government Printing Office, 1897.

———. *Memorial of a Committee on Behalf of the Colored People of the Choctaw and Chickasaw Tribes of Indians.* Sen. Misc. Doc. 106, 41st Cong., 2nd sess. Washington, D.C.: Government Printing Office, 1870.

———. *Papers Relating to the Rights of Freedmen under the Third Article of the Treaty with the Choctaw and Chickasaw Nations of Indians, Concluded April 28, 1866.* Sen. Exec. Doc. 82, 40th Cong., 2nd sess. Washington, D.C.: Government Printing Office, 1868.

———. *Report from the Committee on Territories.* Sen. Rpt. 744, 45th Cong., 3rd sess. Washington, D.C.: Government Printing Office, 1879.

———. *Report of the Commission to the Five Civilized Tribes.* Sen. Misc. Doc. 24, 53rd Cong., 3rd sess. Washington, D.C.: Government Printing Office, 1894.

———. *Report of the Committee on Indian Affairs.* Sen. Rpt. 1278, Pt. 1, 49th Cong., 1st sess. Washington, D.C.: Government Printing Office, 1886.

———. *Report of the Select Committee to Investigate Matters Connected with Affairs in the Indian Territory.* Sen. Rpt. 5013, Pt. 1, 59th Cong., 2nd sess. Washington, D.C.: Government Printing Office, 1907.

———. *Status and Rights of Choctaw and Chickasaw Freedmen.* Sen. Doc. 84, 55th Cong., 2nd sess. Washington, D.C.: Government Printing Office, 1898.

PUBLISHED PRIMARY SOURCES

Acts and Resolutions of the General Council of the Choctaw Nation, at the Called Sessions Thereof, Held in April and June 1858, and the Regular Session Held in October, 1858. Fort Smith, Ark.: J. Dotson, 1859; reprint, Wilmington, Del.: Scholarly Resources, Inc., 1975.

Alden, Joseph Warren. *Emancipation and Emigration: A Plan to Transfer the Freedmen of the South to the Government Lands of the West.* Principia Club Papers, no. 9. Boston: The Principia Club, 1878.

American Board of Commissioners for Foreign Missions. *Report of the American Board of Commissioners for Foreign Missions, Presented at the Thirty-Ninth Annual Meeting, Held in Boston, Massachusetts, Sept. 12–15, 1848.* Boston: T. R. Marvin, 1848.

American Colonization Society. *Thirty-Sixth Annual Report of the American Colonization Society: With the Proceedings of the Board of Directors and of the Society, and the Addresses Delivered at the Annual Meeting, January 18, 1853.* Washington, D.C.: C. Alexander, Printer, 1853.

———. *Thirty-Seventh Annual Report of the American Colonization Society: With the Proceedings of the Board of Directors and of the Society, and the Addresses Delivered at the Annual Meeting, January 17, 1854.* Washington, D.C.: C. Alexander, Printer, 1854.

———. *Fortieth Annual Report of the American Colonization Society: With the Proceedings of the Board of Directors and of the Society, January 20, 1857.* Washington, D.C.: C. Alexander, Printer, 1857.

Baker, T. Lindsay, and Julie P. Baker, eds. *The WPA Oklahoma Slave Narratives.* Norman: University of Oklahoma Press, 1996.

Benson, Henry Clark. *Life among the Choctaw Indians, and Sketches of the South-West.* Cincinnati: R. P. Thompson, Printer, 1860; reprint, New York: Johnson Reprint Corporation, 1970.

Bibb, Henry. *Narrative of the Life and Adventures of Henry Bibb, an American Slave, Written by Himself.* New York: self-published, 1849. Available online at the University of North Carolina–Chapel Hill, Documenting the American South, http://docsouth.unc.edu/neh/bibb/bibb.html.

Byington, Cyrus. *A Dictionary of the Choctaw Language.* Edited by John R. Swanton and Henry S. Halbert. Washington, D.C.: Government Printing Office, 1915.

Carter, Clarence Edwin, ed. *The Territory of Mississippi, 1809–1817.* Vol. 6 of *The Territorial Papers of the United States.* Washington, D.C.: Government Printing Office, 1938.

Constitution, Laws, and Treaties of the Chickasaws. Tishomingo City: E. J. Foster, 1860; reprint, Wilmington, Del.: Scholarly Resources, Inc., 1975.

The Constitution and Laws of the Choctaw Nation. Park Hill, Cherokee Nation: John Candy, Printer, 1840; reprint, Wilmington, Del.: Scholarly Resources, Inc., 1975.

The Constitution and Laws of the Choctaw Nation. Park Hill, Cherokee Nation: Mission Press, 1847; reprint, Wilmington, Del.: Scholarly Resources, Inc., 1975.

The Constitution and Laws of the Choctaw Nation. Doaksville, 1852; reprint, Wilmington, Del.: Scholarly Resources, Inc., 1975.

Crawford, W. D. "Oklahoma and the Indian Territory." *New England Magazine* 8 (June 1890): 454–57.

Davies, K. G., comp. *Documents of the American Revolution, 1770–1783*. Shannon, Ireland: Irish Universities Press, 1972.

Dawes, Henry L. "Have We Failed with the Indians?" *Atlantic Monthly* 84 (August 1899): 280–85.

Deloria, Vine, and Raymond J. DeMallie, comps. *Documents of American Indian Diplomacy: Treaties, Agreements, and Conventions, 1775–1979*, vol. 1. Norman: University of Oklahoma Press, 1999.

De Tonti, Henri. "Henri de Tonti to M. d'Iberville, 23 February 1702." In "Henri de Tonti du village des Chacta, 1702: The Beginning of the French Alliance," translated and transcribed by Patricia K. Galloway. In *La Salle and His Legacy: Frenchmen and Indians in the Lower Mississippi Valley*, edited by Patricia K. Galloway, 166–73. Jackson: University Press of Mississippi, 1982.

Dilliard, Irving, comp. "Dred Scott Eulogized by James Milton Turner: A Historical Observance of the Turner Centenary, 1840–1940." *Journal of Negro History* 25 (January 1941): 1–11.

Durant, A. R., comp. *Constitution and Laws of the Choctaw Nation: Together with the Treaties of 1837, 1855, 1865, and 1866*. (Dallas: John F. Worley, Printer and Publishers, 1894).

Foreman, Grant, ed. "Colbert Letters." *Arrow Points: Monthly Bulletin of the Alabama Anthropological Society* 16 (1930): 67–72.

Grant, Ulysses S. *1866*. Vol. 16 of *Ulysses S. Grant Papers*, edited by John Y. Simon. Carbondale: Southern Illinois University Press, 1988.

Hitchcock, Ethan Allen. *A Traveler in Indian Territory: The Journal of Ethan Allen Hitchcock, Late Major-General in the United States Army*. Edited by Grant Foreman. Cedar Rapids, Iowa: Torch Press, 1930.

The Home and Foreign Record of the Presbyterian Church in the United States of America. Philadelphia: Presbyterian Board of Publication, vol. 7, April 1856.

Hoole, William Stanley, ed. "A Southerner's Viewpoint of the Kansas Situation, 1856–1857: The Letters of Lieut. Col. A. J. Hoole, C.S.A." *Kansas Historical Quarterly* 3 (February 1934): 43–56.

Jacobs, Harriet. *Incidents in the Life of a Slave Girl, Written by Herself*. Edited by Jean Fagan Yellin. Boston, 1861; reprint, Cambridge, Mass.: Harvard University Pres, 2000.

Jefferson, Thomas. *Notes on the State of Virginia*. Edited by William Peden. Chapel Hill: Published for the Institute of Early American History and Culture at Williamsburg, Virginia, by the University of North Carolina Press, 1954; 1982.

Kappler, Charles, comp. *Treaties*. Vol. 2 of *Indian Affairs: Laws and Treaties*. Washington, D.C.: Government Printing Office 1904. Available online through Oklahoma State University Library, http://digital.library.okstate.edu/Kappler/.

Kingsbury, Cyrus. "Diary of Rev. Cyrus Kingsbury." Edited by W. B. Morrison. *Chronicles of Oklahoma* 3 (June 1925): 152–57.

Lowrie, Walter, ed. *American State Papers, Class VIII, Public Lands*, vol. 7. Washington, D.C.: Gales and Seaton, 1860.

Lowrie, Walter, and Walter S. Franklin. *American State Papers: Class 2, Indian Affairs*. Washington, D.C.: Gales and Seaton, 1834.

Matthews, James M., ed. *The Statutes at Large of the Provisional Government of the Confederate States of America, from the Institution of the Government, February 8, 1861, to its Termination, February 18, 1862, Inclusive. Arranged in Chronological Order Together with the Constitution for the Provisional Government, and the Permanent Constitution of the Confederate States, and the Treaties Concluded by the Confederate States with Indian Tribes*. Richmond, Va.: R. M. Smith, 1864.

McAdam, R. W. "An Indian Commonwealth." *Harper's New Monthly Magazine* 87 (1893): 884.

McClinton, Rowena, ed. *The Moravian Springplace Mission to the Cherokees*, vol. 1, *1805–1813*. Lincoln: University of Nebraska Press, 2007.

McKenney, Thomas. *Memoirs, Official and Personal*. Reprint of vol. 1 of the 1846 edition. Lincoln: University of Nebraska Press, 1973.

Miller, Nyle H., ed. "Surveying the Southern Boundary Line of Kansas: From the Private Journal of Colonel Joseph E. Johnston." *Kansas Historical Quarterly* 1 (February 1932): 104–39.

Miller, Randall M., ed. *"Dear Master": Letters of a Slave Family*. Ithaca, N.Y.: Cornell University Press, 1978.

Moore, Alexander, ed. *Nairne's Muskhogean Journals: The 1708 Expedition to the Mississippi River*. Jackson: University Press of Mississippi, 1988.

Morrison, James D., ed. "Notes from the *Northern Standard*, 1842–1849, Part 1." *Chronicles of Oklahoma* 19 (March 1941): 82–98.

————. "Notes from the *Northern Standard*, 1842–1849, Part 2." *Chronicles of Oklahoma* 19, (September 1941): 269–83.

Morrison, W. B., ed. "Colbert Ferry on Red River, Chickasaw Nation, Indian Territory: Recollections of John Malcolm, Pioneer Ferryman." *Chronicles of Oklahoma* 16 (September 1938): 302–14.

Moseley, John W., ed. *Record of Missionary Meetings Held in the Chahta and Chikasha Nations and the Records of the Tombigbee Presbytery from 1825 to 1838*. West Point Leader Printery [between 1838 and 1864].

Norris, John. "Profitable Advice for Rich and Poor." London, 1712. In *Selling a New World: The Colonial South Carolina Promotional Pamphlets*, by Jack P. Greene, 128–32. Columbia: University of South Carolina Press, 1989.

Olmsted, Frederick Law. *A Journey in the Back Country*. New York: Mason Brothers, 1860; New York: Schocken Books, 1970.

Parsons, John E., ed. "Letters on the Chickasaw Removal of 1837." *New York Historical Society Quarterly* 37 (1953): 273–83.

Phelps, Dawson A., ed. "Excerpts from the Journal of the Reverend Joseph Bullen, 1799 and 1800." *Journal of Mississippi History* 17 (October 1955): 254–81.

Rawick, George. *Oklahoma Narratives*. Vol. 12 of *The American Slave: A Composite Autobiography*. Westport, Conn.: Greenwood Press, 1977.

Rowland, Dunbar, and A. G. Sanders, comps., trans., eds. *Mississippi Provincial Archives: French Dominion*, vols. 1 and 3. Jackson: Press of the Mississippi Department of Archives and History, 1927–32; New York: AMS Press, 1973.

Short, Peyton. "Tour to Mobile, Pensacola &c. by Peyton Short of Kentucky." *Quarterly Publication of the Historical and Philosophical Society of Ohio* 5 (January-March 1910): 4–15.

Storm, Colton, ed. "Up the Tennessee in 1790: The Report of Major John Doughty to the Secretary of War." *East Tennessee Historical Society: Publications* 17 (1945): 119–32.

Washington, Booker T. "Boley, a Negro Town in the West." In *The Booker T. Washington Papers*, vol. 9, edited by Louis R. Harlan and Raymond Smock, 430–35. Urbana: University of Illinois Press, 1980.

Whipple, Charles K. *Relation of the American Board of Commissioners to Foreign Missions to Slavery*. Boston: R. F. Wallcut, 1861.

Windley, Lathan, comp. *South Carolina*. Vol. 3 of *Runaway Slave Advertisements*. Westport, Conn.: Greenwood Press, 1983.

Young, Jacob. *Autobiography of a Pioneer; or, The Nativity, Experience, Travels, and Ministerial Labors of Reverend Jacob Young.* Cincinnati: Poe & Hitchcock, 1860.

Secondary Sources

ARTICLES AND ESSAYS

Akers, Donna L. "Removing the Heart of the Choctaw People: Removal from a Native Perspective." In *Medicine Ways: Disease, Health, and Survival among Native Americans,* edited by Clifford Trafzer and Diane Weiner, 1–15. Walnut Creek, Calif.: AltaMira Press (Rowan Littlefield Publishers), 2001.

Albers, Patricia. "Labor and Exchange in American Indian History." In *A Companion to American Indian History,* edited by Philip J. Deloria and Neal Salisbury, 269–86. Malden, Mass.: Blackwell Publishers, 2002.

Barone, John A. "Historical Presence and Distribution of Prairies in the Black Belt of Mississippi and Alabama." *Castanea* 70 (September 2005): 170–83.

Bieder, Robert E. "Scientific Attitudes toward Indian Mixed-Bloods in Early Nineteenth-Century America." *Journal of Ethnic Studies* 8 (Summer 1980): 17–30.

Billington, Monroe Lee. "Buffalo Soldiers in the American West, 1865–1900." In *African Americans on the Western Frontier,* edited by Monroe Lee Billington and Roger D. Hardaway, 54–72. Niwot: University Press of Colorado, 1998.

Biolsi, Thomas. "The Birth of the Reservation: Making the Modern Individual among the Lakota." In *American Nations: Encounters in Indian Country, 1850 to the Present,* edited by Frederick E. Hoxie, Peter C. Mancall, and James H. Merrell, 110–39. New York: Routledge, 2001.

Blassingame, John. "Using the Testimony of Ex-Slaves: Approaches and Problems." *Journal of Southern History* 41 (November 1975): 473–92.

Braund, Kathryn Holland. "Guardians of Tradition and Handmaidens to Change: Women's Roles in Creek Economic and Social Life during the Eighteenth Century." *American Indian Quarterly* 14 (Summer 1990): 239–58.

Burnham, Margaret A. "An Impossible Marriage: Slave Law and Family Law." *Law and Inequality* 5 (1987): 187–225.

Carson, James Taylor. "From Corn Mothers to Cotton Spinners: Continuity in Choctaw Women's Economic Life, A.D. 950–1830." In *Women of the American South: A Multicultural Reader,* edited by Christie Farnham, 8–25. New York: New York University Press, 1997.

Chapman, Berlin. "Removal of the Osages from Kansas," part 1. *Kansas Historical Quarterly* 7 (August 1938): 287–305.

Cullen, Jim. "'I's a Man Now': Gender and African American Men." In *A Question of Manhood: A Reader in U.S. Black Men's History and Masculinity,* vol. 1, "Manhood Rights": The Construction of Black Male History and Manhood, 1750–1870, edited by Darlene Clark Hine and Earnestine Jenkins, 489–501. Bloomington: Indiana University Press, 1999.

Dann, Martin. "From Sodom to the Promised Land: E. P. McCabe and the Movement for Oklahoma Colonization." *Kansas Historical Quarterly* 40 (Autumn 1974): 370–78.

DeRossier, Arthur H., Jr. "Pioneers with Conflicting Ideals: Christianity and Slavery in the Choctaw Nation." *Journal of Mississippi History* 21 (July 1959): 174–89.

Dilliard, Irving. "James Milton Turner: A Little-Known Benefactor of His People." *Journal of Negro History* 19 (October 1934): 372–411.

Dominguez, Virginia R. "Exporting U.S. Concepts of Race: Are There Limits to the U.S. Model?" *Social Research* 65 (Summer 1998): 369–97.

Doran, Michael F. "Negro Slaves of the Five Civilized Tribes." *Annals of the Association of American Geographers* 68 (September 1978): 335–50.

———. "Population Statistics of Nineteenth-Century Indian Territory." *Chronicles of Oklahoma* 53 (Winter 1975–76): 492–515.

Dykstra, Robert R., and Harlan Hahn. "Northern Voters and Negro Suffrage: The Case of Iowa, 1868." *Public Opinion Quarterly* 32 (Summer 1968): 202–15.

Etheridge, Robbie. "The Making of a Militaristic Slaving Society: The Chickasaws and the Colonial Indian Slave Trade." In *Indian Slavery in Colonial America*, edited by Alan Gallay, 251–76. Lincoln: University of Nebraska Press, 2009.

Fields, Barbara J. "Ideology and Race in American History." In *Region, Race, and Reconstruction*, edited by J. Morgan Kousser and James M. McPherson, 143–77. New York: Oxford University Press, 1982.

Fite, Gilbert. "Development of Cotton Industry by the Five Civilized Tribes in Indian Territory." *Journal of Southern History* 15 (August 1949): 342–53.

Foner, Eric. "The Meaning of Freedom in the Age of Emancipation." *Journal of American History* 81 (September 1994): 435–60.

Galloway, Patricia K. "The Chief Who Is Your Father." In *Powhatan's Mantle: Indians in the Colonial Southeast*, edited by Gregory A. Waselkov, Peter H. Wood, and Tom Hatley, 345–70. Lincoln: University of Nebraska Press, 1989; 2006.

Grinde, Donald A., and Quintard Taylro. "Red vs. Black: Conflict and Accommodation in the Post–Civil War Indian Territory, 1865–1907." *American Indian Quarterly* 8 (Summer 1984): 211–27.

Guyatt, Nicholas. " 'The Outskirts of Our Happiness': Race and the Lure of Colonization in the Early Republic." *Journal of American History* 95 (March 2009): 986–1011.

Halbert, Henry S. "The Last Indian Council on Noxubee River." *Publications of the Mississippi Historical Society* 4 (1901): 271–80.

———. "Story of the Treaty of Dancing Rabbit Creek." *Publications of the Mississippi Historical Society* 6 (1902): 373–402.

Halliburton, R., Jr. "Chief Greenwood Leflore and His Malmaison Plantation." In *After Removal: The Choctaw in Mississippi*, edited by Samuel J. Wells and Roseanna Tubby, 56–63. Jackson: University Press of Mississippi, 1986.

Harmon, Alexandra. "American Indians and Land Monopolies in the Gilded Age." *Journal of American History* 90 (June 2003): 106–33.

Harris, Cheryl I. "Whiteness as Property." *Harvard Law Review* 106 (June 1993): 1710–88.

Hodes, Martha. "The Mercurial Nature and Abiding Power of Race: A Transnational Family Story." *American Historical Review* 108 (February 2003): 84–118.

Horsman, Reginald. "The Indian Policy of an 'Empire for Liberty.' " In *Native Americans and the Early Republic*, edited by Frederick E. Hoxie, Ronald Hoffman, and Peter J. Albert, 37–61. Charlottesville: University of Virginia Press, 1999.

James, Winston. "The Wings of Ethiopia: The Caribbean Diaspora and Pan-African Projects from John Brown Russwurm to George Padmore." In *African Diasporas in the New and Old Worlds: Consciousness and Imagination*, edited by Klaus Benesch and Geneviève Fabre, 121–60. Cross/Cultures: Readings in the Post/Colonial Literatures in English Series, vol. 69. Amsterdam, New York: Rodopi, 2004.

Jeltz, Wyatt F. "The Relations of Negroes and Choctaw and Chickasaw Indians." *Journal of Negro History* 33 (January 1948): 24–37.

Johnston, James Hugo. "Documentary Evidence of the Relations of Negroes and Indians." *Journal of Negro History* 14 (January 1929): 21–43.

Kaczorowski, Robert J. "To Begin the Nation Anew: Congress, Citizenship, and Civil Rights after the Civil War." *American Historical Review* 92 (February 1987): 45–68.

Kidwell, Clara Sue. "The Choctaw Struggle for Land and Identity in Mississippi, 1830–1918." In *After Removal: The Choctaw in Mississippi*, edited by Samuel J. Wells and Roseanna Tubby, 64–93. Jackson: University Press of Mississippi, 1986.

King, F. R. "George Colbert—Chief of the Chickasaw Nation." *Arrow Points* 7 (October 1923): 53–57.

Krauthamer, Barbara. "A Particular Kind of Freedom: Black Women, Kinship, Slavery, and Freedom in the American Southeast." In *Women and Slavery*, vol. 2, *The Modern Atlantic*, edited by Gwyn Campbell, Suzanne Miers, and Joseph C. Miller, 100–127. Athens: Ohio University Press, 2008.

Lincecum, Gideon. "Life of Apushimataha." *Publications of the Mississippi Historical Society* 9 (1906): 415–85.

Littlefield, Daniel F., Jr. "Juneteenth and August Fourth Celebrations: Political Rally Days in Indian Territory." Unpublished paper, 2006.

———. "The Treaties of 1866: Reconstruction of Re-Destruction?" In *Proceedings: War and Reconstruction in Indian Territory*. Fort Smith, Ark.: Fort Smith National Historic Park, 1996.

Littlefield, Daniel F., Jr., and Lonnie E. Underhill. "Slave 'Revolt' in the Cherokee Nation, 1842." *American Indian Quarterly* 3 (Summer 1977): 121–31.

Littlefield, Daniel F., Jr., and Mary Ann Littlefield. "The Beams Family: Free Blacks in Indian Territory." *Journal of Negro History* 61 (January 1976): 16–35.

Love, William A. "Mingo Moshulitubbee's Prairie Village." *Publications of the Mississippi Historical Society* 7 (1903): 373–78.

Lovett, Laura. "'African and Cherokee by Choice': Race and Resistance under Legalized Segregation." In *Confounding the Color Line: The Indian-Black Experience in North America*, edited by James F. Brooks, 192–222. Lincoln: University of Nebraska Press, 2002.

Mack, Kenneth W. "Law, Society, Identity, and the Making of the Jim Crow South: Travel and Segregation on Tennessee Railroads, 1875–1905." *Law and Social Inquiry* 24 (Spring 1999): 377–409.

McLoughlin, William G. "The Choctaw Slave Burning: A Crisis in Mission Work among the Indians." *Journal of the West* 13 (January 1974): 113–27.

———. "'The First Man Was Red': Cherokee Responses to the Debate over Indian Origins, 1760–1860." *American Quarterly* 41 (June 1989): 243–64.

———. "A Note on African Sources of American Indian Racial Myths." *Journal of American Folklore* 89 (July-September 1976): 331–35.

Merrell, James H. "The Racial Education of the Catawba Indians." *Journal of Southern History* 50 (August 1984): 363–84.

Meserve, John Bartlett. "Chief Allen Wright." *Chronicles of Oklahoma* 19 (December 1941): 314–21.

Metcalf, Warren R. "Lambs of Sacrifice: Termination, the Mixed-Blood Utes, and the Problem of Indian Identity." *Utah Historical Quarterly* 64 (Fall 1996): 322–343.

Miles, Tiya, and Barbara Krauthamer. "Africans and Native Americans." In *The Blackwell Companion to African American History*, edited by Alton Hornsby, 121–40. Malden, Mass.: Blackwell Publishing, 2005.

Morrison, James D. "News for the Choctaws." *Chronicles of Oklahoma* 27 (1949): 207–22.

———. "Note on Abolitionism in the Choctaw Nation." *Chronicles of Oklahoma* 38 (1960): 76–84.

Perdue, Theda. "Native Women in the Early Republic: Old World Perceptions, New World Realities." In *Native Americans and the Early Republic*, edited by Frederick E. Hoxie,

Ronald Hoffman, and Peter J. Albert, 85–122. Charlottesville: University of Virginia Press, 1999.

———. "Race and Culture: Writing the Ethnohistory of the Early South." *Ethnohistory* 51 (Fall 2004): 701–23.

Porter, Kenneth Wiggins. "Notes Supplementary to 'Relations between Negroes and Indians.'" *Journal of Negro History* 18 (July 1933): 282–321.

———. "Relations between Negroes and Indians within the Present Limits of the United States." *Journal of Negro History* 17 (July 1932): 287–367.

Powers, E. W. "Notes on Doaksville, Choctaw Nation." *Chronicles of Oklahoma* 53 (1955): 541–47.

Ronda, James P. "'We Have a Country': Race, Geography, and the Invention of Indian Territory." *Journal of the Early Republic* (Winter 1999): 739–55.

Saunt, Claudio. "The Paradox of Freedom: Tribal Sovereignty and Emancipation during the Reconstruction of Indian Territory." *Journal of Southern History* 60 (January 2004): 63–94.

Saunt, Claudio, Barbara Krauthamer, Tiya Miles, Celia E. Naylor, and Circe Sturm. "Rethinking Race and Culture in the Early South." *Ethnohistory* 53 (Spring 2006): 399–405.

Shaw, Stephanie J. "Using the WPA Ex-Slave Narratives to Study the Impact of the Great Depression." *Journal of Southern History* 69 (August 2003): 623–58.

Shoemaker, Nancy. "How Indians Got to Be Red." *American Historical Review* 102 (June 1997): 625–44.

Soltow, Lee. "Economic Inequality in the United States in the Period from 1790 to 1860." *Journal of Economic History* 31 (December 1971): 822–39.

Strickland, Rennard. "The Genocidal Premise in Native American Law and Policy: Exorcising Aboriginal Ghosts." *Journal of Gender, Race, and Justice* 1 (Spring 1998): 325–33.

Strong, Pauline Turner. "Transforming Outsiders: Captivity, Adoption, and Slavery Reconsidered." In *A Companion to American Indian History*, edited by Philip J. Deloria and Neal Salisbury, 339–56. Malden, Mass.: Blackwell Publishers, 2002.

Strong, Pauline Turner, and Barrik Van Winkle. "'Indian Blood': Reflections on the Reckoning and Refiguring of Native North American Identity." *Cultural Anthropology* 11 (1996): 547–76.

———. "Tribe and Nation: American Indians and American Nationalism." *Social Analysis* 33 (September 1993): 9–26.

Van Hoak, Stephen P. "Untangling the Roots of Dependency: Choctaw Economics, 1700–1860." *American Indian Quarterly* 23 (Summer-Autumn 1999): 113–28.

Vorenberg, Michael. "Abraham Lincoln's 'Fellow Citizens'—Before and after Emancipation." In *Lincoln's Proclamation: Emancipation Reconsidered*, edited by William A. Blair and Karen Fisher Younger, 151–69. Chapel Hill: University of North Carolina Press, 2009.

Warren, Henry. "Some Chickasaw Chiefs and Prominent Men." *Publications of the Mississippi Historical Society* 8 (1904): 555–70.

White, William W. "The Texas Slave Insurrection of 1860." *Southwestern Historical Quarterly* 52 (January 1949): 259–85.

Willis, William S. "Divide and Rule: Red, White, and Black in the Southeast." *Journal of Negro History* 48 (July 1963): 157–76.

Wilson, Terry P. "Blood Quantum: Native American Mixed Bloods." In *Racially Mixed People in America*, edited by Maria P. P. Root, 108–25. Newbury Park, Calif.: Sage Publications, 1992.

Wood, Peter. "Slave Labor Camps in Early America: Overcoming Denial and Discovering the Gulag." In *Inequality in Early America*, edited by Carla Gardina Pestana and Sharon V. Salinger, 222–38. Hanover, N.H.: University Press of New England, 1999.

Woodson, Carter G. "The Relations of Negroes and Indians in Massachusetts." *Journal of Negro History* 5 (January 1920): 45–57.

Wright, Muriel H. "Early Navigation and Commerce along the Arkansas and Red Rivers in Oklahoma." *Chronicles of Oklahoma* 8 (March 1930): 65–88.

———. "John Hobart Heald." *Chronicles of Oklahoma* 2 (September 1924): 311–18.

———. "Organization of Counties in the Choctaw and Chickasaw Nations." *Chronicles of Oklahoma* 8 (September 1930): 315–44.

BOOKS

Abel, Annie Heloise. *The American Indian and the End of the Confederacy, 1863–1866.* Cleveland: A. H. Clark Co., 1925; reprint, Lincoln: University of Nebraska Press, 1993.

———. *The American Indian as Slaveholder and Secessionist.* Cleveland: A. H. Clark Company, 1915; reprint, Lincoln: University of Nebraska Press, 1992.

———. *The American Indian in the Civil War, 1862–1865.* Cleveland: A. H. Clark Co., 1919; reprint, Lincoln: University of Nebraska Press, 1992.

Akers, Donna. *Living in the Land of Death: The Choctaw Nation, 1830–1860.* East Lansing: Michigan State University Press, 2004.

Armstrong, William H. *Warrior in Two Camps: Ely S. Parker, Union General and Seneca Chief.* Syracuse, N.Y.: Syracuse University Press, 1978.

Atkinson, James. *Splendid Land, Splendid People: The Chickasaw Indians to Removal.* Tuscaloosa: University of Alabama Press, 2004.

Ayers, Edward L. *The Promise of the New South: Life after Reconstruction.* New York: Oxford University Press, 1992.

Bailey, Minnie Thomas. *Reconstruction in Indian Territory: A Story of Avarice, Discrimination, and Opportunism.* Port Washington, N.Y.: Kennikat Press, 1972.

Baird, W. David. *Peter Pitchlynn: Chief of the Choctaws.* Norman: University of Oklahoma Press, 1972.

Banner, Stuart. *How the Indians Lost Their Land: Law and Power on the Frontier.* Cambridge, Mass.: Harvard University Press, 2005.

Basson, Lauren L. *White Enough to Be American? Race Mixing, Indigenous People, and the Boundaries of State and Nation.* Chapel Hill: University of North Carolina Press, 2008.

Bay, Mia. *The White Image in the Black Mind: African American Ideas about White People, 1830–1925.* New York: Oxford University Press, 2000.

Berkhofer, Robert F., Jr. *The White Man's Indian: Images of the American Indian from Columbus to the Present.* New York: Knopf, 1978.

Berlin, Ira. *Generations of Captivity: A History of African American Slaves.* Cambridge, Mass.: Harvard University Press, 2003.

Berry, Mary Frances. *Black Resistance, White Law: A History of Constitutional Racism in America.* New York: Prentice-Hall, 1971; reprint, New York: Penguin Books, 1994.

Braund, Kathryn Holland. *Deerskins and Duffels: The Creek Indian Trade with Anglo-America, 1685–1815.* Lincoln: University of Nebraska Press, 1993.

Brooks, James F. *Captives and Cousins: Slavery, Kinship, and Community in the Southwest Borderlands.* Chapel Hill: University of North Carolina Press, 2002.

Brophy, Alfred L. *Reconstructing the Dreamland: The Tulsa Riot of 1921; Race Reparations, and Reconciliation.* New York: Oxford University Press, 2002.

Burke, Diane Mutti. *On Slavery's Border: Missouri's Small Slaveholding Households, 1815–1865.* Athens: University of Georgia Press, 2010.

Burrowes, Carl Patrick. *Power and Press Freedom in Liberia, 1830–1870: The Impact of Globalization and Civil Society on Media-Government Relations.* Trenton, N.J.: Africa World Press, 2004.

Burton, Jeffrey. *Indian Territory and the United States, 1866–1906: Courts, Government, and the Movement for Oklahoma Statehood*. Norman: University of Oklahoma Press, 1995.

Camp, Stephanie M. H. *Closer to Freedom: Enslaved Women and Everyday Resistance in the Plantation South*. Chapel Hill: University of North Carolina Press, 2004.

Campbell, Randolph B. *An Empire for Slavery: The Peculiar Institution in Texas, 1821–1865*. Baton Rouge: Louisiana State University Press, 1989.

Carroll, John M., ed. *The Black Military Experience in the American West*. New York: Liveright Publishing, 1973.

Carson, James Taylor. *Searching for the Bright Path: The Mississippi Choctaws from Prehistory to Removal*. Lincoln: University of Nebraska Press, 1999.

Chang, David A. *The Color of the Land: Race, Nation, and the Politics of Landownership in Oklahoma, 1832–1929*. Chapel Hill: University of North Carolina Press, 2010.

Cornelius, Janet Duitsman. *Slave Missions and the Black Church in the Antebellum South*. Columbia: University of South Carolina Press, 1999.

———. *"When I Can Read My Title Clear": Literacy, Slavery, and Religion in the Antebellum South*. Columbia: University of South Carolina Press, 1991.

Creel, Margaret Washington. *"A Peculiar People": Slave Religion and Community-Culture among the Gullahs*. New York: New York University Press, 1988.

Curtin, Philip D. *The Atlantic Slave Trade: A Census*. Madison: University of Wisconsin Press, 1969.

Cushman, Horatio Bardwell. *History of the Choctaw, Chickasaw, and Natchez Indians*. N.p., 1899; abridged edition by Angie Debo, 1962; Norman: University of Oklahoma Press, 1999.

Debo, Angie. *And Still the Waters Run: The Betrayal of the Five Civilized Tribes*. N.p., 1940; reprint, Norman: University of Oklahoma Press, 1984.

———. *The Rise and Fall of the Choctaw Republic*. The Civilization of the American Indian Series, vol. 6. 2nd edition. Norman: University of Oklahoma Press, 1961.

———. *The Road to Disappearance*. Norman: University of Oklahoma Press, 1941.

Deloria, Philip Joseph. *Indians in Unexpected Places*. Lawrence: University Press of Kansas, 2004.

Deloria, Vine. *Custer Died for Your Sins: An Indian Manifesto*. New York: Macmillan, 1969.

Du Bois, W. E. B. *The Souls of Black Folk*. Edited by Brent Hayes Edwards. N.p., 1903; reprint, New York: Oxford University Press, 2009.

Duthu, N. Bruce. *American Indians and the Law*. New York: Viking, 2008.

Ellison, Ralph. *Going to the Territory*. New York: Random House, 1986.

Feimster, Crystal Nicole. *Southern Horrors: Women and the Politics of Rape and Lynching*. Cambridge, Mass.: Harvard University Press, 2009.

Feldman, Jay. *When the Mississippi Ran Backwards: Empire, Intrigue, Murder, and the New Madrid Earthquakes*. New York: Free Press, 2005.

Fisher, Kirsten. *Suspect Relations: Sex, Race, and Resistance in Colonial North Carolina*. Ithaca, N.Y.: Cornell University Press, 2002.

Foner, Eric. *The Fiery Trial: Abraham Lincoln and American Slavery*. New York: W. W. Norton, 2010.

———. *Free Soil, Free Labor, Free Men: The Ideology of the Republican Party before the Civil War*. New York: Oxford University Press, 1970.

———. *Nothing but Freedom: Emancipation and Its Legacy*. Baton Rouge: Louisiana State University Press, 1983; 2007.

———. *Reconstruction: America's Unfinished Revolution, 1863–1877*. New York: Harper and Row, 1988.

Forbes, Jack D. *Africans and Native Americans: The Language of Race and the Evolution of Red-Black Peoples*. 2nd edition. Urbana: University of Illinois Press, 1993.

Foreman, Grant. *Indian Removal*. The Civilization of the American Indian Series, vol. 2. Norman: University of Oklahoma Press, 1932; reprint, 1972.

Forret, Jeff. *Race Relations at the Margins: Slaves and Poor Whites in the Antebellum Southern Countryside*. Baton Rouge: Louisiana State University Press, 2006.

Fowler, Arlen. *The Black Infantry in the West, 1869–1891*. Westport, Conn.: Greenwood Press, 1971.

Frederickson, George. *The Black Image in the White Mind: The Debate on Afro-American Character and Destiny, 1817–1914*. New York: Harper and Row, 1971.

Freehling, William. *The Secessionists at Bay*. Vol. 2 of *The Road to Disunion*. New York: Oxford University Press, 2007.

Gallay, Alan. *The Indian Slave Trade: The Rise of the English Empire in the American South, 1670–1717*. New Haven: Yale University Press, 2002.

Galloway, Patricia Kay. *Choctaw Genesis, 1500–1700*. Lincoln: University of Nebraska Press, 1998.

Gibson, Arrell Morgan. *The Chickasaws*. Norman: University of Oklahoma Press, 1971; 1978.

Gomez, Michael. *Exchanging Our Country Marks: The Transformation of African Identities in the Colonial and Antebellum South*. Chapel Hill: University of North Carolina Press, 1998.

Greenwald, Emily. *Reconfiguring the Reservation: The Nez Perces, Jicarilla Apaches, and the Dawes Act*. Albuquerque: University of New Mexico Press, 2002.

Gross, Ariela J. *What Blood Won't Tell: A History of Race on Trial in America*. Cambridge, Mass.: Harvard University Press, 2008.

Guterl, Matthew Pratt. *American Mediterranean: Southern Slaveholders in the Age of Emancipation*. Cambridge, Mass.: Harvard University Press, 2008.

Hadden, Sally E. *Slave Patrols: Law and Violence in Virginia and the Carolinas*. Cambridge, Mass.: Harvard University Press, 2001.

Hahn, Steven. *A Nation under Our Feet: Black Political Struggles in the Rural South, from Slavery to the Great Migration*. Cambridge, Mass.: Belknap Press of Harvard University Press, 2003.

Hall, Gwendolyn Midlo. *Africans in Colonial Louisiana: The Development of Afro-Creole Culture in the Eighteenth Century*. Baton Rouge: Louisiana State University Press, 1992.

Hargrove, Hondon B. *Black Union Soldiers in the Civil War*. Jefferson, N.C.: McFarland and Co., Inc., 1988.

Harmon, Alexandra. *Rich Indians: Native People and the Problem of Wealth in American History*. Chapel Hill: University of North Carolina Press, 2010.

Harrold, Stanley. *Border War: Fighting over Slavery before the Civil War*. Chapel Hill: University of North Carolina Press, 2010.

Hirsch, James S. *Riot and Remembrance: The Tulsa Race War and Its Legacy*. Boston: Houghton Mifflin, 2002.

Horsman, Reginald. *Race and Manifest Destiny: The Origins of American Racial Anglo-Saxonism*. Cambridge, Mass.: Harvard University Press, 1981.

Hoxie, Frederick E. *A Final Promise: The Campaign to Assimilate the Indians, 1880–1920*. Lincoln: University of Nebraska Press, 1984.

Ingersoll, Thomas. *To Intermix with Our White Brothers: Indian Mixed Bloods in the United States from Earliest Times to the Indian Removals*. Albuquerque: University of New Mexico Press, 2005.

Jacobson, Matthew Frye. *Whiteness of a Different Color*. Cambridge, Mass.: Harvard University Press, 1998.

Jones, Martha S. *All Bound Up Together: The Woman Question in African American Public Culture*. Chapel Hill: University of North Carolina Press, 2007.

Kachun, Mitch. *Festivals of Freedom: Memory and Meaning in African American Emancipation Celebrations, 1808–1915*. Amherst: University of Massachusetts Press, 2003.

Kantrowitz, Stephen. *Ben Tillman and the Reconstruction of White Supremacy*. Chapel Hill: University of North Carolina Press, 2000.

Kaye, Anthony E. *Joining Places: Slave Neighborhoods in the Old South*. Chapel Hill: University of North Carolina Press, 2007.

Kidwell, Clara Sue. *Choctaws and Missionaries in Mississippi, 1818–1918*. Norman: University of Oklahoma Press, 1995.

———. *The Choctaws in Oklahoma: From Tribe to Nation, 1855–1970*. Norman: University of Oklahoma Press, 2007.

King, Wilma. *Stolen Childhood: Slave Youth in the Nineteenth Century*. Bloomington: University of Indiana Press, 1995.

Klein, Laura, and Lillian Ackerman, eds. *Women and Power in Native North America*. Norman: University of Oklahoma Press, 1995.

Laurie, Bruce. *Beyond Garrison: Antislavery and Social Reform*. New York: Cambridge University Press, 2005.

Lawson, Gary, and Guy Seidman. *The Constitution of Empire: Territorial Expansion and American Legal History*. New Haven: Yale University Press, 2004.

Libby, David J. *Slavery in Frontier Mississippi, 1720–1835*. Jackson: University Press of Mississippi, 2004.

Littlefield, Daniel F. *The Chickasaw Freedmen: A People without a Country*. Westport, Conn.: Greenwood Press, 1980.

———. *Seminole Burning: A Story of Racial Vengeance*. Jackson: University Press of Mississippi, 1996.

Lubet, Steven. *Fugitive Justice: Runaways, Rescuers, and Slavery on Trial*. Cambridge, Mass.: Harvard University Press, 2010.

Martini, Don. *Chickasaw Empire: The Story of the Colbert Family*. Ripley, Miss.: n.p., 1986.

McCurry, Stephanie. *Masters of Small Worlds: Yeoman Households, Gender Relations, and the Political Culture of the Antebellum South Carolina Low Country*. New York: Oxford University Press, 1995.

McLaurin, Melton A. *Celia, a Slave*. Athens: University of Georgia Press, 1991.

McLoughlin, William. *The Cherokees and Christianity, 1794–1870: Essays on Acculturation and Cultural Persistence*. Athens: University of Georgia Press, 1994.

Meyer, Melissa L. *Thicker than Water: The Origins of Blood as Symbol and Ritual*. New York: Routledge, 2005.

Miles, Tiya. *The House on Diamond Hill: A Cherokee Plantation Story*. Chapel Hill: University of North Carolina Press, 2010.

———. *Ties That Bind: The Story of an Afro-Cherokee Family in Slavery and Freedom*. Berkeley and Los Angeles: University of California Press, 2005.

Minges, Patrick N. *Slavery in the Cherokee Nation: The Keetowah Society and the Defining of a People, 1855–1867*. New York: Routledge, 2003.

Montoya, Maria. *Translating Property: The Maxwell Land Grant and the Conflict over Land in the American West, 1840–1900*. Berkeley: University of California Press, 2002.

Morgan, Edmund. *American Slavery, American Freedom: The Ordeal of Colonial Virginia*. New York: Norton, 1995.

Morgan, Jennifer. *Laboring Women: Sex and Reproduction in New World Slavery*. Philadelphia: University of Pennsylvania Press, 2004.

Morgan, Philip D. *Slave Counterpoint: Black Culture in the Eighteenth-Century Chesapeake and Lowcountry*. Chapel Hill: University of North Carolina Press, 1998.

Mulroy, Kevin. *The Seminole Freedmen: A History*. Norman: University of Oklahoma Press, 2007.

Naylor, Celia E. *African Cherokees in Indian Territory: From Chattel to Citizens*. Chapel Hill: University of North Carolina Press, 2008.

Nobles, Melissa. *Shades of Citizenship: Race and the Census in Modern Politics*. Palo Alto, Calif.: Stanford University Press, 2000.

O'Brien, Greg. *Choctaws in a Revolutionary Age, 1750–1830*. Lincoln: University of Nebraska Press, 2002.

Paige, Amanda L., Fuller L. Bumpers, and Daniel F. Littlefield, Jr. *Chickasaw Removal*. Ada, Okla.: Chickasaw Press, 2010.

Penningroth, Dylan. *The Claims of Kinfolk: African American Property and Community in the Nineteenth-Century South*. Chapel Hill: University of North Carolina Press, 2003.

Perdue, Theda. *Cherokee Women: Gender and Culture Change*. Lincoln: University of Nebraska Press, 1998.

———. *"Mixed Blood" Indians: Racial Construction in the Early South*. Athens: University of Georgia Press, 2003.

———. *Sifters: Native American Women's Lives*. New York: Oxford University Press, 2001.

———. *Slavery and the Evolution of Cherokee Society, 1540–1866*. Knoxville: University of Tennessee Press, 1979.

Piker, Joshua. *Okfuskee: A Creek Indian Town in Colonial America*. Cambridge, Mass.: Harvard University Press, 2004.

Portnoy, Alisse. *Their Right to Speak: Women's Activism in the Indian and Slave Debates*. Cambridge, Mass.: Harvard University Press, 2005.

Prucha, Francis Paul. *American Indian Treaties: The History of a Political Anomaly*. Berkeley: University of California Press, 1994.

Raboteau, Albert. *Slave Religion: The Invisible Institution in the American South*. New York: Oxford University Press, 1978.

Reeves, Carolyn Keller, ed. *The Choctaw before Removal*. Jackson: University Press of Mississippi, 1985.

Rhodes, Jane. *Mary Ann Shadd Cary: The Black Press and Protest in the Nineteenth Century*. Bloomington: Indiana University Press, 1998.

Richardson, Heather Cox. *West from Appomattox: The Reconstruction of America after the Civil War*. New Haven, Conn.: Yale University Press, 2007.

Rothman, Adam. *Slave Country: American Expansion and the Origins of the Deep South*. Cambridge, Mass.: Harvard University Press, 2005.

St. Jean, Wendy. *Remaining Chickasaw in Indian Territory*. Tuscaloosa: University of Alabama Press, 2011.

Saunt, Claudio. *Black, White, and Indian: Race and the Unmaking of an American Family*. New York: Oxford University Press, 2005.

———. *A New Order of Things: Property, Power, and the Transformation of the Creek Indians, 1733–1816*. New York: Cambridge University Press, 1999.

Savage, W. Sherman. *Blacks in the West*. Westport: Greenwood Press, 1976.

Saville, Julie. *The Work of Reconstruction: From Slave to Wage Laborer in South Carolina, 1860–1870*. New York: Cambridge University Press, 1994.

Schechter, Patricia A. *Ida B. Wells-Barnett and American Reform, 1880–1930*. Chapel Hill: University of North Carolina Press, 2001

Schwalm, Leslie A. *Emancipation's Diaspora: Race and Reconstruction in the Upper Midwest*. Chapel Hill: University of North Carolina Press, 2009.

———. *A Hard Fight for We: Women's Transition from Slavery to Freedom in South Carolina.* Urbana: University of Illinois Press, 1997.

Schwartz, Marie Jenkins. *Birthing a Slave: Motherhood and Medicine in the Old South.* Cambridge, Mass.: Harvard University Press, 2006.

———. *Born in Bondage: Growing Up Enslaved in the Antebellum South.* Cambridge, Mass.: Harvard University Press, 2000.

Semmes, John Edward. *John H. B. Latrobe and His Times, 1803–1891.* Baltimore: The Norman, Remington Co., 1917.

Sheehan, Bernard W. *Seeds of Extinction: Jeffersonian Philanthropy and the American Indian.* Chapel Hill: University of North Carolina Press, 1973.

Shoemaker, Nancy. *A Strange Likeness: Becoming Red and White in Eighteenth-Century North America.* New York: Oxford University Press, 2004.

———, ed. *Negotiators of Change: Historical Perspectives of Native American Women.* New York: Routledge, 1995.

Sidbury, James. *Becoming African in America: Race and Nation in the Early Black Atlantic.* New York: Oxford University Press, 2007.

Sobel, Mechal. *Trabelin' On: The Slave Journey to an Afro-Baptist Faith.* Westport, Conn.: Greenwood Press, 1979.

Stanley, Amy Dru. *From Bondage to Contract: Wage Labor, Marriage, and the Market in the Age of Slave Emancipation.* New York: Cambridge University Press, 1998.

Stepan, Nancy Leys. *"The Hour of Eugenics": Race, Gender, and Nation in Latin America.* Ithaca, N.Y.: Cornell University Press, 1991.

Stuckey, Sterling. *Slave Culture: Nationalist Theory and the Foundations of Black America.* New York: Oxford University Press, 1987.

Sturm, Circe. *Blood Politics: Race, Culture, and Identity in the Cherokee Nation of Oklahoma.* Berkeley: University of California Press, 2002.

Sydnor, Charles S. *Slavery in Mississippi.* Baton Rouge: Louisiana State University Press, 1933; 1966.

Thoburn, Joseph B., and Muriel H. Wright. *Oklahoma: A History of the State and Its People.* New York: Lewis Publishing Co., 1928.

Usner, Daniel H. *Indians, Settlers, and Slaves in a Frontier Exchange Economy: The Lower Mississippi Valley before 1783.* Chapel Hill: Published for the Institute of Early American History and Culture, Williamsburg, Virginia, by the University of North Carolina Press, 1992.

Vorenberg, Michael. *Final Freedom: The Civil War, the Abolition of Slavery, and the Thirteenth Amendment.* New York: Cambridge University Press, 2001.

Washington, Margaret. *Sojourner Truth's America.* Urbana: University of Illinois Press, 2009.

Wells, Samuel J., and Roseanna Tubby, eds. *After Removal: The Choctaw in Mississippi.* Jackson: University Press of Mississippi, 1996.

White, Deborah Gray. *Ar'n't I a Woman? Female Slaves in the Plantation South.* 2nd edition. New York: Norton, 1999.

White, E. Frances. *Dark Continent of Our Bodies: Black Feminism and the Politics of Respectability.* Philadelphia: Temple University Press, 2001.

White, Richard. *The Roots of Dependency: Subsistence, Environment, and Social Change among the Choctaws, Pawnees, and Navajos.* Lincoln: University of Nebraska Press, 1983.

Wicket, Murray R. *Contested Territory: Whites, Native Americans, and African Americans in Oklahoma, 1865–1907.* Baton Rouge: Louisiana State University Press, 2000.

Wiethoff, William E. *The Insolent Slave.* Columbia: University of South Carolina Press, 2002.

Wilentz, Sean. *The Rise of American Democracy: Jefferson to Lincoln.* New York: W. W. Norton, 2005.

Wilkins, David E., and K. Tsianina Lomawaima. *Uneven Ground: American Indian Sovereignty and Federal Law*. Norman: University of Oklahoma Press, 2001.

Wilson, Joseph T. *The Black Phalanx: A History of the Negro Soldiers of the United States*. Hartford, Conn.: American Publishing Co., 1890; reprint, New York: Arno Press, 1968.

Wood, Peter. *Black Majority: Negroes in Colonial South Carolina from 1670 to the Stono Rebellion*. New York: W. W. Norton, 1974.

Wunder, John, ed., *Native American Sovereignty*. New York: Garland Publishing, 1996.

Yarbrough, Fay A. *Race and the Cherokee Nation: Sovereignty in the Nineteenth Century*. Philadelphia: University of Pennsylvania Press, 2008.

Dissertations

St. Jean, Wendy. "Trading Paths: Chickasaw Diplomacy in the Greater Southeast, 1690s–1790s." Ph.D. diss., University of Connecticut, 2004.

Spalding, Arminta Scott. "Cyrus Kingsbury: Missionary to the Choctaws." Ph.D. diss., University of Oklahoma, 1974.

Index

Page numbers in *italic* type indicate illustrations.

Biloxi, Miss., 18
Black, William, 72
Black churches, 54, 55
Black Codes, 108
Black people. *See* African Americans; Free blacks; Freedpeople; Slaves
"Bleeding Kansas," 9, 92
Blue, James, 40
Blue, King, 145, 146
Boggy Depot, 121
Boggy River, 80
Boudinot, Cornelius, 128
Brandon, Gerard, 38
Brashears (as free black surname), 72
Brashears, Richard, 124, 125
Britain, 65, 66; colonists from, 7, 18, 19, 20, 21, 24
Brown, Anderson, 121, 122
Brown, Charley, 128
Buffalo soldiers, 136
Bullen, Joseph, 25–26, 49, 57, 59
Bureau of Refugees, Freedmen and Abandoned Lands. *See* Freedmen's Bureau
Burnham, Margaret, 81
Burris, Adam, 150–52
Burris, Suckey, 150–52
Burton, Daniel, 128
Bushwackers, 98
Butler, B. F., 91
Butler, Lemon, 124, 128, 132
Butler, Squire, 121
Byington, Cyrus, 64, 88, 158 (n. 58)

Caddo convention (1879), 139–40
Calhoun, John C., 50
Camp, Stephanie, 60–61, 82, 85
Campbell, Jack, 44, 120
Canada, 65, 66; free blacks' flight to, 71, 75
Caney Creek mission school, 50
Caribbean. *See* West Indies
Carson, James Taylor, 7, 39
Catawba Nation, 156 (n. 17)
Cattle rustlers, 111
Census records, 29–40, 43, 72, 144, 147, 149, 154, 160–61 (n. 92), 161 (nn. 94, 106), 175 (n. 1)
Chang, David, 80, 150, 160 (n. 85), 172 (n. 84)
Charity Hall (Chickasaw mission school), 49
Charleston, S.C., 28, 54

Chattel slavery. *See* Slaveholding; Slaves
Cherokee Advocate, 133
Cherokee Nation, 106, 113, 115, 116, 128, 132; antiassimilation/antislavery society, 62; Civil War and, 98, 99, 104, 105; Dawes Commission and, 141–44; federal removal of, 8, 41; federal termination of sovereignty/ land titles of, 142–43; freedpeople's status and, 102, 113, 133; insurrection conspiracy and, 97; map of Indian Territory, 94; matrilineal descent and, 26; missionizing of, 48–49; slave emancipation by, 10, 101; slaveholding by, 40, 43; war captives of, 18–19
Chickasaw Freemen's Association, 145
Chickasawhay River, 6, 49
Chickasaw Old Fields, 156 (n. 9)
Choctaw and Chickasaw Nations: antialcohol codes of, 85; as autonomous nations, 10, 101, 133; black slaves' religious lives and, 47, 55–56; blood quanta classification and, 147; census records and, 39–40, 43, 72, 144, 154, 160–61 (n. 92), 161 (nn. 94, 106), 175 (n. 1); centralized self-government of, 6, 7; Chickasaw political autonomy and, 93; Chickasaw warrior reputation and, 18; Choctaw and Chickasaw differences and, 7, 9, 39, 92, 99, 140–41; Choctaw constitutions and, 34, 35, 93, 95, 96, 154, 171 (n. 76); Choctaw murder statutes and, 87; Choctaw political factionalism and, 93, 95–96; citizenship definition of, 71 (*see also* Citizenship); common elements of, 8; Confederacy alliance of, 10, 14, 98–99, 101, 104, 105, 107, 125, 133; consolidation of Choctaw chiefdoms and, 7; critiques of lifestyle of, 143; Dawes Act and, 141–42, 147; farming and, 3–4, 80, 126, 128–29; federal compulsory relocation of (*see* Indian removal); federal erosion of sovereignty of, 92, 101, 116; federal financial dispute with, 116–17; federal fraud allegations by, 131–32; federal push for lands of, 6, 48; federal termination of sovereignty and land titles of, 142–43; federal treaties and, 7, 39, 50, 93 (*see also* Treaty of 1866); Fort Smith treaty council (1865) and, 105–7, 109, 114, 117, 120, 134, 174–75 (n. 35); free blacks and, 70, 71, 72; freedpeople enumeration in,

149–50; freedpeople's right of return and, 113, 134–35; freedpeople's self-identification with, 12–13, 123–25, 134, 146, 150–52; freedpeople's status and citizenship rights with, 13, 15, 101–18, 119–38, 139–52, 154; Fugitive Slave Act (1850) and, 9–10, 14, 170 (n. 62); fugitive slaves and, 89–91, 97; gender role changes and, 33–34; hiring of white farmworkers by, 128, 143; hiring out of slaves by, 64; hunting and trading by, 3, 24, 26; intermarriage with white settlers of, 29, 30, 57, 130, 143, 161 (n. 94); as joint nation, 80; joint U.S. treaty with (*see* Treaty of 1866); land cessions by, 26, 50, 52, 48, 114, 116 (*see also* Indian lands); land communal ownership of, 6, 42, 114, 115, 127–28, 143; land-use privatization and, 80–81; language dictionary of, 158 (n. 58); legal code adoption by, 34–35; map of Choctaw Nation, *102*; map of Indian Territory holdings of, *94*; map of Mississippi territory of, *51*; matrilineal descent and, 26, 30–32, 130, 161 (n. 94); merger and separation of governments of (1830–55), 8–9, 39, 93; missionary relations with, 14, 34, 47–50, 52–58, 60–63, 65, 69, 87–88, 166 (n. 74); Mississippi/Alabama former lands of, 2, 3–7, 13, 18–38, 47, 50, *51*, 57; Net Proceeds claims (1830s) and, 116–17, 131, 132; New Madrid earthquakes and, 57–58, 163 (n. 27); property ownership by (*see* Property); proslavery stance of, 71; racial ideology and, 4–5, 12, 13, 17–18, 21, 32–35, 45, 71, 107–8, 120, 121, 126, 129, 130, 133, 134, 140, 141, 145, 147, 149; as separate entities, 101; slave codes of, 71, 83, 84, 93; slave emancipation and, 10, 11, 15, 126; slaveholding/personal wealth equation and, 17–18, 39–40, 42, 78; slave interpreters for, 57; slave labor adopted by, 1, 2, 3, 4, 6, 9, 10, 13, 17–45, 126; slave legal ownership and, 37–38; slave purchases by, 54; slave refugees from, 103–4, 108–9; slave resistance and, 14, 77–78, 82–88, 93, 96–97, 100; slavery's geographic expansion and, 92–93, 95; slave subordination and, 107–18; southern state laws and, 38; war captive treatment by, 18–19; wariness of white enterprises by, 129–30; wealth of, 17–18, 32, 39–40, 42, 78,

80, 128–29. *See also* Indian Territory
Choctaw constitution: of 1826, 34; of 1840, 35; of 1857, 93, 95, 171 (n. 76); of 1983, 154
Choctaw General Council, 71, 93, 95, 139, 140, 145
Choctaw Intelligencer, 83, 90
Choctaw Telegraph, 62
Cholera, 44, 75
Chollar, Martin, 121
Christianity, 26, 46, 53–54, 57, 61–62, 63, 73; slaveholding and, 52, 59. *See also* Missionaries; *specific denominations*
Citizenship, 12, 35, 119–38, 139–52; black vs. Indian distinction and, 147; Choctaw/Chickasaw definition of, 71; Choctaw/Chickasaw differences on, 140–41; in Choctaw/Chickasaw Nations, 119, 122, 123, 124, 133–34; Choctaw/Chickasaw racial views and, 1, 12, 35, 45, 120, 121, 126, 133, 134, 140; Choctaw/Chickasaw rights of, 119, 120; cultural affinity and, 124–25; federal land allotments and, 147; freedpeople's status and, 4, 10, 11, 12, 15, 101, 113–24, 128, 129, 131, 132–34, 137–38, 139, 140, 144–50, 154; by marrying Choctaw or Chickasaw woman, 130; as reparation for slavery, 137; treaties of 1866 differing terms of, 113, 115, 116–17, 144; in United States, 119, 122, 123, 124, 131, 148, 150; unresolved questions of, 119–20, 128
"Civilization" programs. *See* Assimilation policy
Civil War, 62, 70, 117; beginning of, 97–98; black refugees and, 103–4, 109, 114, 134–35; black Union loyalists and, 103–4, 125; buildup to, 9, 10, 78, 80, 91–93, 95, 96, 103; end of, 101, 104; Indian nations and, 10, 14, 98–99, 101, 104, 105, 107, 125. *See also* Confederacy
Clark, S. N., 135–36
Clay, Henry, 53
Cob, Henry, 121
Coffee, John, 38–39
Cohee, Charles, 121, 145
Colbert (as free black surname), 72
Colbert, Anna (slave), 37
Colbert, Benjamin Franklin, 1, 80
Colbert, Buck, 84
Colbert, Caesar (former slave), 148–49
Colbert, Chaney (slave), 44

113; Treaty of 1866 as confirmation of, 113.
    See also Freedpeople
Emancipation Proclamation (1863), 10, 104
Enlightenment, 25
Enslaved people. *See* Slaves
Equal rights, 114, 115, 150
Ervin, Jessie R., 1
Euro-Americans: Christian belief and, 46;
    Indian intermarriage with, 29–30, 161
    (n. 94); Indian relations with, 3, 6, 7, 18–25,
    30–32, 38; racial ideologies of, 4–5, 6, 53. *See
    also* White settlers; White superiority
Evangelical Protestantism, 47, 55–56, 59. *See
    also* Missionaries
Evarts, Jeremiah, 48, 158 (n. 49)
Ex-slaves. *See* Freedpeople

Farms and plantations, *41*, 48, 78–80, 143;
    Choctaw wealth and, 17–18, 39–42, 78,
    80, 128–29; commodity crops and, 4;
    freedpeople's labor and, 108, 110, 126,
    144; freedpeople's ownership of, 127–28,
    131; freedpeople's remaining on, 126, 132;
    growth of Deep South and, 8, 41; Indian
    collective landholding and, 115; Indian
    gender roles and, 4, 20, 25, 26, 33–34, 45,
    66, 159 (n. 70); Indian gradual shift to, 3–4,
    24, 25, 26, 27–28, 48, 115; sharecroppers and,
    69, 108, 110, 119, 126; slave labor and, 1–6,
    8–10, 13, 17–45, 78, 126; white hired workers
    and tenants, 128–29, 130–31, 143; white
    overseers and, 33. *See also* Corn crops;
    Cotton farming
Federal Writers' Project, 1, 58
Fields, Barbara, 12
Fields, Charles, 145–46
Fifteenth Amendment, 131
Filibusters, 98
Financial panic (1870s), 131
Finn, Daniel C., 131–32, 133, 177 (n. 50)
First and Second Kansas Colored Regiments,
    156, 177 (n. 63)
Fischer, Kirsten, 157 (n. 33)
Five Tribes. *See* Cherokee Nation; Choctaw
    and Chickasaw Nations; Creek Nation;
    Seminole Nation
Flint, Edmond, 58
Florida, 21, 28, 117
Folsom (as free black surname), 72

Folsom, David, 7, 30–31, 38–39, 78
Folsom, Edmond, 85
Folsom, Henry, 89
Folsom, Israel, 62, 82, 96
Folsom, Jacob, 97
Folsom, Loring, 32, 84, 87, 89, 111, 169
    (nn. 35, 42)
Folsom, Malvina Pitchlynn, 84, 126, 128, 130,
    169 (n. 37)
Folsom, Nathaniel, 30–31, 161 (n. 94)
Folsom, Sampson, 92–93, 98, 131
Folsom, Sophia, 31
Foner, Eric, 11
Fort Adams, 26
Fort Gibson, 90, 99, 111, 174 (n. 28)
Fort Leavenworth, 136
Fort Rosalie, 21
Fort St. Stephen, 27
Fort Smith, 98, 99, 103–4, 105, 112, 120, 122, 124
Fort Smith Treaty council (1865), 105–7, 109,
    114, 117, 120, 134, 174–75 (n. 35)
Fort Towson, 80
Forty-acres allotment, 1, 15, 112, 115, 140, 142,
    145
Fourteenth Amendment, 150
Franklin, Treaty of (1830), 39
Frederick Douglass's Paper (abolitionist
    periodical), 97
Free blacks (pre-emancipation), 97; African
    colonization movement and, 53, 73–76, 116;
    Choctaw/Cherokee repression/expulsion
    (1840) of, 70–71, 72, 73; in Choctaw/
    Chickasaw census, 40, 72; evangelical
    movements and, 55; Fugitive Slave Act
    threat to, 10, 71–75, 170 (n. 62); kidnapping
    of, 72–73; purchase of freedom of, 64,
    68–70, 75, 166 (n. 74); racial hierarchy
    and, 84; repayment of purchase price by,
    69–70; shared surnames with prominent
    Choctaws/Chickasaws, 72
Freedmen's Bureau, 104, 109, 110, 112, 135–36
Freedpeople (postemancipation), 101–18, 119–
    38, 139–52; annual freedom celebrations of,
    136–37; Atoka Agreement and, 142, 145–46;
    autonomy valuation by, 126–27; Choctaw/
    Chickasaw census (early 1900s) of, 175
    (n. 1); Choctaw/Chickasaw cultural ties of,
    12–13, 123–25, 134, 146, 150–52; Choctaw/
    Chickasaw residency permit required for,

Harrison, Simon, 76, 122
Harrold, Stanley, 100
Hayes, Rutherford B., 103
Historical memory, 153
Hitchcock, Ethan Allen, 30
Holy Spirit, 58, 60, 61
Homastubbee, Mingo, 27
Homestead Act (1862), 112
Honey Springs, Battle of (1863), 99
House Committee on Indian Affairs, U.S., 132
Howell, Cal, 127
Hunt, Major General, 109
Hunting and trapping, 3, 24, 25, 26, 27, 48, 50

Indian Affairs commissioner. *See* Office of
    Indian Affairs
Indian agents. *See* U.S. Indian agents
Indian lands, 3, 5–7; Choctaw/Chickasaw
    cessions of, 26, 39, 48, 50, 52, 114, 116,
    140; Choctaw/Chickasaw claims and
    annuity payments and, 102; Choctaw/
    Chickasaw leases to white tenants of, 128;
    Choctaw/Chickasaw original holdings,
    3, 5–6; communal ownership of, 6, 24,
    42, 114, 115, 127–28, 143; encroachment
    by Euro-American settlers on, 3, 24;
    federal allotment policies and (*see* Land
    allotments); federal appropriation of, 10,
    11, 15, 24, 25, 38–39, 48, 50, 62, 93, 101, 114;
    federal forced privatization of, 141, 148;
    freedpeople's claims to, 112, 114, 115, 119, 122,
    123, 127–28, 129, 134, 142, 143; Indian use of,
    24–25; shift to privatization of, 80–81
Indian nations. *See* Native American; *specific
    nations*
Indian removal, 7–14, 38–45, 50; Choctaw/
    Chickasaw census and, 39–40, 43;
    Choctaw/Chickasaw consequences of,
    8–13, 44–45; disease and privation and,
    44–45, 78, 150; independent parties and,
    43–44; Jackson's plan for, 38; from Kansas
    Territory, 9, 78; missionary denunciation
    of, 48, 73; Net Proceeds claims and, 116–17,
    131, 132; remaining Indians and, 41; slaves
    accompanying, 1, 8, 41–44, 150. *See also*
    Indian Territory; Land allotments
Indian Removal Act (1830), 38
Indian Territory: agricultural profit in, 78–80;
    black migrants to (late 1800s), 153–54;

borders of, 77; characterizations of, 153–54;
    Choctaw/Chickasaw boundary disputes
    and, 93; Civil War and, 98–99, 134–35;
    concerns about political future of, 91–92;
    congressional investigative visit to, 131–32;
    critiques of land use in, 143; Dawes Act
    and, 141–42; districts of, 78; Emancipation
    Proclamation and, 104; federal designs on,
    92, 101, 105–6, 116, 122, 131, 133, 137; federal
    dissolution of tribal governments in, 148–
    49, 150; federal power over, 112, 116; federal
    takeover of, 139, 140, 142–43, 148–50; free
    black emigrants to Liberia from, 74–76;
    freedpeople and (*see* Freedpeople); Fugitive
    Slave Act and, 9–10, 14, 91, 98, 170 (n. 62);
    Indian relocation to (Indian removal), 7–8,
    13–14, 38–39; Kansas-Nebraska Act and,
    9, 14, 78, 92; Leased District and, 114, 116;
    map of Choctaw and Chickasaw territories,
    94; missionaries and, 3, 14, 47–76, 146;
    narratives of black experience in, 1,
    153–54; as nonhomogenous, 102; Oklahoma
    statehood and, 105, 150, 153; post–Civil
    War violence and lawlessness in, 109–12;
    racial classification of, 147–50; railroads
    and, 114, 129–30; Reconstruction policies
    and, 10, 11, 12, 105, 116; runaway slaves from
    and into, 90–91, 97, 98; self-liberated slaves
    from, 103–4; slave population growth in,
    81–82, 168 (n. 11); slave resistance in, 14,
    77–78, 83, 96–97, 100; slavery's protracted
    demise in, 97–98, 104–5; slaves brought
    into, 8, 9–10, 13–14, 17–18, 30–31, 42–45,
    78–80; surrounding slave states of, 77,
    79; Thirteenth Amendment exemption
    of, 104–5; U.S. sectional crisis and, 9–10,
    92–93, 95; white influx into, 112, 123,
    128–31, 133, 134. *See also* Cherokee Nation;
    Choctaw and Chickasaw Nation; Creek
    Nation; Seminole Nation
Interior Department, U.S., 105, 110, 112, 121
Intermarriage: children of, 30–31; Indian-
    black, 140; Indian-black ban, 35; Indian-
    white, 29–32, 57, 130, 143, 161 (n. 94). *See
    also* Mixed blood
Ischomer (as free black surname), 72

Jackson, Andrew, 7, 8, 38, 39, 50
Jackson, Martha, *151*

Riverside (Colbert home), *81*

Runaway slaves, 21, 77, 83–85, 89–91, 97; Civil War and, 103–4, 109; resistance role of, 100; retrieval from Indian Territory of, 91, 98. *See also* Fugitive Slave Act

Russwurm, John, 74

St. Domingue, 28

St. Jean, Wendy, 7

Sanborn, John, 110–11, 112

Saunt, Calauio, 24

Savannah, Ga., 54, 55, 56

Schools, mission, 34, 48, 49, 50

Scullyville Constitution (1857), 93, 95

Scullyville conventions (1869 and 1870), 122, 123, 124, 135

Secession, 97

Second Colored Church (Savannah), 55

Sectional crisis (1840s–1850s), 9, 10, 72, 78, 91–93, 95; Compromise of 1850 and, 91

Segregation, 144, 148, 150

Sells, Elijah, 105, 111

Seminole Nation, 99, 104, 106, 115, 116; Civil War and, 104, 105; Dawes Commission and, 142–44; federal removal of, 8, 41; federal termination of sovereignty and land titles of, 142–43; freedpeople's status and, 102, 113, 117; map of Indian Territory, *94*; slave emancipation by, 10, 101

Senate Committee on Indian Affairs, U.S., 148–49

Senate Judiciary Committee, U.S., 107

Seneca Nation, 105, 106

79th U.S. Colored Infantry Regiment, 177 (n. 63)

Shanks, P. C., 132, 133

Sharecroppers, 69, 108, 110, 119, 126

Shawnee Nation, 106

Shawnee prophet, 163 (n. 27)

Sherman, William, 112

Shields, Bob, 42, 161 (n. 106)

Shields, James, 161 (n. 106)

Shoemaker, Nancy, 32, 157 (n. 32)

Skullyville, 80

Skullyville Constitution (1857), 93, 95, 171 (n. 76)

Slave codes, 63, 71, 83, 84, 93, 112

Slaveholding: abolition of, 10 (*see also* Emancipation; Treaty of 1866); boundaries of, 40; Choctaw census racial categories and, 161 (n. 94); Choctaw inception of, 23; Christian belief and, 52, 59; defense of, 62; federally expanded rights of (1850), 71, 91; Indian practices of, 28–29, 30, 32, 52, 54, 153, 178 (n. 21); Indian racial identity and, 30; Indian Territory and, 40, 43, 80; Indian Territory dismantling of, 108–9; Indian-white conflicts and, 77, 90, 91; sectional crisis over (1840s–1850s), 9, 10, 72, 78, 91–93, 95; southern white-owned plantations and, 2, 8, 9, 18, 41; territorial expansion of, 8, 9, 10, 14, 78, 91; women's reproductive capacity and, 44–45, 81–82. *See also* Slave trade

Slave patrols, 83–84

Slave resistance, 14, 72, 77–78, 82–89, 93, 100; communication networks and, 77; insurrection rumors and, 96–97; missionaries and, 88; self-liberation plots and, 97; types of, 77, 82, 83, 84; violence and, 85–89. *See also* Runaway slaves

Slaves, 17–45; African-born vs. American-born, 54; as agricultural labor, 1–6, 8–10, 13, 17–45, 78, 126; alcohol possession ban for, 85; Choctaw/Chickasaw buying and selling of, 43; Choctaw/Chickasaw census (1860) of, 175 (n. 1); Choctaw/Chickasaw subordination of, 107–18; Choctaw/Chickasaw wealth in, 17–18, 32, 39–40, 42, 78; as Civil War refugees, 103–4, 109, 114, 134–35; colonial America and, 19–21; communication networks among, 90, 96, 97; deaths and births and, 44–45; disputes among, 84–86; female reproductive value of, 44–45, 81–82; freeing of (*see* Emancipation); fugitive (*see* Runaway slaves); gendered labor and, 33; hard labor of, 82; Indian removal/movement to Indian Territory of, 1, 8, 9–10, 13–14, 17–18, 30–31, 42–45, 78–80; Indians as, 20; Indian Territory population growth of, 81–82, 168 (n. 11); Indian war captives contrasted with, 13, 18–19; laws governing, 8, 9 (*see also* Fugitive Slave Act; Slave codes); lifelong service and heritability of, 13, 17, 44–45, 81; literacy of, 56–57, 58, 59, 63; missionary ethical conflicts over, 14, 52; missionary hiring of, 64, 65, 66–70,

Vicksburg, Battle of (1863), 99
Vigilante Commission, 174 (n. 28)
Vigilantes, 111, 112
Violence: against former slaves, 109–12, 120, 123, 174 (n. 28); Indian abuse of slaves and, 35–36; slave resistance and, 85–89; slavery status in Kansas and, 9, 92
Vorenberg, Michael, 124
Voting rights. *See* Suffrage

Walker, Tandy, 95
Ward, William, 28
Ware, Thomas, 40
Washington, George, 24
Western territories: Compromise of 1850 and, 91; expansion of slavery into, 8, 9, 10, 14, 78, 91; freedpeople's proposed colonization in, 117; Indian removal and, 78; Kansas-Nebraska Act and, 9, 78; missionaries and, 47, 50; white settlers in, 103, 112, 116. *See also* Indian Territory
West Florida, 21, 28
West Indies, 28–29, 55, 136
Wet nurses, 82
Wheelock mission, 66, 67, 70, 79, 84
White, Richard, 3

White settlers, 6, 7, 18–25, 26, 62, 98, 103; federal settlement in South of, 24–25; Indian intermarriage with, 29–30; in Indian Territory, 112, 123, 128–30, 131, 133, 134; in western territories, 103, 112, 116
White superiority, 5, 30, 32, 45, 57, 143
Whooping cough, 45
Williams, Loring, 49, 53, 59, 63, 64, 158 (n. 49)
Williams, Matilda, 49, 53
Wills and estates, 37
Wilson, Billy, 90
Wistar, Thomas, 105
Wolf, James Squire, 121, 122
Wolf, Jonas, 141
Women. *See* Gender practices
Worcester, Reverend, 34
Wright, Allen, 92, 122, 129–30
Wright, John, 20
Wright, Mrs. (missionary), 69–70, 75
Wyandot Nation, 106

Yalobusha River, 49
Yeoman farmers, 25
Young, Jacob, 28, 29, 39

Zebra (ship), 75